The Forgotten Heroes of Liberty

The Forgotten Heroes of Liberty

The Chaplains and Clergy of the American Revolution

Joel Tyler Headley

Solid Ground Christian Books
Birmingham, Alabama USA

Solid Ground Christian Books
2090 Columbiana Rd, Suite 2000
Birmingham, AL 35216
205-443-0311
sgcb@charter.net
http://solid-ground-books.com

The Forgotten Heroes of Liberty
The Chaplains and Clergy of the American Revolution

Joel Tyler Headley (1813-1897)

Solid Ground Classic Reprints

First printing of new edition June 2005

Cover work by Borgo Design, Tuscaloosa, AL
Contact them at nelbrown@comcast.net

Cover image is a likeness of Rev. James Caldwell handing out copies of Watts' Hymns and Psalms to use for wadding against the British troops. This incident is recorded on page 227 of this volume.

SPECIAL THANKS to Rick Berryman of Jacksonville, FL for his willingness to permit us to use his personal copy of *The Chaplains and Clergy of the American Revolution*. Your willing sacrifice is greatly appreciated.

ISBN: 1-932474-92-7

AUTHOR'S PREFACE

In writing the biographies of the chaplains and clergymen who bore a prominent part in our revolutionary struggle, I have thought proper to devote a few pages at the outset to the influence of *the pulpit as an institution*. In New England especially, which inaugurated the rebellion, and on which fell so heavily the burden of carrying it forward, the pulpit was a recognized power in the State, and its aid formally and earnestly invoked.

It was necessary to do this to carry out the entire object I had in view, which was not merely to give a series of biographical sketches, but to exhibit the religious element—in other words, present the religious *phase* of the Revolution. Individual clergymen might have been devoted patriots, and rendered efficient service to their country, and yet the *pulpit* as such deserve no more prominent place in the struggle than the profession of law or medicine because many of its members bore a distinguished part in it. The clergy, however, wielded twofold power—as *individuals* and as *representatives* of a profession which in New England dominated the State.

In writing the biographical sketches, I have restricted myself almost exclusively to events and actions embraced by the revolutionary period. This was necessary, not only to give definiteness and unity to the work, but because *full* biographies of some of the distinguished chaplains would make separate volumes in themselves. Hence I have not professed to write the *life* of any one individual, but as far as I could obtain the facts, the *revolutionary* history of all.

The details and incidents necessary to carry out this design not being found in public documents, it will readily occur to the reader that the most serious difficulties had to be surmounted in obtaining them. I have had to rely chiefly of course on family papers and traditions, with such additional items as I could pick up in my researches among old pamphlets, letters, etc, found in antiquarian societies. I mention this to explain the absence of all references to authorities in the body of the work. To have given the multifarious sources, such as individuals, letters, pamphlets, magazines, historical collections, etc., would have burdened the work with a vast amount of useless matter. For some of the fuller sketches, such as Allen, Avery, Cotton Smith, Gallo, Champion and Ker, I have been indebted almost exclusively to the kindness of the immediate descendants of these men. In others, in part to family relatives of the chaplains, and in part to various miscellaneous sources. For many of the shorter biographies I am greatly indebted to Dr. Sprague's admirable work, "The American Pulpit."[1] Without this I should not have been able to give the birth, nativity, and date of death of a large portion of those whose names will be entirely new to the reader. Of course many who ought to be embraced in this collection are omitted, because I could not obtain the facts necessary to make a biography. In some cases the personal diaries, which would have furnished these, have been lost by the families who once had them in their possession—in others they having lived only in tradition, have passed away with time, or are so dimly remembered as to be comparatively valueless.

I have regretted especially that I could obtain nothing satisfactory respecting the Lutheran Church, which rendered the country good service.

But notwithstanding the necessary incompleteness of the work, I feel I have done something towards giving the clergy and the pulpit the place which they ought to have in the history of the Revolution, and furnished a book which will benefit the generation now rising into manhood, by directing the mind not only to religious influences, but to the great source of all national blessings, as well as to battle fields and the strong legions.

This diversion of the mind from armies to the God of armies is especially needed in our present crisis.

---

[1] William B. Sprague (1795-1876) complied eight volumes of *The Annals of the American Pulpit*. Solid Ground Christian Books has just published Volume Six of this work in two volumes, called *The Annals of the American Baptist Pulpit*.

Enthusiasm and numbers will not deliver us from the troubles that now overwhelm us. Penitence and humility will go farther than either, and whether the State turns as it did in the Revolution to the Church as its strongest support or not, we may rest assured, if its prayers do not save us, whatever success we may achieve will in the end prove a sad failure.

J.T. Headley, 1861

CONTENTS.

CHAPTER I.

RELIGIOUS ELEMENT OF THE REVOLUTION.—NOT SUFFICIENTLY DWELT ON BY HISTORIANS.—INFLUENCE AND ACTION OF PASTORS.—EXAMPLE IN STOCKBRIDGE, MASS.—INTERESTING SCENE.................................... 13

CHAPTER II.

SYSTEMATIC INFLUENCE OF THE CLERGY.—ELECTION SERMONS BEFORE THE REVOLUTION.—ELECTION SERMONS A PART OF THE PROCEEDINGS OF THE PROVINCIAL LEGISLATURE.—SAMUEL COOK'S SERMON'S, 1770.—MR. TUCKER'S, IN 1771.—CHARLES TURNER'S, IN 1773.—GAD. HITCHCOCK'S, IN 1774.—"THE TEA OVERBOARD."—PRESIDENT LANGDON'S, IN 1775.—"BUNKER HILL, MONITIONS OF THE COMING STORM."—THESE SERMONS THE POLITICAL PAMPHLETS OF THE TIMES.. 21

CHAPTER III.

ELECTION SERMONS, PREACHED AFTER THE ASSEMBLING OF THE CONTINENTAL CONGRESS AND ORGANIZATION OF COLONIAL GOVERNMENT.—REV. WM. GORDON.—REV. SAMUEL WEST, OF DARTMOUTH, IN 1776.—BOLD APPEAL. 35

CHAPTER IV.

SERMONS DURING THE WAR.—SERMON OF SAMUEL WEBSTER, IN 1777.—BOLD AND PATRIOTIC PRAYER.—DISCOURSE OF PHILLIP PAYSON, OF CHELSEA, 1778.—ELOQUENT APPEAL.—PROPHETIC VISION........................ 48

CHAPTER V.

PERSONAL INFLUENCE OF THE CLERGY.—APPOINTMENTS OF CHAPLAINS.—CORRESPONDENCE BETWEEN THE MINISTERS OF CONNECTICUT AND MASSACHUSETTS.—THAXTER, FOSTER AND PAYSON FIGHTING AT LEXINGTON AND CONCORD.—WASHINGTON ASKS CONGRESS FOR CHAPLAINS.—NUMBER AND NAMES OF, IN THE ARMY AT CAMBRIDGE.—WASHINGTON'S SECOND LETTER TO CONGRESS ON THE SUBJECT.—HIS ORDER RESPECTING CHAPLAINS.—DAVID ELY.—JOSEPH FISH.—JONAH STEARNS.—JOHN MILIS.—DAVID CALDWELL.—THOMAS READ.—ROBERT DAVIDSON.—ELIZUR GOODRICH.—WM. GORHAM.—JOHN STEELE.—FRANCIS CUMMINGS.—AZEL ROE.—HEZEKIAH BALCH.—CHARLES McKNIGHT.—MANASSEH CUTLER.—NATHAN STRONG.—NATHANIEL PORTER.—ANNIE ROBINS.—JOHN CLEVELAND.—SAMUEL McCLINTOCK.—HEZEKIAH RIPLEY.—ISAAC LEWIS.—DR. LATTA.—DR. ARMSTRONG...... 56

CHAPTER VI.

JONAS CLARK.—THE PASTOR OF LEXINGTON.—HIS MINISTERIAL LIFE.—EARLY TEACHINGS.—PATRIOTIC CONDUCT AND ABILITY AS A STATESMAN.—HANCOCK AND ADAMS FIND REFUGE IN HIS HOUSE.—NEWS OF THE APPROACH OF THE ENEMY.—HIS ACCOUNT OF IT.—SUMMONING OF THE MILITIA.—SCENE ON THE GREEN.—APPROACH OF THE ENEMY.—THE SLAUGHTER.—MR. CLARK AMONG HIS SLAIN PARISHIONERS.—HIS FEELINGS AND PREDICTION...... 74

CHAPTER VII.

JACOB DUCHÉ.—OPENS THE FIRST CONTINENTAL CONGRESS WITH PRAYER.—JOHN ADAMS'S DESCRIPTION OF THE SCENE.—HIS PATRIOTIC SERMONS.—GIVES HIS PAY AS CHAPLAIN TO THE FAMILIES OF THOSE SLAIN IN BATTLE.—BECOMES ALARMED, AND TURNS AGAINST HIS COUNTRY.—HIS INSULTING LETTER TO WASHINGTON.—FLEES THE COUNTRY.—HIS RETURN TO PHILADELPHIA.—HIS DEATH.—HIS CHARACTER............................... 83

CONTENTS.

CHAPTER VIII.
                                                                    PAGE
SAMUEL SPRING, D.D.—HIS EARLY LIFE.—BECOMES CHAPLAIN IN THE ARMY.—THE ONLY CHAPLAIN IN ARNOLD'S EXPEDITION ACROSS THE NORTHERN WILDERNESS.—HIS DESCRIPTION OF ITS FORMATION.—PREACHES AT NEWBURYPORT TO THE ARMY.—VISITS THE TOMB OF WHITFIELD.—DESCRIPTION OF THE MARCH THROUGH THE WILDERNESS.—HIS SUFFERINGS AND LABORS.—FAMINE.—HIS DESCRIPTION OF SHOOTING A MOOSE.—HIS LABORS AT POINT AUX TREMBLES.—STORMING OF QUEBEC.—HE LEADS ARNOLD OUT OF THE FIGHT.—LEAVES THE ARMY.—SETTLED AT NEWBURYPORT.—HIS INTERVIEW WITH AARON BURR.—HIS DEATH.................................... 89

CHAPTER IX.
EBENEZER PRIME.—HIS PATRIOTISM.—DRIVEN FROM HIS CHURCH.—HIS LIBRARY DESTROYED.—HIS DEATH.—INSULT TO HIS GRAVE................ 107

CHAPTER X.
SAMUEL EATON.—IS SETTLED IN HARPSBURG, MAINE.—PRACTICES THREE PROFESSIONS.—ATTENDS A POLITICAL MEETING.—HIS STIRRING ADDRESS.—NARROW ESCAPE OF AN OFFICER OF THE KING.—RECRUITING OFFICER SEEKS HIS AID.—EATON ADDRESSES THE PEOPLE ON SABBATH EVENING.—THRILLING SCENE.—SOLDIERS OBTAINED.—HIS DEATH................... 110

CHAPTER XI.
WILLIAM TENNENT.—HIS BIRTH AND EDUCATION.—SETTLED AT NORWALK, CONN.—REMOVES TO CHARLESTON, S. C.—HIS PERSONAL APPEARANCE.—HIS ELOQUENCE AND ZEAL IN THE CAUSE OF THE COLONIES.—MAKES PATRIOTIC APPEALS ON THE SABBATH.—IS ELECTED MEMBER OF THE PROVINCIAL CONGRESS OF SOUTH CAROLINA.—SENT WITH HENRY DRAYTON TO BACK SETTLEMENTS TO BAFFLE TORIES.—LETTERS TO HENRY LAURENS AND CONGRESS.—AGAIN SENT TO CONGRESS.—HIS CHARACTER... 115

CHAPTER XII.
PETER GABRIEL MUHLENBURG.—FIGHTING CLERGYMEN.—MUHLENBURG'S BIRTH AND EDUCATION.—GOES TO ENGLAND.—SETTLES IN VIRGINIA.—TAKES A PROMINENT PART IN POLITICAL MOVEMENTS.—BECOMES MEMBER OF THE HOUSE OF BURGESSES.—RAISES A REGIMENT, OF WHICH HE IS CHOSEN COLONEL.—PREACHES HIS FAREWELL SERMON.—ORDERS THE DRUM TO BEAT FOR RECRUITS AT THE CHURCH DOOR.—MARCHES TO CHARLESTON.—CAMPS AT VALLEY FORGE.—FIGHTS BRAVELY AT BRANDYWINE.—AT MONMOUTH.—COMMANDS THE RESERVE AT STONY POINT.—MAKES A DESPERATE ASSAULT AT YORKTOWN.—IS MADE MAJOR GENERAL.—POLITICAL CAREER AFTER THE WAR.—DEFENCE OF COURSE IN ABANDONING PROFESSION..... 121

CHAPTER XIII.
THOMAS ALLEN.—HIS BIRTH AND EDUCATION.—SETTLES IN PITTSFIELD.—TAKES DECIDED PART WITH THE COLONIES.—IS MADE CHAIRMAN OF THE COMMITTEE OF SAFETY AND CORRESPONDENCE.—HIS LABORS.—HIS INTEREST IN THE CONQUEST OF TICONDEROGA.—NEW AND INTERESTING LETTER TO GEN. SETH POMROY.—JOINS THE ARMY AS CHAPLAIN.—HIS DIARY AT THE BATTLE OF WHITE PLAINS.—GOES TO TICONDEROGA.—ADDRESS TO THE SOLDIERS WHEN EXPECTING AN ATTACK.—HIS DISGUST AT THE RETREAT.—RALLIES THE MILITIA TO THE AID OF STARKE, AT BENNINGTON.—SUMMONS THE ENEMY TO SURRENDER, AND IS FIRED AT.—FIGHTS IN THE RANKS.—FIRST OVER THE BREAST-WORK.—HIS CARE FOR THE WOUNDED.—RETURNS TO HIS PARISH.—DIALOGUE WITH A PARISHIONER.—VOYAGE TO ENGLAND AFTER AN INFANT GRANDCHILD.—PRAYS WITH AND ADDRESSES THE CREW IN EXPECTATION OF AN ATTACK.—HIS CONDUCT IN THE SHAY'S REBELLION.—HIS STATESMANSHIP.—HIS DEATH........................ 128

CHAPTER XIV.
JOHN ROSSBURGH.—AN IRISHMAN BY BIRTH.—HIS EDUCATION.—IS SETTLED AT THE " FORKS OF THE DELAWARE."—HIS PATRIOTISM.—JOINS A COMPANY FORMED IN HIS OWN PARISH AS A SOLDIER.—HIS PAINFUL PARTING WITH

CONTENTS. ix

PAGE

HIS WIFE.—MAKES HIS WILL.—CHAPLAIN OF A REGIMENT.—MARCHES AGAINST THE ENEMY.—IS TAKEN PRISONER, AND MURDERED WHILE PRAYING FOR HIS ENEMIES.—THE MUTILATED CORPSE STEALTHILY BURIED.—HIS LETTERS TO HIS WIFE JUST BEFORE A SKIRMISH.—HIS CHARACTER......... 158

CHAPTER XV.

ABNER BENEDICT.—HIS BIRTH AND EDUCATION.—SETTLED AT MIDDLETOWN.—BECOMES CHAPLAIN IN THE ARMY AT NEW YORK.—DESCRIPTION OF A TERRIFIC THUNDER-STORM.—THE BATTLE OF LONG ISLAND.—HIS FEELINGS.—THE LAST TO LEAVE THE SHORE IN THE RETREAT.—INVENTIONS IN SUBMARINE NAVIGATION.—MANUFACTURES SALTPETER FOR POWDER.—ELECTED PROFESSOR IN YALE COLLEGE.—HIS CHARACTER AND DEATH.......... 164

CHAPTER XVI.

WILLIAM WHITE, D.D.—HIS BIRTH AND EARLY STUDIES.—GOES TO ENGLAND.—FRIEND OF GOLDSMITH AND JOHNSON.—SETTLED IN PHILADELPHIA.—TAKES THE OATH OF ALLEGIANCE.—NOBLE DETERMINATION.—ELECTED CHAPLAIN OF CONGRESS.—HIS CONDUCT AFTER THE REVOLUTION.—IS MADE BISHOP.—HIS CHARACTER AND DEATH........................... 171

CHAPTER XVII.

TIMOTHY DWIGHT.—PATRIOTISM OF OUR COLLEGES.—DWIGHT'S BIRTH.—HIS EARLY LIFE.—TUTOR OF YALE COLLEGE.—IS LICENSED TO PREACH.—HIS PATRIOTISM.—BECOMES CHAPLAIN.—ADVOCATES COMPLETE INDEPENDENCE.—DESOLATE APPEARANCE OF WESTCHESTER COUNTY.—SERMON AFTER THE VICTORY AT SARATOGA.—ANECDOTE OF PUTNAM.—COMPOSES THE ODE TO COLUMBIA.—DEDICATES A POEM TO WASHINGTON.—SHARES THE SUFFERINGS OF THE SOLDIERS AT WEST POINT IN THE WINTER OF 1778.—HIS FAITH.—DEAD UNBURIED AT FORT MONTGOMERY.—DEATH OF HIS FATHER.—LEAVES THE ARMY.—SETTLES AT NORTHAMPTON.—GOES TO LEGISLATURE.—PUBLISHES SEVERAL POEMS.—ELECTED PRESIDENT OF YALE COLLEGE.—A FEDERALIST IN 1812.— EMINENCE AS A THEOLOGIAN.—HIS DEATH........ 175

CHAPTER XVIII.

NAPHTHALI DAGGET.—PROFESSOR OF DIVINITY IN YALE COLLEGE.—THE COLLEGE BROKEN UP.—INVASION OF TRYON.—TERROR OF THE INHABITANTS.—A COMPANY OF A HUNDRED YOUNG MEN RAISED TO RESIST HIM.—DR. DAGGET AND HIS BLACK MARE.—ADVANCES ALONE TO RECONNOITER.—THE FIGHT.—THE RETREAT.—DR. DAGGET REFUSES TO RUN.—INTERVIEW WITH THE BRITISH OFFICER.—FORCED TO GUIDE THE COLUMN.—BRUTAL TREATMENT.—RESCUED BY A TORY.—HIS SICKNESS.—DEATH............. 199

CHAPTER XIX.

EZRA STYLES.—HIS PROPHECY RESPECTING THE COLONIES, IN 1760.—PRESIDENT OF YALE COLLEGE.—CHANCELLOR KENT'S EULOGY OF HIM.—HIS PATRIOTISM.—KEEPS A DIARY OF REVOLUTIONARY EVENTS.—HIS DEATH.. 205

CHAPTER XX.

JOEL BARLOW.—EARLY EDUCATION.—A FRIEND OF DWIGHT.—HIS POEM, "THE PROSPECT OF PEACE."—BECOMES CHAPLAIN.—WRITES PATRIOTIC BALLADS.—"HYMNS FOR YANKEE REBELS."—THE BURNING OF CHARLESTOWN."—OCCUPATION IN THE ARMY.—FRIEND OF WASHINGTON.—SERMON ON ARNOLD'S TREASON.—BECOMES LAWYER AND EDITOR AT HARTFORD, CONNECTICUT.—REVISES WATT'S PSALMS AND HYMNS—AGENT OF SCIOTO LAND COMPANY.—VISITS ENGLAND AND FRANCE.—IN FRENCH REVOLUTION.—OCCUPATIONS IN EUROPE.—CONSUL AT ALGIERS.—MAKES A FORTUNE IN FRANCE.—RETURNS TO AMERICA.—REMARKABLE PROPHECIES IN HIS COLUMBIAD.—MINISTER TO FRANCE.—CHARGE OF RELIGIOUS APOSTACY... 207

CHAPTER XXI.

JAMES CALDWELL.—HIS BIRTH AND ANCESTRY.—PERSONAL APPEARANCE.—POWER OF HIS VOICE.—HIS CHARACTER.—HIS CONGREGATION AT ELIZABETHTOWN.—MADE CHAPLAIN.—HIS TOAST ON THE RECEPTION OF THE DECLARATION OF INDEPENDENCE.—HIS ACTIVITY.—REWARDS OFFERED

FOR HIS CAPTURE.—REMOVES TO CONNECTICUT FARMS.—GOES ARMED.—HIS SERVICES.—LETTER TO LEE.—ASSISTANT COMMISSARY GENERAL.—LAST INTERVIEW WITH HIS WIFE.—HER MURDER.—FIGHT AT SPRINGFIELD.—"GIVE 'EM WATTS."—MURDER OF CALDWELL.—HIS FUNERAL.—HIS CHILDREN.—MONUMENT TO HIM............................... 217

CHAPTER XXII.

BENJAMIN TRUMBULL.—HIS BIRTH AND EDUCATION.—TAKES SIDES WITH THE COLONIES.—ENTERS THE ARMY AS CHAPLAIN.—FIGHTS IN THE RANKS.—CURIOUS INTERVIEW WITH WASHINGTON.—FIGHTS AT WHITEPLAINS.—ANECDOTE.—FIGHTS AT NEW HAVEN.—RETURNS TO HIS PARISH.—WRITES THE HISTORY OF CONNECTICUT.—HIS DEATH.—HIS PUBLICATIONS........ 233

CHAPTER XXIII.

SAMUEL KIRKLAND.—HIS BIRTH AND EDUCATION.—A TEACHER IN DR. WHEELOCK'S SCHOOL.—GOES A MISSIONARY TO THE INDIANS OF NEW YORK STATE.—HIS LABORS AND PERILS.—HIS MISSION BROKEN UP BY THE REVOLUTION.—EMPLOYED BY CONGRESS TO KEEP THE INDIANS FROM JOINING THE BRITISH.—PREVENTED BY BRANDT.—A CHAPLAIN IN SULLIVAN'S BRIGADE.—ACCOMPANIES IT TO GENESEE FLATS.—HIS SERVICES REWARDED BY CONGRESS.—SETTLES AMONG THE ONEIDAS AFTER THE WAR.—FOUNDS HAMILTON COLLEGE.—IS THROWN FROM HIS HORSE.—HIS DEATH......... 239

CHAPTER XXIV.

JAMES HALL.—HIS BIRTH AND EDUCATION.—SETTLED IN NORTH CAROLINA.—ROUSES HIS PEOPLE TO OPPOSE THE MOTHER COUNTRY.—IS MADE CAPTAIN OF A COMPANY OF CAVALRY.—ACTS ALSO AS CHAPLAIN.—MARCHES TO SOUTH CAROLINA.—OFFERED THE COMMISSION OF BRIGADIER GENERAL BY GREENE.—DECLINES.—HIS AFTER LIFE................................ 255

CHAPTER XXV.

JOHN GANO.—THE BAPTISTS OF VIRGINIA.—GANO'S EARLY LIFE.—VISITS THE SOUTH AND PREACHES.—ARRAIGNED FOR IT, BUT IS ACQUITTED AND LICENSED.—ANECDOTES OF HIS COOLNESS AND COURAGE.—SETTLED IN NORTH CAROLINA.—OFFERED A CAPTAIN'S COMMISSION IN THE ARMY AGAINST THE CHEROKEES.—DECLINES.—RETURNS NORTH.—FINALLY SETTLES IN NEW YORK.—HIS CONGREGATION BROKEN UP.—JOINS THE ARMY AS CHAPLAIN.—UNDER FIRE AT WHITE PLAINS.—AT TRENTON.—CHAPLAIN UNDER CLINTON AT FORT MONTGOMERY.—HIS DESCRIPTION OF THE TAKING OF THE FORT.—WITH CLINTON'S BRIGADE AT ALBANY.—ITS CHAPLAIN.—IN THE EXPEDITION AGAINST THE INDIANS.—ANECDOTES OF HIM IN THIS CAMPAIGN.—SERMON ON THE FOURTH OF JULY.—HIS FAITHFULNESS.—GOES SOUTH WITH THE ARMY.—ADVANCING AGAINST CORNWALLIS.—RETURNS TO HIS CHURCH AT THE CLOSE OF THE WAR.—REMOVES TO KENTUCKY.—HIS DEATH.. 250

CHAPTER XXVI.

CHARLES CUMMINGS.—AN IRISHMAN BY BIRTH.—SETTLES IN VIRGINIA.—ENTERS THE MINISTRY.—FIGHTS THE INDIANS.—GOES ARMED TO HIS CHURCH.—TAKES THE LEAD IN THE POLITICAL MOVEMENTS OF THE PEOPLE.—CHAPLAIN TO THE ARMY IN THE EXPEDITION AGAINST THE CHEROKEES.—HIS DEATH.. 273

CHAPTER XXVII.

DANIEL MCCALLA.—HIS BIRTH.—GRADUATES AT PRINCETON WHEN EIGHTEEN YEARS OF AGE.—STUDIES FOR THE MINISTRY.—SETTLES IN PENNSYLVANIA.—APPOINTED CHAPLAIN UNDER GENERAL THOMSON.—IS TAKEN PRISONER IN THE ATTACK ON "THREE RIVERS."—THROWN INTO A PRISON SHIP.—HIS SUFFERINGS AND FORTITUDE.—RELEASED ON PAROLE.—FLEES TO VIRGINIA.—SETTLES IN SOUTH CAROLINA.—HIS DEATH................. 276

CHAPTER XXVIII.

JOHN WITHERSPOON, D.D.—THE CLERGY AS STATESMEN.—WITHERSPOON A SCOTCHMAN BY BIRTH.—HIS EARLY LIFE.—IS LICENSED TO PREACH.—JOINS THE ARMY OF THE PRETENDER.—TAKEN PRISONER AT THE BATTLE OF FAL-

CONTENTS. xi

PAGE

KIRK.—EMINENCE AS A THEOLOGIAN.—ELECTED PRESIDENT OF PRINCETON COLLEGE.—FLATTERING RECEPTION IN THIS COUNTRY.—TAKES SIDES WITH THE COLONIES.—ELECTED MEMBER OF THE NEW JERSEY LEGISLATURE.—SCATHING ATTACK ON GOVERNOR FRANKLIN.—ELECTED MEMBER OF CONGRESS.—HIS SPEECH ON THE DECLARATION OF INDEPENDENCE. HIS GREAT SERVICES IN CONGRESS.—HIS DEATH........................ 280

CHAPTER XXIX.

DAVID AVERY.—HIS BIRTH AND CHARACTER.—CONVERTED UNDER WHITFIELD. —LEAVES HIS TRADE TO STUDY FOR THE MINISTRY.—ENTERS DR. WHEELOCK'S CHARITY SCHOOL.—GRADUATES AT YALE COLLEGE.—STUDIES DIVINITY.—A MISSIONARY AMONG THE INDIANS.—SETTLED AT GAYSBORO, VERMONT.—HIS PATRIOTISM.—RAISES A COMPANY AND MARCHES TO BOSTON.— MADE CHAPLAIN.—NODDLE'S ISLAND.—PRESENT AT THE BATTLE OF BUNKER HILL.—PRAYING FOR VICTORY.—ACCOMPANIES WASHINGTON THROUGH THE JERSEYS.—WOUNDED AT TRENTON.—AT VALLEY FORGE.—AT TICONDEROGA.—AT BENNINGTON.—HIS DEATH............................. 287

CHAPTER XXX.

ISRAEL EVANS.—HIS CHARACTER.—ORDAINED CHAPLAIN IN THE ARMY.—REMAINS WITH THE NEW HAMPSHIRE BRIGADE THROUGH THE WAR.—STANDS BESIDE WASHINGTON AT YORKTOWN.—ANECDOTE OF HIM AND WASHINGTON.—HIS SERMON ON THE FIELD OF BATTLE.—SETTLED AT CONCORD, NEW HAMPSHIRE.—HIS DEATH.. 300

CHAPTER XXXI.

COTTON MATHER SMITH.—HIS BIRTH AND PARENTAGE.—A TEACHER AMONG THE INDIANS.—STUDIES THEOLOGY.—IS SETTLED AT SHARON, CONN.—INFLUENCE OF THE CLERGY OF CONNECTICUT IN BRINGING ABOUT THE REVOLUTION.—HIS VIEWS OF THE STRUGGLE BETWEEN THE COLONIES AND MOTHER COUNTRY.—THE PART HE TOOK IN IT.—PATRIOTISM OF HIS CONGREGATION.—IS MADE CHAPLAIN, AND MARCHES TO TICONDEROGA.—HIS DEVOTION TO THE SICK.—SEIZED WITH THE CAMP FEVER.—RETURNS HOME.—INVASION OF BURGOYNE.—HIS SERMON JUST BEFORE THE FINAL VICTORY AT SARATOGA.—THRILLING SCENE.—HIS CHARACTER.—HIS DEATH... 305

CHAPTER XXXII.

JUDAH CHAMPION, THE PASTOR OF LITCHFIELD, CONNECTICUT.—HIS PRAYERS FOR HIS COUNTRY.—EXTRAORDINARY SCENE IN CHURCH ON THE ARRIVAL OF NEWS FROM THE ARMY.—WOMEN WORKING ON THE SABBATH TO PREPARE GARMENTS FOR THE SOLDIERS.—THE PASTOR ON THE FIELD OF BATTLE... 318

CHAPTER XXXIII.

ALEXANDER MCWHORTER.—HIS EARLY LIFE.—ZEAL IN THE CAUSE OF LIBERTY.—SENT SOUTH BY CONGRESS TO ROUSE THE INHABITANTS.—ACCOMPANIES WASHINGTON IN HIS RETREAT THROUGH NEW JERSEY.—MADE CHAPLAIN OF KNOX'S BRIGADE.—LEAVES THE ARMY.—SETTLES IN NORTH CAROLINA.—HIS LIBRARY AND FURNITURE DESTROYED BY THE BRITISH.— FLEES TO PENNSYLVANIA.—SENT TO ENGLAND TO RAISE FUNDS FOR PRINCETON COLLEGE.—REVISITS HIS NATIVE PLACE.—HIS DEATH............... 327

CHAPTER XXXIV.

MOSES ALLEN.—HIS EARLY LIFE.—A FRIEND OF MADISON.—SETTLES IN MIDWAY, GEORGIA.—HIS PATRIOTIC EFFORTS.—CHAPLAIN IN THE ARMY.— HIS HOUSE AND CHURCH BURNED.—IN THE BATTLE BEFORE SAVANNAH.— IS TAKEN PRISONER.—CONFINED ON BOARD A PRISON SHIP.—HIS SUFFERINGS.—BRUTALITY OF HIS CAPTORS.—ATTEMPTS TO ESCAPE.—IS DROWNED. —DENIED DECENT BURIAL... 331

CHAPTER XXXV.

BENJAMIN POMEROY.—HIS EARLY LIFE.—BECOMES A "NEW LIGHT."—IS PERSECUTED BY THE STATE, AND FINALLY DEPRIVED OF HIS SALARY.—BECOMES CHAPLAIN IN THE FRENCH WAR.—HIS LETTER TO HIS WIFE

CONTENTS.

DESCRIBING THE EXECUTION OF A CRIMINAL.—AT SEVENTY BECOMES CHAPLAIN IN THE REVOLUTIONARY ARMY.—HIS VENERABLE APPEARANCE.—TOUCHING APPEALS.—HIS DEATH............................ 341

CHAPTER XXXVI.

JOHN ROGERS.—HIS REPUTATION ABROAD.—HIS PATRIOTISM.—INTRODUCTION TO WASHINGTON.—CHAPLAIN IN HEATH'S BRIGADE.—RESIGNS AND GOES TO GEORGIA.—ON HIS RETURN MADE CHAPLAIN TO THE NEW YORK PROVINCIAL ASSEMBLY.—BECOMES MEMBER OF THE LEGISLATURE.—CHANCELLOR OF THE REGENTS OF THE UNIVERSITY.......................... 347

CHAPTER XXXVII.

GEORGE DUFFIELD.—DESCENDED FROM THE HUGUENOTS.—STUDIES FOR THE MINISTRY.—IS SETTLED IN CARLISLE.—HIS PARISHIONERS GO ARMED TO CHURCH.—HIS PATRIOTISM.—SETTLES IN PHILADELPHIA.—KING'S MAGISTRATE ATTEMPTS TO STOP HIS PREACHING.—IS BROUGHT UP BEFORE THE MAYOR ON CHARGE OF RIOT.—EXCITEMENT OF THE PEOPLE.—HIS POPULARITY WITH MEMBERS OF CONGRESS.—STIRRING ADDRESS.—BECOMES CHAPLAIN IN THE ARMY.—PREACHES TO THE SOLDIERS FROM THE FORKS OF A TREE.—BURIES A BROTHER CHAPLAIN WHO HAS BEEN MURDERED.—NARROW ESCAPE.—EXAMPLE OF HIS FAITH.—HIS DEATH.............. 350

CHAPTER XXXVIII.

DAVID SANDFORD.—HIS PATRIOTISM.—HIS PERSONAL APPEARANCE.—HIS ELOQUENCE.—GIVES HIS SALARY TO THE CAUSE OF LIBERTY.—BECOMES CHAPLAIN.—EXPRESSIVE COUNTENANCE.—ANECDOTE ILLUSTRATING IT.—STERN REBUKES.—HIS PIETY.—HIS DEATH.. 361

CHAPTER XXXIX.

NATHAN KER.—HIS BIRTH AND ANCESTRY.—ANECDOTE OF HIS GRANDFATHER.—HIS PATRIOTISM.—ABJURES ALL ALLEGIANCE TO GREAT BRITAIN.—TORIES AND INDIANS.—MASSACRE AT MINISINK.—SLAUGHTER OF MR. KER'S CONGREGATION.—ANECDOTE OF HIM AND LAFAYETTE.—A FRIEND OF WASHINGTON.—LOANS THE GOVERNMENT EIGHT THOUSAND DOLLARS, FOR WHICH HE RECEIVED NOTHING BUT "OLD LIBERTY."—CELEBRATION AT THE CLOSE OF THE WAR... 365

CHAPTER XL.

JOHN HURST.—HIS PATRIOTISM.—SERMON TO THE SOLDIERS................. 372

CHAPTER XLI.

WILLIAM MCKAY TENNENT.—UNCERTAINTY AS TO HIS IDENTITY WITH THE SUBJECT OF THE FOLLOWING SKETCH.—PATRIOTIC SERMON DELIVERED BEFORE THE TROOPS AT TICONDEROGA.—HIS CAREER AFTER THE WAR.—HIS DEATH, 376

CHAPTER XLII.

MR. BOARDMAN.—CHAPLAIN TO DURKEE'S REGIMENT.—HIS DIARY.......... 382

CHAPTER XLIII.

MR. MAGOON.—EXTRACTS FROM HIS ADDRESS TO HASLETT'S BATTALION...... 389

CHAPTER XLIV.

THOMAS COOMBS.—SERMON ON FAST-DAY AND PATRIOTIC SENTIMENTS....... 392

CHAPTER XLV.

A ROMAN CATHOLIC CHAPLAIN.—CATHOLICS HAVE FOUGHT WITH PROTESTANTS FROM THE FIRST FOR LIBERTY.—CAUSE OF THIS SINGULAR COINCIDENCE.—FOURTH OF JULY ADDRESS... 394

CHAPTER XLVI.

A CHAPLAIN AT BRANDYWINE.—ADDRESS BEFORE THE BATTLE.............. 398

CHAPTER I.

Religious Element of the Revolution.—Not sufficiently dwelt on by Historians.—Influence and Action of Pastors.—Example of in Stockbridge, Mass.—Interesting Scene.

Notwithstanding the numberless books that have been written on the American Revolution, there is one feature of it which has been sadly overlooked. I mean the religious element. In this respect there is not a single history of that great struggle which is not so radically defective as to render the charge against it of incompleteness a valid one. This omission on the part of historians, seems the more remarkable from the fact that common belief, the universal impression, is against it. There has scarcely been a celebration of the day on which our independence was declared, in which this religious element is not referred to as constituting one of the chief features of the Revolution, yet it receives a subordinate place in history. One reason of this, doubtless, is, that it did not enter into the *machinery* of political or military life. It was not an organized force that could be numerically calculated or physically disposed of in making outward achievements.

To omit Religion in a history of the Crusades, would be like building a structure without laying a foundation, for that great movement was begun and carried forward by religious feeling alone. The banner that moved at the head of crowding millions was the Cross of Christ, and he that bore it a priest, while the great object to be accomplished was the rescue of the Sepulchre of the Saviour from infidel hands.

So of the English Revolution under Cromwell: no one would dream of writing its history without making religion and religious men a prominent and perpetual force. In short, a history that should ignore them, would be false and worthless. The reason is, that here, too, they formed a part of the physical machinery by which the revolution was carried on. The camp was a prayer-meeting—its passwords Scriptural phrases, and the dread slogan of the army the language of the sanctuary. Freedom and equal rights, was not the warcry of the Invincible Ironsides; but when they, with their helmets on, and their eyes bent in wrath on their enemies, swept like a thunder-cloud to battle, the charge-cry that rolled so terribly over the field was "Religion!"

In our Revolution the religious element was not paramount, and hence did not give shape and character to the whole physical structure and organization. It kept more within its appropriate sphere, and stood behind and sustained the political and military organizations of the land, rather than formed a part of them. But it is not on that account to be overlooked. He who forgets or under-estimates the moral forces that uphold or bear on a great struggle, lacks the chief qualities of a historian.

It is unquestionably true that, if the clergy of New England had from the outset taken the decided and determined stand *against* the cause of the colonies, which they did for it, *the result would have been totally different.* Why then should not they and their sermons, addresses, and prayers, have as prominent a place it the history of the Revolution, as town committees of safety, and local petitions, and resolutions, and remonstrances, which the historian thinks so necessary to the completeness of his narrative? That omission in our histories I design in these pages as far as possible to fill up.

There is some excuse for the historian in not giving a greater prominence to the religious element of the Revolution, for its development, force, and the efforts it caused to be put forth, did not take the shape of town meetings, and form part of the political and military records of the times. It is impossible, therefore, to collect together the unreported harangues, and sermons, and unorganized efforts that lay at the bottom of its power. I have had this difficulty to contend with an every step.

It is difficult in these days, when chaplains in the army are looked upon simply as a necessary part of its methodical organization, a set of half officers, half civilians who are not allowed to fight, and often can not preach, to get a proper conception of those times when their appeals thrilled the ranks, and made each hand clutch its weapon with a firmer grasp, and when their prayers filled each heart with a lofty enthusiasm. Then the people composed the army; and when the man of God addressed the crowding battalions, he addressed the young men and old men of his flock, who looked up to him with love and reverence, and believed him almost as they did the Bible. Could the history of each volunteer band, as it left its native valley—the enthusiasm kindled by the pastor's address, the courage imparted by his solemn parting blessing, and assurance that God smiled on them—be given, we should have a revolutionary page that would thrill the heart.

The religious sentiment was stronger in New England than in the other colonies, from the fact that the original settlers were driven there by religious persecution. Having fled across the ocean to secure religious freedom, it was natural they should consider it to be the chief end and purpose of all government. Hence all rules, regulations, and laws for their government, were, figuratively speaking, first baptized before they were allowed to become a part of the civil system. Hence, too, in the early wars of the colonies, chaplains became a necessary part of the army. Men who had been in the conventicles of Cromwell's troops, and heard Baxter preach and pray, would not be apt to forget a chaplain when organizing an expedition. The office at that time was no sinecure, nor unattended with danger, and men of nerve and force, as well as piety, were sought after.

Those who were chaplains during the French and Indian war became at its close pastors of churches, and although most of those who were alive at the breaking out of the Revolution were too old to become chaplains once more, they still held to their former belief in the right of resistance, and taught it in their congregations. The same was true of the entire clergy throughout the New England Colonies, and though some were not so positive and aggressive in their action as others, yet they were equally decided, and exerted though a quiet, a deep influence on the Revolution. They were humble pastors, from whose flocks were drawn the numberless little companies of minute-men, who formed the first army against which the tides of British valor rolled in vain on the heights of Bunker Hill. In every quiet little valley and sequestered nook in New England, the pastor had taught the doctrines of freedom, and preached the duty of resistance to oppression.

The farmers and mechanics listened with reverence and confidence to these teachings, and showed their faith by their works when the hour of trial came. At the battle-cry, that rolled over the land from Lexington and Concord, they shouldered their muskets, and went forth with the blessing of their pastor on their heads and his fervent prayers for their success following their footsteps. If the scenes that transpired in the countless villages and hamlets of New England, when the news of the first blood, shed by British troops, swept over the colonies, and the first uprising of the people took place, could be described, just as they occurred, in all the beauty, pathos, patriotism, and religion that characterized them, the Revolutionary struggle would possess an interest that all its thrilling battles and perilous marches, deeply as they enlist our sympathies, can never impart. The description of a single one, that took place in one of the remotest towns of Massachusetts — Old Stockbridge — must answer as an illustration of what transpired every where throughout the country.

For a long time matters had been drawing to a crisis; the colonists refused to yield their sacred rights, and the mother country steadily increased the pressure of her power to force obedience, till she could go no farther unless she resorted to military force. Hence the whole country was in a state of the most painful suspense and expectation. But firmly resolved to meet open force with force, they had arranged relays of horses and couriers along the highways and byeways of New England, to speed the news of the first shedding of American blood. To be ready for these fearful tidings, minute-men had been enrolled in every town, prepared to march on a moment's notice.

In Stockbridge, Berkshire County, Mass., Deacon Cleveland and another leading member of the church had been selected, for their positions in the centre of the valley and of the village, to spread the note of alarm. The son of the Deacon, a young man only seventeen years of age at the time, gave to a friend of the writer a description of the reception of the news in that little village.

One quiet Sabbath morning, when all was still, as it ever was in that peaceful valley on that holy day, he was suddenly startled by the report of a musket. On going out to ascertain what it meant, he saw his father in the back yard with the discharged piece in his hand. Before he had time to express his wonder, another report broke the stillness of the Sabbath morning, and as the smoke curled up in the damp atmosphere, he saw in the neighboring yard one of the chief pillars of the church, standing with his musket in his hand. He paused astounded, not knowing what awful phenomenon this strange event portended. He said that he thought the judgment day had come. But in a few moments he noticed men hurrying along the hitherto deserted street, with weapons in their hands. One by one they entered his father's gate, and gathered on the low stoop. The flashing eye and flushed cheek told that something eventful had transpired—and there had.

When the report of those two muskets echoed along the sweet valley of the Housatonic and up the adjacent slopes, the sturdy farmers knew what it meant. The father, just preparing for the duties of the sanctuary, heard it, and, flinging aside his Sabbath garments, hastily resumed his work-day dress, and taking down his musket strained his wife and children in one long farewell embrace to his bosom, then turned from the home he might never see again. The young man buckled on his knapsack, and amid sobs and tears shut the little farm gate behind him, the fire in his eye drying up the tears as fast as they welled to the surface. Although the heart heaved with emotion, the step was firm and the brow knit and resolute.

In a short time the little porch was crowded with men. A moment after, Dr. West, the pastor, was seen slowly descending the hill toward the same place of rendezvous. It was a cold, drizzly morning, and as, with his umbrella over his head, and the Bible under his arm, he entered the dooryard, his benevolent face revealed the emotion that was struggling within. He, too, knew the meaning of those shots; they were the signals agreed upon to inform the minute-men of Stockbridge that their brethren in the East had closed with the foe in battle. He ascended the steps, and, opening the Bible, read a few appropriate passages, and then sent up a fervent prayer to Heaven. When he ceased, the rattling of arms was heard. A short and solemn blessing closed the impressive scene, and before twelve o'clock twenty men, with knapsacks on their backs and muskets on their shoulders, had started on foot for Boston, nearly two hundred miles distant.

Oh, how deep down in the consciences of men had the principles of that struggle sunk, when they made those Puritans forget the solemn duties of the sanctuary for the higher duties of the battle-field. They had been taught from the pulpit that it was the cause of God, and they took it up in the full belief they had His blessing and His promise. Such scenes as these were enacted every where, and from the consecrating hand of the man of God went forth the thousand separate bands that soon after met and stood shoulder to shoulder on the smoking heights of Bunker Hill.

CHAPTER II.

Systematic Influence of the Clergy.—Election Sermons before the Revolution.—Election Sermons a part of the Proceedings of the Provincial Legislature.—Samuel Cook's Sermon, 1770.—Mr. Tucker's, in 1771.—Charles Turner's, in 1773.—Gad. Hitchcock's, in 1774.—"The Tea Overboard."—President Langdon's, in 1775.—"Bunker Hill,—Monitions of the Coming Storm."—These Sermons the Political Pamphlets of the Times.

THERE was one way in which the clergy of New England acted directly and systematically on the popular judgment and heart, in producing and sustaining the revolution which, it seems a little strange, should have escaped the attention of those historians, who have investigated so carefully the means by which it was brought about. I refer to the annual "election sermon," as it was called, that was preached before the Governor and House of Representatives, especially in Massachusetts, at the election of His Majesty's Council.

These sermons were as much a part of the stately and imposing ceremonies as the election itself. The ablest divines in the Colony were invited to deliver them—not as a mere compliment to religion, nor were they listened to simply with that quiet decorum and respectful attention, which is accorded in ordinary worship, but with the deep interest of those seeking light and instruction. The preachers did not confine themselves to a dissertation on doctrinal truths nor mere exhortation to godly behavior. They grappled with the great question of the rights of man, and especially the rights of the colonists in their controversy with the mother country. In reading these discourses one is struck with the thorough knowledge those divines possessed of the origin, nature, object, character and end of all true government. They dealt in no high sounding phrases of liberty and equality; they went to the very foundations of society, showed what the natural rights of man were, and how those rights became modified when men gathered into communities; how all laws and regulations were designed to be for the good of the governed; that the object of concentrated power was to protect not invade personal liberty, and when it failed to do this, and oppressed instead of protected, assailed instead of defended rights, resistance became lawful, nay, obligatory. They showed also the nature of compacts and charters, and applied the whole subject to the case of the Colonies.

The profound thought and unanswerable arguments, found in these sermons, show that the clergy were not a whit behind the ablest statesmen of the day in their knowledge of the great science of human government. In reading them one gets at the true pulse of the people, and can trace the steady progress of the public sentiment. They are like the hands of a clock that, at regular intervals, tell the time of day. The publication of these sermons in a pamphlet form was a part of the regular proceedings of the assembly, and being scattered abroad over the land, clothed with the double sanction of their high authors and the endorsement of the legislature, became the text books of human rights in every parish. They were regarded as the political pamphlets of the day. Thus the thorough indoctrination of the people into the duties and powers of government, the reciprocal obligations resting on them and the mother country were reduced to a system.

It must be remembered that newspapers at that day were a novelty, and ideas were not so easily disseminated as now. The pulpit, therefore, was the most direct and effectual way of reaching the masses. The House of Representatives of Massachusetts knew this, and passed resolutions requesting the clergy to make the question of the rights of the Colonies and the oppressive conduct of the mother country a topic of the pulpit on week days. They thus proclaimed to all future time their solemn convictions of their dependence on the pulpit for that patriotic feeling and unity of action, which they knew to be indispensable to success. Here, then, the historian can lay his hand on the deep, solid substratum that underlaid the Revolution.

Thus as far back as 1770 we can see in the election sermons of Massachusetts the dim foreshadowings of the coming contest. In that year Samuel Cook, of the Second Church of Cambridge, preached the sermon before Gov. Hutchinson, the Council and House of Representatives. He took for his text, 2 Samuel, xxiii. 3d and 4th verses: "He that ruleth over men must be just ruling in the fear of God. And he shall be as the light of the morning, when the sun riseth, even a morning without clouds, as the tender grass springing out of the earth by clear shining after rain." He did not apply this text primarily or chiefly to the duty of rulers to be just, virtuous and God fearing, but to them as *law makers*. As I remarked of the sermons in general, he began by describing the rights which man possessed in a state of nature, showed in what way they became modified when men were collected into communities, and framed laws for the protection of all. He thus gradually brought before them the design and end of true government, viz., the protection of the rights of all. Hence followed the necessity of obedience to laws and constitutions. While on this topic, he uttered a truth which men would do well to ponder at this day: "A free state," he says, "will no longer *continue so than while the constitution is maintained entire in all its branches and connections.*" He then quotes the New England Charter, and asserts that it is not an "act of *grace*, but a *compact*," a mutual agreement, the conditions of which, while the Colonies observe, the government at home must respect. He then speaks of the present indications of an attempt to concentrate the power in the hands of the governor, and declares, when that is accomplished, "the days of liberty are over." "America," he exclaims, now pleads her right to her possessions, which she can not resign while she apprehends she has truth and justice on her side." After thus ably explaining the rights of man by nature, the necessity of laws in communities, the object and end of government, the sacred nature of constitutions and compacts, and the duty of freemen to guard with jealous care the liberty guaranteed by them—he speaks of the present claims of the Colonists, which the government hesitates to acknowledge, and then turns to His Majesty's Governor and Council and the House of Representatives, and rings in their attentive listening ears, "These their claims the Americans consider not as novel and wantonly made, but founded in nature and in compact, in their rights as men and British subjects — the same which their forefathers, the first occupants, made and asserted at the time of their removal with their effects into this wilderness;" and winds up with, "Let every attempt to secure our liberties be conducted with manly fortitude, but with the respectful decency which reason approves, and which alone gives weight to the most salutary measures." Let His Majesty's Governor and Council hear that and ponder it well—let His Majesty across the ocean read it, for his subjects on this side will, and lay it to heart, and every pulpit will echo it. Thus five years before the children of a common stock closed in deadly conflict at Lexington and Concord did such ominous truths fall on the hearts of ruler and ruled.

[1771.]

The next year, on the 29th of May, John Tucker, of the First Church of Newbury, preached the sermon, taking his text from 1 Peter, ii. 13, 14, 15, 16: "Submit yourselves to every ordinance of man for the Lord's sake, whether it be the king as supreme," &c. This sermon reveals the increased excitement in the Colonies, and shows what a more determined and sterner attitude the clergy had taken. He goes over the same ground that Mr. Cook did with regard to the origin and design of government and the sacredness of compacts. While acknowledging that government is the work of man, he declares it derives all its powers from God, and hence its enactments must be in accordance with his will, and boldly asserts that "the people as well as their rulers are the proper judges of the civil constitution they are under and of their own rights and principles." When he comes to apply the text in requiring submission to rulers he enters into a full consideration of what kind of submission is due. He says the duties of ruled and ruler are reciprocal, and "Unlimited submission is not due to government in a free state. There are certain boundaries beyond which submission can not be justly required, and should not be yielded. They have," he says, "an undoubted privilege to complain of unconstitutional measures in government, and of unlawful encroachments upon their rights, and may, while they do it with becoming decency, do it with that noble freedom and firmness which a sense of wrong joined with the love of liberty will inspire." Warming with his subject he goes farther, and declares that they not only have a right to complain, but that resistance may become a duty. He does not, he says, presume to draw the line in the present controversy where resistance should begin, but declares, "Sirs, it is not necessary if our constitutional rights and privileges should be demanded, we should readily yield to the unrighteous claim. Should we thus meanly resign them up, and take in exchange the chains of slavery for ourselves and children, could we forgive ourselves? Would our unhappy posterity forgive us? Would we not deserve the punishment while we felt the guilt of assassins, for having stabbed the vitals of our country?" Well may that grave audience listen in breathless silence, and the Governor and Council look meaningly on each other, for in those swelling tones with which the minister of God pours forth these bold, exciting truths they hear the distant bugle call to rally for freedom. Such truths, sown broadcast over the land, and falling on hearts already on fire, exerted an influence that, at the present day, it is impossible to conceive. It must be remembered they were uttered at the seat of power by men of high standing and influence, and sent abroad by that power to the people.

[1773.]

In 1773 the sermon was preached by Charles Turner from Romans, xiii. 4, in which he meets the objection that ministers should not meddle in politics, and while he concedes its force in mere local matters, he boldly asserts that it is their duty to interfere where the liberties of the land are assailed, not only for the sake of their own posterity as well as that of others, but because "when the civil rights of a country receive a shock, it may justly render the ministers of God deeply thoughtful for the safety of sacred privileges— for religious liberty is so blended with civil, that if one falls it is not to be expected that the other will continue."

[1774.]

The next spring, May 25th, 1774, the tone of the election sermon, preached by Gad Hitchcock, of Pembroke, furnished the key-note of public feeling, and showed clearly the increased state of excitement and the stronger spirit of resistance abroad in the Colonies. He took his text from Prov. xxix. 2 : " When the righteous are in authority the people rejoice, but when the wicked bear rule the people mourn." The very text was like a trumpet call to battle. To appreciate fully its force, and the telling effect of the sermon on those who listened to it, and the people who read it, we must recall the exciting scenes of the autumn and winter that had passed. First came the news that a cargo of tea had been ordered to Boston, when the bells were set ringing, and the people hastened to Liberty Tree to consult on the matter. Exciting harangues were made, and a committee appointed to wait on the consignees, and to request them not to receive the tea. The whole town was in commotion, and Gov. Hutchinson, in alarm, prepared to flee to the " castle" for safety. Persuaded to desist from this rash act, he sat, irresolute and trembling, not knowing what to do. At length the tea came. The people resolved it should not be landed, and in December it went overboard, tumbled into the harbor by citizens disguised as Indians. The people then knew " that they had passed the river, and cut away the bridge." The cold and dreary storms that swept over Boston that winter were but a feeble emblem of the tempests of feeling and indignation that raged in the hearts of the inhabitants. Spring came, but the popular tempest showed no abatement. "Don't put off the boat," said the timid, "till you know where you will land." "We must," replied the bold, "though we *don't* know." "God will bring us into a safe harbor," thundered Hawley. British fleets and troops were on the way to enforce submission. The land rocked with excitement. The fearful undulations at Boston rolled southward to the Carolinas. Amid such fierce commotions within, and the gathering of hostile forces without, the House of Representatives met to choose a council for the coming year. Gad Hitchcock was selected to preach the opening sermon. Fresh from the people, whose excitement and indignation he shared, he arose in the presence of the hushed assemblage, and launched full on the bosom of the astonished Governor, "When the wicked bear rule, the people mourn." Having delivered this startling message, he did not follow it up with fierce denunciations like the preachers who addressed the covenanters, fleeing from the sword of Claverhouse. He was not addressing men about to close in battle with their foes, but a dignified body of law-makers, and his whole sermon was a clear and masterly exposition of government properly organized and administered, and of the sufferings of the people under oppressive rulers. He then stated boldly the grievances of the colonies, and the cause of the turbulent feeling and loud complaints that filled the land. Making each point tell on the present condition of things, he wound up his eloquent discourse in the following bold and startling language, "Our danger is not visionary but real; our contention is not about trifles, but about liberty and property, and not ours only, but those of posterity to the latest generation. * * * * If I am mistaken in supposing plans are formed and executing, subversive of our natural and chartered rights and privileges, and incompatible with every idea of liberty, *all America is mistaken with me.* Our continued complaints, our repeated humble, but fruitless, unregarded petitions and remonstrances, and, if I may be allowed the sacred allusion, our groanings that can not be uttered, are at once indications of our sufferings, and the feeling sense we have of them." Let the Governor in his chair of state hear it, we not only mourn, but with groanings that can not be uttered, and all because *the wicked rule.* The castle can not shelter him from that scorching thunderbolt. Families are divided, brother is arrayed against brother, friend against friend. Society is cut from its moorings, and hate and consternation reign on every side, and all because *the wicked bear rule.* King George may say the evils that produce this state of things are imaginary, but I tell you," says Gad Hitchcock, "and I tell the tyrant to his face, it is because *the wicked bear rule.*"

Such sermons had something to do with the Revolution as well as the appointing of committees and the drawing up of resolutions.

[1775.]

The next year, Dr. Langdon, president of Harvard College, was appointed to deliver the election sermon. The contest had then begun—blood had flowed at Lexington and Concord, and only three weeks before the battle of Bunker Hill had been fought. Boston was in possession of the British, and the Colonial Congress assembled at Harvard. There was no election of councillors, but it was the anniversary of the day fixed by charter for the election. The Congress was perplexed and ignorant what course to adopt. His Majesty's Governor was not there, neither would they elect a Council for His Majesty; and yet Congress had taken no decided steps toward the inauguration of an independent government.

Nevertheless until things assumed more definite shape they would fulfill, as far as they were concerned, the conditions of the Charter. They therefore met on the appointed day, and listened to a sermon from the learned Dr. LANGDON.

He took for his text Isaiah, i. 26: "And I will restore thy judges as at the first, and thy counsel as at the beginning. Afterward thou shalt be called the city of righteousness, the faithful city." Nothing could be more appropriate than this text. It shows in what perfect harmony the pulses of the clergy and the people beat. The latter did not now need any instruction as to their rights, or appeals to assert them. They had already asserted them at the point of the bayonet. The die was cast, and every one asked what would the end be. The capital was in the hands of the brutal soldiery, and the patriots were driven from their homes which they might never see again. In such a crisis, in such a state of feeling, how beautiful, how appropriate and encouraging is this full, rich promise.

He commences by saying, " Shall we rejoice, my fathers and brethren, or shall we weep together on the return of this anniversary, which from the first settlement of the Colony has been sacred to liberty, to perpetuate the invaluable privilege of choosing from among ourselves wise men fearing God and hating covetousness, to be honorable counsellors, to constitute an essential branch of that happy government which was established in the faith of royal charters?" He then compares the past joyful day of elections with the present anniversary when the capital is the stronghold of despotism. He goes over the successive acts of tyranny, describes the murder at Lexington and Concord, the slaying of women and infants, and enforces the necessity of repentance and the laying aside of every sin. But, after recounting all the disasters that have befallen them, and the sufferings they have endured, he turns to the cheering promise of the text, and says the past, instead of disheartening, should encourage them. "Let us praise God," he exclaims, in a subdued yet noble enthusiasm, " for the advantages already given us over the enemies of liberty—particularly that they have been so dispirited by repeated experience of the efficacy of our arms in the late action at Chelsea, when several hundred of our soldiery, the greater part open to the fire of so many cannon swivels and musketry from a battery advantageously situated, from two armed cutters full of marines, and from ships of the line in the harbor, not one man on our side was killed, and but two or three wounded, when a great number were killed and wounded on the other side, and one of the cutters taken and burnt. If God be for us, who can be against us? The enemy has reproached us for calling on his name, and professing our trust in him. They have made a mock of our solemn fasts and every appearance of Christianity in the land. On this account, by way of contempt, they call us saints, while their mouths are full of cursing and bitterness. And may we not be confident that the Most High who regards these things will vindicate his own honor, and plead our righteous cause against such enemies to his government as well as to our liberties. O may our camp be free from every accursed thing. May we be truly a holy people, and all our towns and cities of righteousness. Then the Lord will be our refuge and strength, a very present help in time of trouble, and we shall have no reason to be afraid, though thousands of our enemies set themselves against us round about, though all nature should be thrown into tumults and convulsions. He can command the stars in their courses to fight his battles, and all the elements to wage war with his enemies. He can destroy them with innumerable plagues, and send faintness into their hearts, so that the men of might shall not find their hands. May the Lord hear us in the day of trouble, and the name of the God of Jacob defend us, send us help from his sanctuary, and strengthen us out of Zion."

Such patriotic sentiments and noble encouragement by the venerated head of Harvard College, published and scattered through the army and over the country, performed a mission and secured results which have since been attributed to secondary causes only. Much is said of the intelligence, virtue, and submission to law which characterized our Revolution, while those who refer to it with so much pride forget, or at least fail to recognize, the fact that the rebellion in New England rested on the pulpit—received its strongest impulse, indeed its moral character, from it. The people were intelligent and moral, says the historian; but how came they so? Under what system of instruction, or by whose teachings was this state of things brought about? It is not sufficient that he should state the fact, he should give also the causes that produced it. It is not enough to point out to us the phenomenon, we want it explained.

CHAPTER III.

ELECTION SERMONS, PREACHED AFTER THE ASSEMBLING OF THE CONTINENTAL CONGRESS AND ORGANIZATION OF COLONIAL GOVERNMENT.—REV. WM. GORDON.—REV. SAMUEL WEST, OF DARTMOUTH, IN 1776.—BOLD APPEAL.

THE first election sermon, preached after the declaration of independence, shows clearly that the clergy kept *pari passu* with the civil authorities in their steady advance to a complete separation of the Colonies from the mother country; nay, rather with the people, who were constantly urging their representatives to more decided action. Two weeks after the bell at Independence Hall, in Philadelphia, rung out to a breathless multitude in the streets below, and over the excited land, "Proclaim liberty throughout all the land to all the inhabitants thereof," the Massachusetts House of Representatives assembled, by ordinance of the Continental Congress, to elect the annual councillors, and Wm. Gordon, of the Third Church of Roxbury, was called upon to preach the sermon. Acting no longer under the royal charter, but under the higher authority of the Continental Congress, the delegates assembled to elect those who should recognize the new, self-constituted government, and yield obedience to it alone. It was a position well calculated to alarm the timid, and fill all with the most serious reflections. Previous to entering on their duties, they wished to hear what the servant of God had to say. They had heard from the Continental Congress, and before proceeding further it became them to listen to a message from the Lord of Hosts. Mr. Gordon took his text from Jeremiah, xxx. 20, 21: " Their children shall be as aforetime, and their congregation shall be established before me, and I will punish all that would oppress them. And their nobles shall be of themselves." After quoting thus far, he paused for a moment, and then added, in an altered tone, " The sentence is not perfected without the addition of '*and the government shall proceed from the midst of them*,' but the wisdom of the Continental Congress, in which we cheerfully confide, has restrained me from making it a part of the text. In an abler hand, at some fitter time, it may of itself alone suffice for a complete text. *Amen, so let it be.*" It is clear at the outset where *he* stands. He has no hesitation, no misgivings, no fears, but is willing to make a clean sweep, and take the whole text, and apply it in the name of the Lord. He chooses, however, to occupy the high position maintained by the clergy all over the land, and which conduced so much to the regard for law and authority, which was exhibited in such a marvellous degree in the midst of revolution—viz.: supporters of the civil authority, instead of independent leaders. The sentence, however, contains more than a peaceful recognition of the authority of the Continental Congress, it embodies a prophecy, and significantly hints at the near approach of the day when another will preach in the presence of a governor chosen " from the midst of them," and the " *Amen,*

so let it be," reveals the deep enthusiasm of his patriotic heart, and at the same time exhibits the prophet-like boldness of his spirit. After giving that portion of the history of the Jewish nation, to which this text applied, and drawing a parallel between it and that of the Colonies, and showing how repentance for sin was indispensable to the result foretold in the prophecy, and stating that the same was necessary now to obtain like results, he says, "A man of timid make and little faith, no ways conversant with or forgetful of historical facts, may be apprehensive that, though our assembly is gathered, and we are about to have our nobles of ourselves, this government will not be established, and the present appearances are only like those sudden revivals that frequently precede the total extinction of life. He may tremble at the thought of the power, with whom we are to contend. He may be terrified with the notion that sooner or later we must fall before it." * * * * *
Proceeding in this strain, he says, "If the cause of the ministry was the cause of the united nation, were not England in debt, a millstone of £30,000,000 hanging round her neck— did the policy of France and Spain coincide with England, and were there no wide Atlantic separating us—had we no officers of merit— had the Colonies been less united and zealous—had not the individuals of the Continental Congress, regardless of threats and wrath like the roaring of lions, boldly ventured to engage in maintaining our common rights upon forming and supporting a continental army, and in appointing able generals to command it,

in whom we can confide and do rejoice—had they not adopted those measures which will expose them to suffer as rebels unless success prevents them : then we might have a fearful looking for of fiery trials of a long continuance, and might have felt great discouragement. But when, besides the favorable circumstances already hinted at, we reflect upon the military spirit that the Lord of Hosts hath providentially diffused through the continent, and that God has wonderfully appeared for us, crowning our military operations with unusual success, and disconcerting those of the enemy — that the British troops, instead of ranging at large without opposition and driving the country before them, and being at liberty to riot on the fat of the land, and to gratify their brutal lusts upon our wives and daughters, are confined within narrow limits by those whom they have been taught to consider as infamous cowards—that our people, who have suffered the most, and been reduced to hardships before unknown, have been strangely preserved from fainting and dejection, as though by the special interposition of heaven, * * * when we further reflect upon the importance and goodness of our cause, and that on the side of the administration have been all manner of lies, deceit and wicked cunning, corruption, profaneness, and blasphemy, we are justified in hoping that the proceedings of this day, instead of being the last of the kind, will prove the renewal of our constitutional privileges, and that *this* mode of government will be established before the Lord. We should certainly rebel against the Sovereign of the Universe in his providential dispensation, and reject the divine council communicated to us by that medium, did we not resolve to persist in our present opposition to the wicked designs of an arbitrary ministry."

The whole sermon is a clear, logical, and patriotic appeal to the House, and he winds up with this bold, direct declaration; as though he were a judge addressing a jury on a question of law, instead of a clergyman exhorting his hearers to righteousness. "No member can consistently take his place, or sit in the House of Assembly, who hesitates about setting up government, seeing Congress has advised to it, and *he that does not mean to bear a part in the public burdens of the day,* but to escape wholly unhurt in person and *property, is no patriot.*" Enlarging on the duty of each one to help in the common cause, and put his hands to the work, he concludes: "May heaven influence every one of us to contribute our best abilities, according to our several stations and relations, to the defense and support of the common weal. AMEN."

It requires no vivid imagination to conceive the effect of such declarations and sentiments as these on a people who regarded the minister as the oracle of God, speaking not merely with the lofty determination and courage of a patriot, but fortifying his utterance with, "*Thus saith the Lord of Hosts.*" Follow such a sermon as this, published by authority of the Provincial Congress, as it goes into every parish of the Colony, and is read by the pastor and the leading men of his congregation, and you will cease to wonder that the soldiers drawn from those parishes should be law-abiding and not given to excesses in the midst of revolution. Patriotism is grafted on religion, and while, in obedience to the former, they strike for freedom, they do it as God-fearing men. Their duty to their country and to their Maker is so blended that they can not be separated; hence their patriotism becomes tinctured with religion, while their religion embraces patriotism in its circle of obligations. With the Israelite to serve his country was to serve his God. The same doctrine was taught everywhere throughout the New England Colonies, and accepted as truth. Resistance to oppressive laws and edicts was not merely the act of independent freemen struggling for their rights, but obedience to the high mandates of heaven.

[1776.]

In 1776, the attitude of the Colonies had become fixed. A separate government had been organized in them all, and hence there was no longer any need to discuss the general principles of government, and educate the people into the belief that resistance to oppression was a duty. The great object now was to convince all that the *new* government was *legal*, and ought to be obeyed. The right to resist tyranny, and struggle against the attempt to enforce decrees and laws that would reduce them to slavery, had been proved, until all believed in a redress of grievances; but the transfer of allegiance from a sovereign that had long been acknowledged, to a throne or king as it were of their own creation was an entirely different matter. Besides, a few years since the very clergy who now gave in their adherence to the new government, and exhorted the people to follow their example, had preached the same duty of submission to the government of the mother country and to the rulers she appointed over them. It was not so easy to take the very same texts by which they then urged obedience to the king, and prove by them that they no longer owed it, nay, that the divine authority that enforced it then, now demanded its transfer. The clergy felt this difficulty, but they grappled with it boldly. Toryism was the great evil to be eradicated; and hence to prove not merely the right, but the solemn duty to renounce forever all allegiance to the English throne, was the first great step towards success.

It was for this purpose Samuel West, of Dartmouth, in the election sermon of 1776, took for his text the first verse of the 3d chapter of Titus, "Put them in mind to be subject to principalities and powers, to obey magistrates, to be ready to every good work." He commenced by enunciating this great principle, "The great Creator, having designed the human race for society, has made us dependent on one another for happiness—he has so constituted us that it becomes both our interest and duty to seek the public good." He showed that the development of the social affections, the action of the benevolent principle implanted in our natures, and the moral faculties given us to discern the difference between good and evil, right and wrong, all proved the necessity of a civil government. As a consequence, obedience to it was obligatory on all. But the same good will to others and desire for justice, which make us acquiesce in civil government, would oblige us equally to resist tyranny which cares neither for the happiness nor right of the subject; for, said he, "*tyranny and magistracy are so opposed to each other that where one begins the other ends.*" After enlarging with great clearness and force on these propositions, he applied the subject to the controversy between the two countries. "Tyranny and arbitrary power," he says, "are utterly inconsistent with and subversive of the very design of civil government, and all political law, consequently the authority of a tyrant, is null and void." He declared that God never gave any man the right to trample on the liberty of his creatures, and "no number of men can confer a right they do not possess, viz., to take away liberty." After proving conclusively, "that representation and taxation are inseparably connected," he adds, "and when great numbers emigrate to a foreign land, so that they can not properly be represented at home, they have a right to legislate for themselves." He thus goes on, step by step, and proceeds to show that the Colonies have acted not only in strict accordance with the Divine purpose, in organizing civil government, but with the principles of justice and common sense. Having thus cleared every thing from his path, as he advanced in his argument, he closed it by boldly declaring that "*any* people, when cruelly oppressed, had a right to throw off the yoke, and be free." He proved this from the history of the Israelites, quoting the commands of God to break the bonds of oppression, and showed that no people ever had a clearer right to rebel from this cause than ourselves. Acting on it, he said, "we have made our appeal to heaven, and we can not doubt that the judge of all the earth will do right." Having clearly proved that the duty of allegiance ends where tyranny begins, he passes from the discussion of the principle, to the enumeration of those acts of the British government which demonstrate its tyrannical character. After speaking of its violation of charter rights and enactment of oppressive laws, he says, " Need I, upon this occasion, descend to particulars ? Can any one be ignorant what the things are of which we complain ? Does not every one know that the King and Parliament have assumed to tax us without our consent ? And can any one be so lost to principles of humanity and common sense as not to view their conduct in the affair as a very grievous imposition ? Reason and equity require that no one be obliged to pay the tax that he has never consented to. * * * Can any one suppose it to be reasonable that a set of men, that are perfect strangers to us, should have the uncontrollable right to lay the most heavy and grievous burdens upon us, if they please, purely to gratify their unbounded avarice and luxury ? Must we be obliged to perish with cold and hunger to maintain them in idleness, in all kinds of debauchery and dissipation? But, if they have the right to take our property from us without our consent, we must be wholly at their mercy for food and raiment, and we know, by sad experience, that their tender mercies are cruel. But, because we are not willing to submit to such an unrighteous and cruel decree, though we modestly complained, and humbly petitioned for a redress of grievances, instead of hearing our complaints, and granting our requests, they have gone on to add iniquity to transgression, by making several cruel and unrighteous acts. Who can forget the cruel act to block up the harbor of Boston, whereby thousands of innocent persons must have been inevitably ruined had they not been supported by the continent? Who can forget the act for vacating the charter altogether, with many other cruel acts, which it is needless to mention? But, not being able to accomplish their wicked purpose by mere acts of Parliament, they have proceeded to commence hostilities against us, and have endeavored to destroy us by fire and sword—our towns they have burned, our brethren they have slain, our vessels they have taken, and our goods they have spoiled. And after all this wanton exertion of arbitrary power is there the man, that has any of the feelings of humanity left, who is not fired with a noble indignation against such merciless tyrants, who have not only brought upon us all the horrors of civil war, but have also added a piece of barbarity unknown to Turks and Mahommedan infidels; yea, such as would be abhorred and detested by the savages of the wilderness. I mean their cruelly forcing our brethren, whom they have taken prisoners, without any distinction of whig or tory, to serve on board their ships of war, thereby obliging them to fight against their brethren, their wives and children, and to assist in plundering their own estates. This, my brethren, is done by men, who call themselves Christians, against their Christian brethren—against men who till now gloried in the name of Englishmen, and who were ever ready to spend their lives and fortunes in the defence of British rights. Tell it not in Gath, publish it not in the streets of Askalon, lest it cause our enemies to rejoice, and our adversaries to triumph. It is an indispensable duty, my brethren, which we owe to God and our country, to rouse up and bestir ourselves; and being animated with a noble zeal for the sacred cause of liberty, to defend our lives and fortunes to the shedding of the last drop of blood. The love of our country, the tender affection that we have for our wives and children, and the regard that we ought to have for unborn posterity—yea, every thing that is dear and sacred—do now loudly call on us to use our best endeavors to save our country. We must turn our plowshares into swords, and our pruning-hooks into spears, and learn the art of self-defence against our enemies. To be careless and remiss, or to neglect the cause of our country through the base motives of avarice or self-interest, will expose us, not only to the resentments of our fellow-creatures, but to the displeasure of God Almighty. For to such base wretches, in such a time as this, we may apply, with the utmost propriety, the passage in Jer. xlviii. 10: 'Cursed be he that doeth the work of the Lord deceitfully, and *cursed be he that keepeth back his sword from blood.*' To save our country from the hands of our oppressors ought to be dearer to us than our lives, and next the eternal salvation of our souls, the thing of greatest importance—a duty so sacred that it can not be dispensed with for the sake of our secular concerns. Doubtless for this reason God has manifested his anger against those who have refused to assist their country against its cruel oppressors. Hence, in a case similar to our own, when the Israelites were struggling to deliver themselves from the tyranny of Jabin, the King of Canaan, we find a most bitter curse denounced against those who refused to grant their assistance in the common cause. Vide Judges, v. 23: 'Curse ye Meroz (said the angel of the Lord), curse ye bitterly the inhabitants thereof, because they came not up to the help of the Lord, to the help of the Lord against the mighty.' Now, if such a bitter curse is denounced against those who refused to assist their country against oppressors, what a dreadful doom are those exposed to, who have not only refused to assist their country in this time of distress, but have, through motives of interest or ambition, shown themselves enemies to their country, by opposing us in the measures we have taken, and by openly favoring the British Parliament. He, that is so lost to humanity as to be willing to sacrifice his country for the sake of avarice or ambition, has arrived at the highest stage of wickedness that human nature is capable of, and deserves a much worse name *than I at present care to give him;* but I think I may with propriety say that such a person has *forfeited his right to human society, and that he ought to take up his abode, not among the savage men, but among the savage beasts of the wilderness.*" The calm opening of this discourse, the careful, argumentative manner, in which he attempted to justify the course of the Colonies in asserting their independence, and to prove that it was the duty of every one to yield obedience to their authority, gave no forewarning of this terrible peroration. By slow steps, but gathering impetus and power, as he moved on in the path of his great argument, he at last turned in fierce wrath on the enemies of his country; and, prophet-like, hurled the vengeance of God against all who, in this hour of trial and gloom, stood aloof from its holy cause. The very slowness with which the storm had gathered made its bursting the more terrible, and the excited accents of the indignant minister of God rolled like angry thunder over the silent, breathless assembly. Its retiring murmurs left every soul serious and solemn; and a sense of greatly added responsibility rested on all, as, with a changed voice and countenance, he closed the sacred volume, saying, "Let us look upon freedom from the power of tyrants as a blessing that can not be purchased too dear, and let us bless God that he has so far delivered us from the idolatrous reverence which men are so apt to pay to arbitrary tyrants, and let us pray that he would be pleased graciously to perfect the mercy he has begun to show us, by confounding the devices of our enemies, and bringing their counsels to naught, and by establishing our just rights and privileges upon such a firm and lasting basis that the powers of earth and hell shall not prevail against it."

This sermon rung like a trumpet-call through the Colony, strengthening wavering hearts, and giving renewed boldness and fervor to the clergy every where.

CHAPTER IV.

SERMONS DURING THE WAR.—SERMON OF SAMUEL WEBSTER, IN 1777.—BOLD AND PATRIOTIC PRAYER.—DISCOURSE OF PHILIP PAYSON, OF CHELSEA, 1778.—ELOQUENT APPEAL.—PROPHETIC VISION.

I SHALL give but two more of these election sermons, delivered at the center of influence in the New England Colonies, as illustrations of the spirit that animated the clergy as the war progressed, and to show that, as Aaron and Hur upheld the hands of Moses when Joshua smote the Amalekites, so they strengthened and stayed up the hands of the civil power through the long struggle of the Revolution. In the spring of 1777, after the successive disasters that had overtaken the American army — the defeat on Long Island, the fall of New York and Fort Washington, and the flight of Washington and his disorganized army through the Jerseys — a year wrapped in gloom and fraught with sad forebodings, with only one gleam of sunshine—the battle of Princeton—to cheer the desponding hearts of the patriots, we find Samuel Webster preaching the election sermon before the House of Representatives, from Ezekiel, 45th chapter, part of 8th and 9th verses : "My princes shall no more oppress my people, and the rest of the land shall they give to the house of Israel, according to their tribes. Thus saith the Lord God. Let it suffice you, O princes of Israel, remove violence and spoil, and execute judgment and justice, and take away your exactions from my people, saith the Lord God."

He commenced his discourse by congratulating them on the delivery of Boston from the hands of the British. He then enlarged on the duty of princes and rulers, but, ignoring those which the mother country wishes to fasten on them, addresses those appointed by the people, and says: "As to old-fashioned rulers, hackneyed to the ways of the world, the voice from heaven cries to them to oppress no more. It cries most solemnly in my text. But, as such rulers hear neither God nor man, we have no immediate business with them. *And God grant we never may.*" The sermon is full of biting sarcasm on the British government, and solemn appeals to the representatives of the people to be true to their trust, telling them however that, notwithstanding their best endeavors, they will all be in vain, unless they depend on something besides an arm of flesh—that their great reliance must be on the Lord of Hosts, who was always able to deliver Israel in the most discouraging circumstances, and will deliver their country from its oppressors if the people call upon him in truth:—he closed with this remarkable prayer: "*Awake, O Lord, for our help, and come and save us. Awake, O Lord, as in ancient times. Do with them, O Lord, if it be thy will, as thou didst unto the Midianites and their confederates, and to Sisera, and to Jabin, when they unjustly and without provocation invaded thy people, and make their lords, and nobles, and great commanders like Oreb and Zeeb, and like Zeba and Zalmunna. Though these angry brethren* *profess to worship the same God with us, yet because it is in somewhat different mode they seem to have said, come let us take the houses of God in possession. Accordingly they have vented a peculiar spite against the houses of God, defaced and defiled thy holy and beautiful sanctuaries where our fathers worshiped thee, turning them into houses of merchandise and receptacles of beasts, and some of them they have torn in pieces and burned with fire. Therefore we humbly pray that thou wilt hedge up their way, and not suffer them to proceed and prosper. But put them to flight speedily, if it be thine holy will, and make them run fast as a wheel downward, or as fast as stubble and chaff is driven before the furious whirlwind. As the fire consumes the wood, and sometimes lays waste whole forests on the mountains, so let them be laid waste and consumed if they obstinately persist in their bloody designs against us.* Lord, raise a dreadful tempest and affright them, and let thy tremendous storms make them quake with fear, and pursue them with thine arrow, till they are brought to see that God is with us of a truth, and fighteth for us, and so return to their own lands, covered with shame and confusion, and humble themselves before thee, and seek to appease thine anger by a bitter repentance for their murderous designs. And let them have neither credit nor courage to come out any more against us. That so all nations, seeing thy mighty power and thy marvellous works, may no more call themselves supreme, but know and acknowledge that thou art God alone, the only supreme Governor among men, doing whatsoever pleaseth thee.*

And so let thy glorious name be magnified in all the earth, till time shall be no more. And let all the people say AMEN *and* AMEN."

[1778.]

As the clergy performed the most active and important part in the education of the people of New England for the Revolution, as well as strengthened and encouraged them in the darkest hours, by patriotic exhortations and promises of final deliverance, and heaven's richest blessings on them and their posterity, for their noble endeavors and heroic sacrifices; so they rejoiced with them in every success, and declared it to be the sign of God's blessing and the precursor of a glorious morning at hand. Thus, in 1778, at the turning point of the struggle, directly after Burgoyne's overthrow, and while the land was still rocking to the enthusiastic rejoicings of the people, who believed they saw in it the first gleam of the coming dawn, PHILIP PAYSON, of Chelsea, in his sermon before the House of Representatives, gave utterance to the universal feeling. He took for his text Galatians, iv. 26, 27: " But Jerusalem, which is above, is free, which is the mother of us all. For it is written, Rejoice thou barren that bearest not, break forth, and cry thou that travaillest not, for the desolate hath many more children than she which hath a husband."

Like all those who preached on these anniversaries, the main body of the discourse was adapted to meet the character and duties of the audience of rulers before him. He spoke of the blessings of liberty, called their attention to the different forms of government adapted to different states of society, as Greece and Rome, showed that the great requisites of a stable government were education, religion, and patriotism, as well as courage, military discipline, and union ; and then passed to the description of just rulers, their high vocation and responsibility, and pointed out their solemn duties, and said, " When these are the characteristics of our country we shall be like the Jerusalem above."

Fired with the contemplation, and rising with his theme, he suddenly exclaims : " Indulgent heaven seems to invite and urge us to accept the blessing. A kind and wonderful Providence has conducted us, by astonishing steps, as it were, within sight of the promised land. We stand this day upon Pisgah's top, the children of the free woman, the descendants of a pious race, who, from the love of liberty and the fear of God, spent their treasure and spilt their blood. Animated by the same great spirit of liberty, and determined, under God, to be free, these states have made one of the noblest stands against despotism and tyranny that can be met with in the annals of history, ancient or modern. One common cause, one common danger, and one common interest, have united us to the most vigorous exertions. We have been all along the scorn and derision of our enemies—but the care of heaven, and the charge of God. And hence our cause and union, like the rising sun, have shone brighter and brighter. Thanks be to God ! we this day behold, in the fullness of our spirit, the great object of our wishes, of our toils and wars, brightening in our view. The battles we have already fought, and the victories we have won (*vid.* Saratoga), the pride of tyranny that must needs have been humbled, mark the characters of the freemen of America with distinguished honor, and will be read with astonishment by generations yet unborn."

He continued for some time to speak in this strain, of what God had done for us, as an evidence that he watched over our destinies, and would take care of our interests even to the end ; and then, in view of the wrongs we had suffered, exclaimed : " Is it possible for us to behold the ashes, the ruins of large and opulent towns that have been burnt in the most wanton manner ; to view the graves of our dear countrymen, whose blood has been most cruelly spilt ; to hear the cries and screeches of our ravished matrons and virgins, that had the misfortune to fall into the enemies' hands—and think of returning to the cruel and bloody power which has done all these things ? No ; we are not to suppose such a thought can dwell in the mind of a free and sensible American. The same feelings in nature that led a Peruvian prince to choose the *other place,* must also teach us to prefer connection with any other people on the globe rather than with those from whom we have experienced such unrighteous severities and unparalleled cruelties." He then paid a short tribute to the good who had fallen, and who, he said, " shall be held in everlasting remembrance ;" and urged on all the necessity of continued, untiring effort, if they would win the glorious prize of complete independence.

While, in imagination, he thus beheld our final triumph, and called up before his mental vision the spectacle of a free people, guiding and controlling, under God, their own destinies, he seemed suddenly to be filled with prophetic fire, and rapt with the inspiring view that, far beyond the bloody battle-fields, rose on the future, he exclaimed : " To anticipate the future glory of America from our present hopes and prospects is ravishing and transporting to the mind. In this light we behold our country beyond the reach of all oppressors—under the great charter of independence, enjoying the purest liberty, beautiful and strong in its union, the envy of tyrants and devils, but the delight of God and all good men, a refuge to the oppressed, the joy of the earth ; each state happy in a wise model of government, and abounding in wise men, patriots and heroes ; the strength and ability of the whole continent collected in a grave and venerable council, at the head of all, seeking and promoting the good of the present and future generations. HAIL, MY HAPPY COUNTRY, SAVED OF THE LORD ! HAPPY LAND ! EMERGED FROM THE DELUGES OF THE OLD WORLD, DROWNED IN LUXURY AND LEWD EXCESS ! HAIL, HAPPY POSTERITY, THAT SHALL REAP THE PEACEFUL FRUITS OF OUR SUFFERINGS, FATIGUES AND WAR !"

It is needless to dwell on the encouraging, inspiriting effect of such a sermon as this on both the Representatives in Provincial Congress assembled, and on the clergy and their congregations throughout the Colonies ; but the prophecy and invocation at the close are certainly most noteworthy, and seem like a direct inspiration from heaven, not merely as foretelling the future independence and glory of the country, but the exact form and character of the government so boldly sketched. Through three years of doubtful war, and all the troubles, and dangers, and uncertainty, that surrounded and retarded the formation of a new government, he saw the union of states, "*each one happy in a wise model of government,*" while "*the strength and ability of the whole continent, collected in a grave and venerable council, is at the head of all, seeking and promoting the good of the present and future generations.*" This uttered fifty years after would have been literal history. Here was the outline of the great confederacy which was eventually formed with so much labor, and which made us "the refuge of the oppressed, the joy of the earth." One can imagine with what intent attitude and breathless silence the Representatives listened to this prophetic outburst, and for the moment forgot the perils that surrounded them, and the sore trials that awaited them in the contemplation of this vision of their country free and happy. It seemed as if God himself were calling on them to untiring exertion and firm trust by his promise of success.

CHAPTER V.

Personal Influence of the Clergy.—Appointment of Chaplains.—Correspondence between the Ministers of Connecticut and Massachusetts.—Thaxter, Foster and Payson fighting at Lexington and Concord.—Washington asks Congress for Chaplains.—Number and Names of, in the Army at Cambridge.—The Plan of one for two Regiments broken up.—Washington's Second Letter to Congress on the Subject.—His General Order respecting Chaplains.—David Ely.—Joseph Fish.—Jonah Stearns.—John Mills.—David Caldwell.—Thomas Read.—Robert Davidson.—Elizur Goodrich.—Wm. Gorham.—John Steele.—Francis Cummings.—Azel Roe.—Hezekiah Balch.—Charles McKnight.—Manasseh Cutler.—Nathan Strong.—Nathaniel Porter.—Annie Robins.—John Cleveland.—Samuel McClintock.—Hezekiah Ripley.—Isaac Lewis.—Dr. Latta.—Dr. Armstrong.

HAVING endeavored briefly to illustrate the influence of the clergy on the Revolution in New England, by showing the systematic, direct power they brought to bear on the representatives of the people, and through them on every pastor and congregation in the Colony, a power more formidable than could be wielded by solemn acts of associations or synods, and as deserving of special recognition as the organization of town committees and the resolutions of councils of safety; I come now to speak more of *personal* influence and actions, of individual clergymen in their respective circles and stations. The annual sermon preached at the meeting of the representatives of the people was a *representative* sermon. Its sentiments were regarded as those of the great body of the clergy throughout the Colony, and hence went before the people with the highest authority and the most solemn sanctions. They had, besides, the indorsement of the civil power, and hence ceased to be *individual* views, and became those of the clergy and the Provincial Congress united. But as in the army and in the civil government the great results finally reached are not to be attributed exclusively to the official acts of bodies of men or of those in high authority, so the tremendous influence wielded by the clergy was not wholly confined to those acts sanctioned by councils or by Congress. Patriotic, energetic individuals in all departments did their share of the work, and exhibited traits of heroism and a devotion to the common cause which entitle them to a place among the good and great names of the Revolution, that have become embalmed in our memory, and consigned to a glorious immortality.

The appointment of clergymen to official positions in the army and navy, under the designation of chaplains, is a custom of long standing; and, at the present day, among Christian nations is considered necessary to their complete organization. It would have been natural, therefore, for Congress, as a mere matter of custom, and in imitation of the mother country, to appoint chaplains in the American army. They did so; and chaplains, at the present time, form a part of our military organizations, and rank as officers, and draw pay like them. The propriety of this custom is recognized by all—for the sick, the suffering and dying need spiritual advisers as much as they do hospitals and surgeons.

But I do not design to speak of the office exclusively, or of those who simply discharged its duties faithfully. A vast number were appointed more for their outside general influence, than because they were earnest, self-denying ministers of God—not that they were not greatly esteemed and valued in this respect, but they were bold and active patriots besides, stirring up rebellion, encouraging the weak and timid by their example as well as by their teachings, and inspiring the brave and true with confidence by their heroism and lofty trust in the righteousness of the cause they vindicated. It is with this class of chaplains and clergy that I have chiefly to do.

A chaplain, when taken prisoner, is usually treated with great courtesy and consideration, but there was a class of clergymen and chaplains in the Revolution, whom the British, when they once laid hands on them, treated with the most barbarous severity. Dreading them for the influence they wielded, and hating them for the obstinacy, courage and enthusiasm they infused into the rebels, they violated all the usages of war among civilized nations, in order to inflict punishment upon them.

Suffering for their patriotism, as these clergy did, and expecting a halter if the Colonies should fail in their effort to obtain freedom, they deserve to be remembered with honor, and have their names go down to immortality, linked with that most important struggle in the world's history. In the first gathering of the yeomanry at Lexington and Concord, as well as afterwards in the miscellaneous enthusiastic assembling of the army around Bunker Hill, they bore an important part, not merely as servants of God in the discharge of their official duties, but as patriots—haranguing the soldiers, and even leading them into the conflict.

The British were aware of the tremendous influence the clergy wielded in the Colonies, and saw with alarm that it was thrown on the side of rebellion. Indeed they were accused of being at the bottom of it. In 1774, the Governor of Massachusetts refused the request of the Assembly to appoint a fast—"For," said he, "the request was only to give an opportunity for sedition to flow from the pulpit." "The taking away of civil liberty," wrote the ministers of Connecticut to their brethren of Boston, "will involve the ruin of religious liberty also. * * * Bear your heavy load with Christian fortitude and resolution." The answer came back: "While we complain to heaven and earth of the cruel oppression we are under, we ascribe righteousness to God. The surprising union of the Colonies affords encouragement. It is an inexhaustible source of comfort that the Lord omnipotent reigneth."

As before hostilities commenced, there was scarcely a military muster at which they were not present, exhorting the militia to stand up manfully for the cause of God—on some occasions saying, "Behold, God himself is with us for our captain, and his priests with sounding trumpets to cry the alarm"—it was to be expected, when war actually broke out, they would be found in the ranks of the rebels, urging forward what they had so long proclaimed as a religious duty. The first outbreak at Lexington and Concord gave them no opportunity to exhibit their zeal officially, and so some shouldered their muskets, and fought like common soldiers. Among these were Thaxter, of Westford, and Foster, who showed that they could fight as well as pray.

There, too, was the amiable and learned Payson, of Chelsea. He was so adverse to bloodshed and all the horrors of war that he had felt it his duty to preach patience and even submission. His bolder and more resolute brethren near him took such umbrage at this that they refused to let him preach in their pulpits. They wanted no conciliatory doctrines taught to their people. The brutal outrage at Lexington transformed this peaceful scholar and meek divine into the fiery, intrepid soldier, and seizing a musket he put himself at the head of a party, and led them forward to the attack. The gentle voice that had so long spoken only words of peace suddenly rung like that of a prophet of old. A body of British soldiers advancing along the road, he poured into them such a destructive volley that the whole were slain or taken prisoners. He was a man of peace and conciliation, but the first citizen's blood that crimsoned the green sward made a clean sweep of all his arguments and objections, and he entered with his whole soul into the struggle.

At a later day, when Washington assumed command of the army at Cambridge, he found chaplains attached to the different regiments sent from the various Colonies—some of them volunteers without pay, and others regularly appointed by the Provincial Congress. As the organization of the army was perfected, measures were adopted for their provision by the general Congress, and their number and the regiments to which they belonged formed a part of the regular army returns of Washington.

At first they were not numerous, as the government had taken no action on the subject, but its attention was soon called to it, and on May 25th, 1775, we find a committee of the Provincial Congress of Massachusetts reporting:

"*Whereas* it has been represented to this Congress that several ministers of the religious assemblies within this Colony have expressed their willingness to attend the army* in the capacity of chaplain, as they may be directed by the Congress, therefore

Resolved, That it be and is hereby recommended to the ministers of the several religious assemblies within the Colony that, with the leave of their congregations, they attend said army in their several towns to the number of thirteen at one time, during the time the army shall be encamped, and that they make known their resolution to the Congress thereon, or to the committee of safety, as soon as may be."

Washington, who in the French and Indian war had more than once requested the Governor of Virginia to allow him a chaplain for his regiment, saw with the deepest gratification this early determination of the New England Colonies to supply their regiments with regular chaplains, and encouraged it in every way he

---

* Under Artemas Ward.

could. On August 15th, 1775, he reported fifteen chaplains who performed service for twenty-three regiments, while twenty-nine were without any. In September there were twenty regiments supplied and twenty vacancies. On October 17th there were twenty-two against nineteen; November 18th, twenty-one against eighteen; December 13th, nineteen to twenty-two; and January 9th, 1776, nine to eighteen.* On the last of December, 1775, Washington wrote to the Continental Congress as follows:

"I have long had it in my mind to mention it to Congress, that frequent applications have been made to me respecting the chaplains' pay, which is too small to encourage men of abilities. Some of them who have left their flocks are obliged to pay the parson acting for them more than they receive. I need not point out the great utility of gentlemen, whose lives and conversation are unexceptionable, being employed in that service in this army. There are two ways of making it worthy the attention of such. One is an

---

* The warrants varied somewhat in the different Colonies, but the following form, adopted in Connecticut, will answer as a sample of all:—

"To Rev. ———, greeting:—Reposing special trust and confidence in your piety, ability, fidelity and good conduct, I do hereby appoint you, the said ———, a chaplain of the ——— regiment, and do hereby authorize and empower you to exercise the several acts and duties of your office and station as chaplain of the said regiment, which you are faithfully to perform in a due and religious discharge thereof, according to the important trust reposed in you, for which this is your warrant.

"Given under my hand and seal-at-arms, in the Colony aforesaid this — day of ———, A. D. 1776.

advancement of their pay ; the other, that one chaplain be appointed to two regiments. This last, I think, can be done without inconvenience. I beg leave to recommend this matter to Congress, whose sentiments hereon I shall impatiently expect."

At first the names of the chaplains were inserted in the army returns. Thus, on the 8th of January, 1776, we find the following returns :

REGIMENT.	COMMANDER.	CHAPLAIN.
1st (Artillery)	Col. Knox	Abiel Leonard.
2d (Foot)	Col. Reed	Hezekiah Smith.
3d "	Ebenezer Learned	Name not given.
4th "	John Nixon	Hezekiah Smith.
5th "	Stark, of Vermont	Noah Cooke.
6th "	Asa Whitcomb	Isaac Mansfield, jr.
7th "	Col. Prescott	None.
8th "	Enoch Poor	Noah Cooke.
9th "	James M. Varnum	Ebenezer David.
10th "	Samuel H. Parsons	None.
11th "	Daniel Hitchcock	Oliver Noble.
12th "	Moses Little	Oliver Noble.
13th "	Joseph Reed	None.
14th "	John Glover	None.
15th "	John Patterson	David Avery.
16th "	Paul D. Sargeant	None.
17th "	Jedediah Huntington, Conn.	John Ellis.
18th "	Edmund Phinney	None.
19th "	Charles Webb	None.
20th "	Col. Arnold	Abiel Leonard.
21st "	Jonathan Ward	None.
22d "	Samuel Wyllys	John Ellis.
23d "	John Bailey	None.
24th "	John Greator	None.
25th "	Wm. Bond	Ebenezer David.
26th "	Loammi Baldwin	None.
27th "	Israel Hutchinson	Isaac Mansfield.

Here are only nine chaplains to twenty-seven regiments. After this, as before stated, the names were left out in the army returns, and the number and the regiments to which each was attached alone given. When the army took up its march for New York this arrangement was very much broken up. Many clergymen had left their parishes only temporarily, and now rejoined them; while some, unable to be so far from their families, surrendered their positions to others. Besides, the absence of Arnold's regiment in Canada, and the separation of the army—a part being left under Artemas Ward to protect Boston—had rendered the plan by which one chaplain was to serve for two regiments no longer practicable. Washington, deprecating this state of things, wrote to Congress from New York, on the 1st of July, 1776, respecting it. He said: "I would also beg leave to mention to Congress the necessity there is of some new regulation being entered into respecting the chaplains of the army. They will remember that applications were made to increase their pay, which was conceived too low for their support, and that it was proposed, if it could not be done for the whole, that the number should be lessened, and one be appointed to two regiments, with an additional allowance. This latter expedient was adopted, and while the army continued altogether at one encampment, answered well, or at least did not produce many inconveniences; but the army being now differently circumstanced from what it then was, part here, part in Boston, and a third part detached to Canada, has introduced much confusion and disorder in this instance; nor do I know how it is possible to remedy the evil but by affixing one to each regiment, with salaries competent to their support. No shifting, no changing from one to the other, can answer the purpose, and in many cases it could not be done, although the regiments could consent, as when detachments are composed of unequal numbers, or ordered from different posts. Many more inconveniences might be pointed out, but these, it is presumed, will sufficiently show the defect of the present establishment, and the propriety of an alteration. What that alteration shall be Congress will please to determine."

The difficulties surrounding him, the gathering of the hostile forces on every side, and the momentous interests at stake in the great battle he knew to be close at hand, could not divert his mind from the importance of having a full supply of chaplains in the army. As neither in the wilds of the Alleghanies, surrounded by hostile Indians, so neither here, at the head of a great army, did he forget to urge on those in authority to provide him with God-fearing men. Fearless in combat, unshaken where others trembled and were dismayed, and taking without hesitation the fate of the nation on his great heart, he yet turned ever to the arm and protection of Him, without whose favor human exertion is in vain.

Congress immediately adopted his views, and Washington having received a dispatch to that effect, eight days after issued the following general order:

"NEW YORK, July 9th, 1776.

"The honorable Continental Congress having been pleased to allow a chaplain to each regiment, with the pay of thirty-three and one-third dollars per month, the colonels or commanding officers of each regiment are directed to procure chaplains—accordingly persons of good character and exemplary lives—to see that all inferior officers and soldiers pay them a suitable respect, and attend carefully upon religious exercises. *The blessing and protection of Heaven are at all times necessary, but especially is it in times of public distress and danger.* The General hopes and trusts that every officer and man will endeavor so to live and act as becomes a Christian soldier, defending the dearest rights and liberties of his country."

Before his plans, however, for putting the chaplains on a proper footing, could be wholly carried out, the disastrous battle of Long Island, and the fall of New York, almost broke up his imposing army. The capture of Fort Washington, and the flight of the disheartened fugitive band through New Jersey, completed its demoralization, and compelled him to defer further action, till he could once more reorganize his forces.

Of course it is impossible, and would not be desirable if possible, to give a detailed biography of each chaplain who served in the army. Many served only for a short time, others performed simply the prescribed routine of duties faithfully, and a narrative of their actions would be only a recital of their religious services before their respective regiments. Doubtless there are many personal anecdotes and touching incidents connected with these, which would possess deep interest if they had been preserved, but they perished with their authors, or their immediate descendants, and have passed away never to be recalled.

They, therefore, can only be alluded to ; while from the multitude of others, better known, I shall select those specially distinguished for their patriotism and who stand in history as representative men. It is necessary only to mention a few of the names of these clergymen, to show what strong minds and clear heads stood by, and sustained the cause of the Colonies, and furnish abundant proof of the debt of gratitude the country owes them.

There was Dr. David Ely, of Huntington, Conn., who, though surrounded by tories, preached rebellion so warmly and effectually, that the latter declared that, when the rebellion was put down, they would hang him on an oak that stood near his own church.

Joseph Fish, of Duxbury, Mass., who, although seventy-six years of age, when invited to address the people, assembled at the call of Washington, for immediate volunteers, said, after a stirring harangue, "Were it not that my nerves are unstrung, and my limbs enfeebled with age, on such a call as you have, I think I should willingly quit the desk, put off my priestly garments, buckle on the harness, and, with trumpet in hand, hasten to battle."

Jonah Stearns, of New Hampshire, not only preached rebellion, but sacrificed most of his worldly wealth to sustain it: and when returning from a state convention at Exeter, called to decide on a course of action, and to which he was a member, said to his boys assembled to hear his report, after answering their eager questions: "If the cause succeeds, it will be a great blessing to the country; but if it should fail, your old father's head will soon be a button for a halter!" and then sent them into the army, bidding them strike manfully for freedom.

John Mills, of Delaware, though of a nervous, timid temperament, in the cause of liberty knew no fear; and only a few days before the Declaration of Independence preached to his people from 1 Kings, xii. 16, the language used by the revolting tribes in the times of Rehoboam: "What portion have we in David, neither have we an inheritance in the son of Jesse. *To your tents, oh Israel!*"—telling them in impassioned eloquence that they were like the revolting tribes whom the king "refused to hear," though their "cause" was "the Lord's;" and that the time had come to throw off their allegiance to king George, and be free forever.

Dr. David Cauldwell, of Pennsylvania, had his house plundered, his library and furniture burned, while he was hunted like a common felon over the country, on account of his devotion to the cause of liberty.

Thomas Read, D. D., of the same State, in 1776, shouldered his musket, and, with forty or fifty others, marched to Philadelphia to aid in defending it against Howe; and the next year saved Washington from being overwhelmed at Elk Ferry by his knowledge of the country.

Dr. Robert Davidson, of Maryland, addressed at

different places the assembled troops, from 1 Chronicles, v. 22 : "For there fell down many slain, *because the war was of God,*" creating the most intense enthusiasm among officers and men.

William Graham, of Paxton, near Harrisburg, when he saw great backwardness in the young men of his parish to enlist in a company of volunteer riflemen, which the Governor had recommended, stepped out, and had his own name enrolled, and thus, by his example, shamed them into patriotism.

The name of the learned Elizur Goodrich was in every patriot's mouth in Connecticut.

John Steele, of Cumberland, Pa., served as captain, and lead the advance company of nine hundred men in their march to the seat of war, and often preached with his gun standing by his side.

Francis Cummings was present at all the Mecklenburg meetings, and afterwards fought in several battles, and though eighty years of age, when South Carolina threatened nullification, said, with the fire of seventy-six burning in his aged eye, to a brother clergyman who, in a moment of excitement, declared he was ready to draw his sword against the general government: "*If you dare do so, I will draw my sword again, and cut you down!*"

Azel Roe, to make the militia of his parish fight, put himself under the enemy's fire, and refused to retire till he had received their promise that, if he would, they would fight it out; and afterwards was taken prisoner, and thrown into the infamous Sugar House of New York.

Hezekiah James Balch, was member and chief actor in the Mecklenburg Convention, and died soon after that famous declaration was given to the world.

Charles McKnight, of Shrewsbury, who, on account of his devotion to the cause of liberty, and the gallant conduct of his patriotic sons on the field of battle, was thrown into prison, and treated with a brutality that would disgrace a savage. His constitution broke down under it, and soon after his release he died, another victim laid upon the altar of his country.

A similar list of chaplains might be made out, an account of whose services has never been preserved; only here and there an incident snatched from oblivion remains to show what those services must have been, and make us regret that so much has been lost.

There were Manassah Cutler, D. D., of Killingsly, Conn., the friend of Washington and Franklin, who served two campaigns; Dr. Nathan Strong, of Coventry, of the same State, who not only served as chaplain, but wrote stirring papers on the rights of the people, which were circulated far and wide; Dr. Nathaniel Porter, six feet high, with hair black as a raven's wing, who, with Wingate's regiment, marched on foot, like a common soldier, through the wilderness to Fort Independence on Lake Champlain; Rev. Amnie Bulmah Robbins, of Branford, Mass., who accompanied Schuyler's brigade as a volunteer to Canada, and became an angel of mercy to the army when it was stricken down with the small pox — not only praying morning and evening with the regiment, but nursing the sick and relieving the destitute and suffering, till his herculean frame at last broke down under his incessant labors and exposure, and he returned home—adding one more to the number of brave hearts who held their lives of small account, when compared with the welfare of their country.

To these might be added John Cleveland, of Canterbury, Conn., who as far back as 1758 was chaplain to a provincial regiment, and stood amid the raining balls that smote Lord Howe at Ticonderoga, and afterwards, in the same capacity, went to Louisburg, and witnessed the terrific siege of six weeks, which ended in the fall of that Gibraltar of America. Used to the hazards of the battle-field, as soon as the Revolution broke out, he offered his services to the Continental army at Cambridge, and accompanied it to New York, to see it melt away like the frosts of morning before the enemy :—

Dr. Samuel McClintock, of Greenland, N. H., so often represented in the battle of Bunker Hill in his robes of office, and who sent four sons into the army, only one of whom lived to hear the anthems of peace that rolled over the liberated land :—

Dr. Hezekiah Ripley, the friend of Washington, whose commanding form was often seen stooping over the couch of the sick and wounded, and whose eloquent voice never failed to animate the troops, and who heard without a sigh of regret that his house, furniture, and library had been committed to the flames by the exasperated foe.

Neither should Dr. Isaac Lewis, of Stratford, Conn., be forgotten, who, when the British attempted to land at Norwalk, assembled with his people to repel them, and saw a cannon ball smite the earth within three feet of him, without disturbing his serenity. Forced back by superior numbers, they witnessed their town given to the flames. Only one house, too remote to attract the attention of the invaders, was left standing, and into this the pastor gathered his people, and preached to them from Isaiah, lxiv. 11, 12: "Our holy and beautiful house, where our fathers praised thee, is burned with fire, and all our pleasant things are laid waste. Wilt thou refrain thyself for these things, O Lord, wilt thou hold thy peace, and afflict us very sore?" Chaplain to the regiment of Col. Philip P. Brady, at Bergen, he, after seven months of arduous labor, was seized with the camp-fever, and brought so low that his life was despaired of. The good old patriot, however, lived to see the country, for which he had prayed, and toiled, and suffered, free and happy.

The brave Dr. Latta, of Lancaster Co., Pa., not only served as chaplain, but on one occasion, when an unusual number of his parishioners were drafted into the army, in order to encourage them, shouldered his knapsack, and accompanied them as a common soldier on their campaign.

Dr. Armstrong, of Maryland, served first in the ranks as a volunteer, and afterwards, when licensed to preach, became chaplain, and continued with the army till the overthrow of the British at Yorktown.

John Martin, after praying with the soldiers at Bunker Hill, seized a musket and fought gallantly to the close of the battle. A day or two after he preached to the remnants of his shattered regiment from Nehemiah iv. 14: "And I said unto the nobles and to the rulers, and to the rest of the people, *Be ye not afraid of them.*"

Nathaniel Bartlett, of Reading, chaplain awhile to Putnam, was accustomed to make his parochial visits with a musket on his shoulder, to protect himself from the tories who had sworn to hang him, and kept his garret full of gunpowder, for the use of his parishioners in case of an attack.

All these, and a hundred other great and good men, by their example and eloquence fed the fires of liberty, and sustained the courage of the people. Men of learning and culture, they were looked up to for advice and counsel—whose praise was not only in all the churches, but throughout the land, for their integrity, ability and patriotism. These formed a host of devoted laborers in the common cause, but more than this, their prayers arose incessantly, from camp and field, that God would defend the right, and save his people. These last are counted as nothing by the historian, but we may rest assured that they did more than resolutions of Congress, and acts of committees of safety, towards achieving our liberties. One may consider it beneath the dignity of history to put them among the causes that led ultimately to our success: but when that history comes to be read in the light of eternity, the enthusiasm of volunteers, and the steady courage of the disciplined battalions, will sink into insignificance beside the devout prayers and faith of these men of God.

CHAPTER VI.

JONAS CLARK.

THE PASTOR OF LEXINGTON.—HIS MINISTERIAL LIFE.—EARLY TEACHINGS.—PATRIOTIC CONDUCT AND ABILITY AS A STATESMAN.—HANCOCK AND ADAMS FIND REFUGE IN HIS HOUSE.—NEWS OF THE APPROACH OF THE ENEMY.—HIS ACCOUNT OF IT.—SUMMONING OF THE MILITIA.—SCENE ON THE GREEN.—APPROACH OF THE ENEMY.—THE SLAUGHTER.—MR. CLARK AMONG HIS SLAIN PARISHIONERS.—HIS FEELINGS AND PREDICTION.—HIS DEATH.

IN writing the biographies of the illustrious, patriotic clergy and chaplains of the Revolution, I can commence the list with no worthier name than Jonas Clark, the pastor of the quiet town of Lexington. This obscure New England village has become as well known, throughout the civilized world, as Rome is. To human observation there was nothing in passing events to justify a prediction of its future renown, but that inscrutable Providence, that weaves the destinies of nations as well as of men, was preparing to make that unobtrusive spot the beacon light of the world, and its name the watchword of freemen for all time. Among the agents designed to bring about this extraordinary result no better one could have been found than Jonas Clark.

He was born in Newton, Mass., Dec. 25th, 1730. Graduating at Cambridge at the early age of twenty-two, he immediately entered on his theological studies, and when but twenty-five years of age was ordained pastor of Lexington. Here he settled on a little farm, and, with a salary of eighty pounds a year, and twenty cords of wood, pursued the quiet, retired life of a country minister. Grave and dignified in the pulpit, yet earnest in manner, he presented the truths of the Gospel with a fervor and power that always commanded the deepest attention of his hearers. "His voice was powerful and agreeable, and when excited by his subject, which was often the case, it extended far beyond the bounds of the meeting-house, and could be heard distinctly by those who were anywhere in the immediate neighborhood."

Uniting the life of farmer with that of village pastor, his life seemed destined to flow on evenly, and unnoticed by the great world without, to its close. But when the trouble between the Colonies and the mother country commenced, he stepped at once from his obscurity, and became known throughout all the region as one of the most uncompromising patriots of the day. Earnestly, yet without passion, he discussed from the pulpit the great questions at issue, and that powerful voice thundered forth the principles of personal, civil, and religious liberty, and the right of resistance, in tones as earnest and effective as it had the doctrine of salvation by the cross.

Long before it was certain that the quarrel must come to blows, he had so thoroughly indoctrinated his people with these great truths, that no better spot on the continent could have been found for the British first to try the terror of their arms, and make the experiment to subjugate the Colonists by force. His congregation was ripe for revolution, ready to fight and to die rather than yield to arbitrary force. His wife was cousin to John Hancock, and thus the latter became a frequent visitor at his house. Whether the pastor influenced Hancock, or Hancock the pastor, is of little consequence; they were harmonious on the question that agitated the Colonies. The conversation of these two patriots, as they surveyed the vast interests at stake, and the fearful struggle they believed to be unavoidable, and the words of courage uttered in that quiet parsonage, would make a heroic page in American history, could they have been preserved. The Rev. William Ware, of Cambridge, in writing to Dr. Sprague, says, "It would not be beyond the truth to assert that there was no person at that time and in that vicinity —not only no clergyman, but *no other person of whatever calling or profession*, who took a firmer stand for the liberties of the country, or was more ready to perform the duties and endure the sacrifices of a patriot, than the minister of Lexington. He was considered, moreover, not only as a person of great ardor of temperament as a politician—the first to move himself and set others in motion on great emergencies— but also as a person of great abilities, whose judgment was one more than others to be respected and relied upon. No one than he better understood the state of the question as between the Colonies and England; nor were there any who, earlier than he, or with more talent at the town meetings, and at other places and times, argued the great topics on which differences had arisen, and then, through the representatives of the town, presented the arguments and conclusions at which they had arrived, in papers which he had prepared, to the General Court, at their various session."

The people had become so thoroughly indoctrinated in his views, and been so animated by his appeals from the pulpit and in public meetings, that they had them embodied in instructions to their delegate to the Provincial Legislature as the expression of their wishes and determination. Those instructions remain to this day, and are engrossed on the town records as a standing memorial not only of his patriotism, but his ability as a stateman.

Mr. Everett, in speaking of these papers, says, "Although the part taken by Lexington was in full accordance with the course pursued by many other towns in the Province, there is nothing invidious in the remark, that this document, in which the principles and opinions of the town are embodied, has few equals, and no superiors among the productions of that class. They are well known to have proceeded from his pen, who, for many years previous to the Revolution to the close of his life, exercised a well deserved ascendency in the public concerns of the town. Mr. Clark was of a class of citizens who rendered services second to no others in enlightening and animating the popular mind on the great question at issue, *I mean the patriotic clergy of New England.*"

It was to a congregation educated by such a man that Providence allowed to be entrusted the momentous events of the 19th of April, events which were to decide more than the fate of a continent—that of civil liberty the world over. "No single individual," says a distinguished man, "probably did so much to educate the people up to that point of intelligence, firmness, and courage, as their honored and beloved pastor." If he had been opposed to resistance, or an advocate of timorous, non-committal measures, where would have been the fiery cross that flew from limit to limit of the thirteen Colonies, and set the hearts of men on fire, and made the shout, "to arms! to arms!" roll like thunder over the land!

Adams and Hancock, when proscribed by the royal government, found an asylum in his house. They were there when the first verbal message came from Warren, that mischief was afoot. "Then," says Mr. Clark in a note he makes of the event, "came an express in writing stating that eight or nine officers of the king's troops were seen just before night passing the road towards Lexington, in a musing, contemplative posture, and it was suspected they were out upon some evil design. Ten or twelve men, on account of Hancock and Adams, were detailed to guard my house that night. Those officers passed through the town. Three men were sent to watch them. At 10 o'clock said officers stopped on the borders of Lincoln, seized their bridles, put pistols to their hearts, and swore if they stirred another step they were dead men. Between the hours of twelve and one o'clock we received intelligence from Warren that a British detachment was on the way to destroy the stores at Lexington." The three held a hurried consultation, and resolved to fight. At two o'clock, peal after peal from the belfry called the excited inhabitants together on the church green.

There they found their pastor who had arrived before them. The roll was called, and a hundred and fifty answered to their names. The men, the hour, the crisis at hand, made the scene on that quiet green a most solemn and impressive one. The church, the pastor, and his congregation thus standing together in the dim light, while the stars looked tranquilly down from the sky above them, formed a subject for a great historic picture. As the pastor surveyed the silent ranks a strange light gleamed in his eye, for he saw clearly beyond that night's business and his attentive ear caught from afar faint, but distinctly, the clock of destiny striking. The great question with Hancock and Adams had been, would the people fight? Would these humble mechanics and farmers dare resist the drilled troops of England? Clark knew they would. Had he not trained them for this hour? Were his years of labor to be in vain? No, they would fight, and if need be die, too, under the shadow of the house of God!

In the meantime swift riders had been sent along the road towards Boston, to obtain if possible some information of the approaching enemy. These, after going several miles, returned, and reported every thing quiet in that direction. A watch was then set, and the men dismissed to their homes, with orders to come together at beat of drum. Just as day was breaking, an advance company of British marines appeared in sight, marching swiftly and in dead silence on the place. In a moment alarm guns broke the stillness of the morning, the church bell rung its loud and startling peal over the village, and the drum beat to arms. Seizing their firelocks fathers and sons rushed together to the common, and soon the stern browed yeomen stood drawn up in two ranks near the meeting house. The spire rose dimly in the gray dawn, speaking to them silently and solemnly of both earth and heaven, and awakening emotions and resolves that have made the hero and martyr of every age. "How often in that building," says Bancroft, "had they with renewed professions of their faith looked up to God as the stay of their fathers and the protector of their privileges. How often, on that village green, hard by the burial place of their forefathers, had they pledged themselves to each other to combat manfully for their birthright inheritance of liberty. There they now stood side by side under the Provincial banner, with arms in their hands, silent and fearless. The ground on which they stood was the altar of freedom, and they were to furnish its victims." How often, he might have added, had they been told from the pulpit of that sacred building, that resistance to tyranny was obedience to God, and that not merely as freemen to combat "for their birthright inheritance of liberty," but as Christians to defend the altars of their religion, they stood there in stern and silent array. In the sharp rattle of musketry that followed the brutal order, "throw down your arms, and disperse! throw down your arms, and disperse!" Mr. Clark heard only what he knew would be the result of his own teachings.

Still the crash of the sudden volley sent a quick keen pang through his heart for it told of death—

and as the white puffs of smoke lifted in the morning air, he saw the green covered with reeling and falling forms. Hastening thither, after the retreat of the British, a sad sight met his gaze—for there, under the windows of his church, lay seven stalwart men, stretched stark and stiff in death, and many wounded. There lay Jonas Parker, the strongest wrestler in Lexington, pierced with both ball and bayonet. In the morning he had sworn never to run from British troops, and he had kept his word, falling on the very spot where he had taken post at the beat of the drum. There, too, lay old Caleb Monroe, his gray hairs dabbled in blood, and near by Caleb Harrington, fallen on the door-steps of the house of God, into which he had gone for powder, and beside them other well-known forms.

The bright spring morning broke tranquilly over this sad scene—the dew-drops glittered beside the red stains that sprinkled the starting grass—the birds came out and sang upon the budding trees, and nature gave no token of the bloody murder that had just been committed. Clark gazed long and earnestly on this tragic spectacle, but no tear of regret mingled with those of sympathy which he shed. Those lifeless forms before him were holy martyrs in his sight, the first precious sacrifices laid upon the altar of his country, which was yet to groan under its load of victims. He had no misgivings, for "from this day," said he, "*will be dated the liberty of the world.*" No sound broke the stillness of the scene, but *he* heard far up in the dome of the universe a bell tolling the knell of tyranny.

A feeling of exultation filled his bosom in spite of his sympathetic grief; for, while he was looking at the militia formed in a body upon the crimsoned grass, they "fired a volley and gave three cheers," he says, "by way of triumph, and as an expression of the joy of victory and the glory of the conquest."

Notwithstanding his dead and dying parishioners lay around him, his patriotic heart leaped to that shout, for it was prophetic.

He lived to see his predictions prove true. Through all the long struggle that followed his interest in it never suffered a moment's abatement, and his faith in ultimate success never wavered. He believed the war to be as just a one as ever was waged by the Israelites of old, and as much under the direction of God, hence there was no room in his heart for doubt.

After the Revolution he lived a quiet, honored and useful life up to its very close, in 1805. He enjoyed almost uninterrupted health until a few weeks before his death, when he was seized with the dropsy, which suddenly terminated his career in his seventy-sixth year.

The teachings of the pulpit of Lexington caused the first blow to be struck for American Independence.

CHAPTER VII.

JACOB DUCHÈ.

Opens the first Continental Congress with Prayer.—John Adams' Description of the Scene.—His Patriotic Sermons.—Gives his Pay as Chaplain to the Families of those slain in Battle.—Becomes alarmed, and turns against his Country.—His insulting Letter to Washington.—Flees the Country.—His Return to Philadelphia, his Death.—His Character.

Jacob Duche, who opened the old Continental Congress with prayer, and was for a time, in 1776, its chaplain, deserves a passing notice here for the prominent figure he presents in the opening scenes of the great drama of the Revolution, though his after career consigns him to merited disgrace.

He was born in Philadelphia in 1738, and after completing his education in this country, went to England to receive orders. On his return he became a rector in his native city. He early showed a literary turn, and in 1771 published a volume of letters relating chiefly to English politics.

John Adams, in a letter to his wife, dated Sept. 16th, 1774, thus describes the thrilling incidents connected with the prayer he made on the opening of the First Congress.

"When Congress first met, Mr. Cushing made a motion that it should be opened with prayer. This was opposed by Mr. Gay, of New York, and Mr. Rutledge, of South Carolina, because we were so divided in religious sentiments—some Quakers, some Anabaptists, some Presbyterians, and some Congregationalists—that we could not join in the same act of worship. Mr. Samuel Adams arose, and said, 'He was no bigot, and could hear a prayer from a gentleman of piety and virtue, who was at the same time a friend to his country. He was a stranger in Philadelphia, but had heard that Mr. Duchè (Dushay they pronounce it) deserved that character, and he therefore moved that Mr. Duchè, an Episcopal clergyman, might be desired to read prayers to the Congress to-morrow morning.' The motion was seconded, and passed in the affirmative. Mr. Randolph, our President, waited on Mr. Duchè, and received for answer that if his health would permit he certainly would. Accordingly he appeared next morning with his clerk and in his pontifical, and read several prayers in the established form, and then read the Collect for the 7th day of September, which was the thirty-fifth Psalm. You must remember this was the next morning after we heard the terrible rumor of the cannonading of Boston. I never saw greater effect upon an audience. It seemed as if Heaven had ordained that Psalm to be read on that morning. After this, Mr. Duchè, very unexpectedly to every body, struck out into an extemporary prayer, which filled the bosom of every man present. I must confess I never heard a better prayer or one so well pronounced. Episcopalian as he is, Dr. Cooper never prayed with such ardor, such earnestness and pathos, and in language so eloquent and sublime for America, for Congress, for the provinces of Massachusetts Bay, and especially the town of Boston. It has had an excellent effect upon every body here. I must beg you to read that Psalm."

No wonder the effect was great. With the echoes of British cannon still lingering in their ears—solemn in view of the mighty work they had undertaken, gloomy with the dark and bloody future that stretched out before them, the deliberate, earnest petition, "Plead my cause, O Lord, with them that strive with me; fight against them that fight against me; take hold of shield and buckler, and stand up for my help; draw out also the spear, and stop the way against them," must have fallen with startling significance upon their ears. The deep silence, the excited, tremulous tone, the circumstances all combined to make it appear like a voice from Heaven. No wonder, either, that Mr. Duchè, under the solemn influences of the scene, broke forth in an ex tempore prayer, and poured out his heart in strong, earnest, natural language to the great Lord of all. In such hours of peril and conscious weakness, the prayer for help from on high has a meaning and power in it unfelt in times of prosperity.

In the fervor of the moment he exclaimed: "O Lord, our Heavenly Father, high and mighty, King of kings and Lord of lords, who dost from thy throne behold all the dwellers on earth, and reignest with power supreme and uncontrolled over all kingdoms, empires, and governments, look down, we beseech thee, on these our American States, who have fled to thee from the rod of the oppressor, and thrown themselves on thy gracious protection, desiring henceforth to be dependent only on thee—to thee have they appealed for the righteousness of their cause—to thee do they now look up for that countenance and support which thou alone canst give. Take them, therefore, Heavenly Father, under thy nurturing care, give them wisdom in council, and valor in the field. Defeat the malicious designs of our cruel adversaries. Convince them of the unrighteousness of their cause, and if they still persist in their sanguinary purpose, O let the voice of thine own unerring justice sounding in their hearts constrain them to drop the weapons of war from their unnerved hands in the day of battle. Be thou present, O God of wisdom, and direct the councils of this honorable Assembly. Enable them to settle things on the best and surest foundation, that the scene of blood may be speedily closed—that order, harmony, and peace may be effectually restored, and truth and justice, religion and piety may prevail and flourish amongst thy people. Preserve the health of their bodies and the vigor of their minds. Shower on them and the millions they here represent such temporal blessings as thou seeest expedient for them in this world, and crown them with everlasting glory in the world to come. All this we ask in the name and through the merits of Jesus Christ thy Son, our Saviour. Amen."

On the fast day appointed by Congress he preached before it a patriotic sermon. On the 7th of July, 1775, he preached to the First Battalion of the city, from the text: "Stand fast, therefore, in the liberty wherewith Christ hath made us free." In this sermon he exhorted the soldiers to stand fast in their assertion of rights, and act like independent freemen, putting their trust in God, who would assuredly deliver them from the hand of the oppressor.

There was not a clergyman in the land, who at this time held so prominent a position in the cause of liberty as he. Not only did he give his prayers, and lend his eloquence to the cause of the Colonies, but the pay voted him by Congress, for his services as chaplain, he generously gave to the families of the patriots slain in battle.

At this time he was the last man any one would have selected as likely to turn recreant to his country. But the successive disasters that overtook the American army after the battle of Long Island, seemed to fill him with dismay; and when Philadelphia finally fell into the hands of the British, he lost all hope, and in a moment of weakness and timidity, presumed to address Washington a letter, in which he speaks with an insolence about Congress and the army, that does little credit to his head or heart. He urges him, with a cool effrontery, to abandon the American cause, and resign his command of the army, or at the head of it to force Congress immediately to desist from hostilities, and to rescind their declaration of independence. "If this is not done," he says, "you have an infallible resource still left—*negotiate for America at the head of your army.*" He describes Congress as composed of weak, obscure men—speaks contemptuously of the New England delegates—says the officers are destitute of principle and courage, unfit to occupy a seat at his excellency's table, etc., etc.

One can imagine the astonishment of Washington at this deliberate attempt of a clergyman—one, too, who had been so loud in his patriotism—to make him perjure himself before the world, and trample under foot the very Congress from which he held his commission. He told Mr. Ferguson, the bearer of the letter, to inform Mr. Duchè that, had he been aware of its contents, he should have returned it unopened; but, having read it, he felt it his duty to lay it before Congress, that they might be aware of the sentiments of the man they had honored with their confidence. Francis Hopkinson, a brother-in-law of Duchè, replied to this letter with a power and pungency that left the traitorous chaplain in a most unenviable position.

This desertion of his country, and nefarious attempt to corrupt Washington, made it dangerous for him to remain in his native city, and he fled to England.

In 1790 he returned to Philadelphia, where he died four years after. Of a brilliant imagination and impulsive nature, he yet lacked the stern integrity and high courage of a true man, and in an evil hour took counsel of his fears, and for ever tainted a reputation that otherwise would have shone with brilliant luster.

CHAPTER VIII.

SAMUEL SPRING, D.D.

His Early Life.—Becomes Chaplain in the Army.—The only Chaplain in Arnold's Expedition across the Northern Wilderness.—His Description of its Formation.—Preaches at Newburyport to the Army.—Visits the Tomb of Whitfield.—Description of the March through the Wilderness.—His Sufferings and Labors.—Famine.—His Description of shooting a Moose.—His Labors at Point aux Tremble.—Storming of Quebec.—He leads Arnold out of the Fight.—Leaves the Army.—Settled at Newburyport.—His Interview with Aaron Burr.—His Death.

CHAPLAINS are usually regarded as mere adjuncts of an army, not expected to share the perils and sufferings of the common soldier, and in ordinary wars they do not, except to a limited extent; but in the Revolutionary war it was not so. The unparalleled sufferings which the American army was compelled to undergo, the chaplains submitted to with cheerfulness, and in many cases were found in the thickest of the fight, steadying and encouraging the men. Thus we find them hutted at Valley Forge—facing the storm in the wintry march on Trenton, covered with the smoke of the conflict at Bennington, standing under the enemy's fire at Yorktown, and attached to every expedition, no matter how hazardous or exhausting, that was set on foot.

In the fight at Lexington, we have seen the pastor of the church on the green where the first blood flowed, encouraging his parishioners to resist, and three clergymen handling the musket like common soldiers. So in that marvellous expedition of Arnold's, through the northern wilderness to Quebec, so fraught with peril and hardships that none but volunteers were asked to form it, we find a chaplain sharing its vicissitudes and sufferings.

Samuel Spring was born at Northbridge, Mass., February 27th, 1746. His father was a farmer, and wished the stout lad to stay and assist him on the farm; but the latter was determined to obtain an education, and having at length received the parental consent, commenced his studies, and in time entered the College of New Jersey. He was not a professing Christian at that period, but, while in college, had his mind directed to the subject of religion by a singular incident. The character of the Deity as shown in his works, especially in the external universe, had often impressed him profoundly, and he was selected by his class, on a certain occasion, to explain and defend the Copernican system. In doing this, his mind became so overwhelmed by the vastness of the theme, and the greatness and majesty of God, the Creator and sovereign Ruler of the universe, that he suddenly stopped awe-struck, and bursting into tears sat down. He graduated in 1771, and entered at once upon his theological studies. He was licensed to preach in 1774, and the next year, fired with the patriotism that drew such a host of God-fearing men into the struggle of the Colonies, hastened to Boston, and offered his services as chaplain. In the fall he accompanied Arnold in his march through the wilderness, the only chaplain attached to the perilous expedition.

He thus describes the manner in which it was formed:* "Congress had in secret session decided upon an expedition for the conquest of Quebec. General Arnold, as its commander-in-chief, with his orders in his pocket, was directed to Dorchester Heights, to select his troops from the main Continental army then in camp in that place. It was in the gray of the morning. The drum beat in every regiment for an instant, and general parade of the whole army, as for review, was ordered. All was bustle. In a very brief space the whole army was paraded in continued line of companies. With one continued roll of drums the general-in-chief with his staff passed along the whole line— regiment after regiment presenting arms. Then came the order, 'Officers, to the front ten paces—march!' then, in quick succession, 'Officers, to the center—face! Officers, to the center—march! Form hollow square!' Arrived at the center, and the square formed, the secret orders of Congress were read. The regiments were designated. It was a perilous service, and not compulsory upon the officers. Volunteers were called for. Not one but when the order came, 'Volunteers, step one step in advance!' but took that step."

Among those who took that step was the young chaplain. Thirty years of age, over six feet high, and finely proportioned, he towered like a young giant over the troops. The force was to march to Newburyport, and there embark in boats for the mouth of the Kennebec, where two hundred bateaux had been collected,

---

* I am indebted for this and other incidents to a member of his family.

to carry the troops, provisions, etc. Arriving at this place in the latter part of the week, the army remained there over the Sabbath, which gave the chaplain a good opportunity to commence his official duties, and he preached to the troops in one of the churches of the place.

He thus graphically describes the circumstances attending this interesting event: "On the Sabbath morning the officers and as many of the soldiers as could be crowded on to the floor of the house, were marched into the Presbyterian Church in Federal street. They marched in with colors flying, and drums beating, and formed two lines, through which I passed—they presenting arms and the drums rolling, until I was seated in the pulpit. Then the soldiers stacked their arms all over the aisles, and I preached to the army and to the citizens, who crowded the galleries, from this text: 'If thy spirit go not with us, carry us not up hence.'"

He spoke without notes, yet there was no hesitation in the choice of words or in his manner, but the stream of his eloquence rolled on unchecked to the close. His commanding figure, clear, distinct utterance, animated gestures, and earnest expression, riveted every eye upon him; while the subject of his discourse—the marvellous and daring expedition, on which they were about to set forth—enlisted every faculty of his hearers, and the profoundest silence rested on the audience, filling the remotest corners of the closely packed building.

There sat the fearless Arnold, the bold rifleman, Morgan, and a host of other brave men, who, notwithstanding their dauntless courage, felt that the perils of the untrodden, mysterious wilderness, they were about to penetrate, might be too great for human energy and endurance, and the hour come, that their only hope would rest in the God whose spirit the chaplain invoked as their guide and stay. The citizens, who crowded the gallery, never forgot that sermon. It became the talk of the place, and was the cause of his eventually settling over them as their pastor. In speaking of the circumstance afterwards Mr. Spring said, "*I preached over the grave of Whitfield.* After the service the general officers gathered around me. Some one requested a visit to Whitfield's tomb. The sexton was hunted up, the key procured, and we descended to his coffin. It had lain in the tomb six years, but was in good preservation. The officers induced the sexton to take off the lid of the coffin. The body had nearly all returned to dust. Some portions of his grave-clothes remained. His collar and wristbands, in the best preservation, were taken and carefully cut in little pieces, and divided among them." The chaplain, with the haughty Arnold, the chivalrous Morgan, and group of officers, gathered in the dark vault around the tomb of Whitfield, formed a scene worthy of a painter. The clank of steel had a strange sound around the sainted sleeper, while the hallowed atmosphere filled all hearts with solemn awe and reverence.

At length every thing being ready, the army of eleven hundred men took its departure, and arriving at the mouth of the Kennebec, unmoored the two hundred boats, and began slowly to ascend the stream. Morgan led the advance guard, and having reached Norridgewock Falls, halted to await the arrival of Arnold. Here the river was so broken into rapids that it was necessary to carry all the boats and baggage and artillery a mile and a quarter through the woods. First the bushes had to be hewn away, and the trees cut down, to make a passage; then the boats to be hoisted upon men's shoulders, and placed on sleds, and carried forward; and finally all the baggage, ammunition, and stores dragged across. In the meantime the boats had sprung aleak, and between repairing them and transporting the materials of war it took seven days to go this mile and a quarter. The boats were finally launched again, while the soldiers took to the water, and nearly to their armpits slowly shoved them against the rapid current. At night they would tie up, and kindling a blazing fire in the forest, lie down to rest. At some of the carrying places the boats had to be dragged up precipices, at others borne on men's shoulders through the swamps. The young chaplain gazed on this struggling army, swallowed up in the wilderness, with strange emotions. Though wading the streams and swamps, and climbing the rocks like the meanest soldier, he would often pause in his toil to watch the novel spectacle. The October frosts soon set in, and all the autumnal glories of our high latitudes were spread upon the forest. The dark fir trees of the low grounds retained their sombre hue, but the undergrowth of bushes made a flooring of gold beneath. The tall pine tree lifted its green crown from the lofty ridges, while farther down, along the vast slopes, all the colors of the rainbow were spread in endless profusion. The scene at night was picturesque in the extreme. Huge fires blazed through the forest as far as the eye could reach, while the tall trees receded away in the gloom, like the columns of some vast cathedral, amid which the slumbering host lay in deep and silent repose. The moonbeams stole dimly through the fretted arches above them, and the rapidly flowing stream seemed chanting a low anthem to the solitude. But the first blast of the bugle in the morning, sending its loud notes far through the forest, stirred this deep repose as by magic — the silent woods witnessed a sudden resurrection, and soon all was bustle and confusion. The bright October days and bracing autumnal air made the toilsome march at first comparatively cheerful; but the long, drenching rains of November told sadly on the troops, and soon the army was burdened with the sick. To visit these, and give spiritual advice and comfort, and encourage those who in their weakness and despondency felt that they should leave their bones in the wilderness, took up much of Mr. Spring's time, and made his duties by no means the least onerous, where the severest toil was the lot of every one.

It was pleasant to see the devotion of the soldiers to their young chaplain. Cheerfully sharing all their privations and hardships he became endeared to them, and when Sunday came, they would pile together their knapsacks, tier upon tier, for a pulpit, on which an orderly would help him mount, while they gathered round to listen, forming a strange congregation in a strange temple.

Standing thus in nature's great cathedral, he would deliver the messages of salvation to his hearers, sending his voice through the solitude, and reminding one of him who styled himself "the voice of one crying in the wilderness."

At length provisions began to grow scarce, and every one had to be put on short allowance. Mr. Spring took his three quarters of a pound of pork per day cheerfully with the rest.

After incredible hardships, and the loss of a hundred and fifty men, by sickness and desertion, the army at last reached the great carrying place, fifteen miles long, extending from the Kennebec to the Dead River. Only three small ponds occurred the whole distance, on which the boats could be launched. The rest of the way they and the provisions, ammunitions, etc., had to be carried on men's shoulders. This was a terrific strain on the army, and the dispiriting effect upon the soldiers was not relieved by the appearance of the Dead River, when they reached it, for it moved sluggish and dark like the waters of oblivion through the silent and motionless forest. Day after day they toiled up this sluggish stream, between the monotonous walls of forest that lined its banks, until it seemed as if there was no outlet or opening to the apparently interminable wilderness. At every bend, the eye strained forward to catch some indication of change, and when at last they came in sight of a snow-covered mountain in the distance, telling them there was an outer world after all, the men sent up a shout that woke the echoes far and wide.

Near its base they encamped three days, and Spring spent most of the time in visiting the sick, and praying with them. The army had scarcely got under way again, when the heavens became overcast; dark and angry clouds swept the heavens, and the heavy winds sobbed and moaned through the forest. Soon the rain came down in torrents. Side by side with the drenched soldier the tall chaplain trudged uncomplainingly on, and lay down like him on the wet ground at night. It poured without cessation for three days, shedding still deeper gloom over the army. The river rose steadily the whole time, till the sluggish current at length swept down with such velocity and power that the boats could with difficulty stem it. On the third night, just as the soldiers had lain down to rest, after having kindled a huge fire, Mr. Spring heard a roar in the forest above them like the sound of the surf beating upon the shore, and the next moment the glancing waters were seen sweeping through the trees on both sides of the stream. In an instant the camp was alive with shouts and cries rising above the turbulent flood that deluged the ground on which they stood. The fires were extinguished, and in the tumult, and confusion, and darkness, no one knew which way to flee for safety, or what to do. In this state of uncertainty and dread the night wore away. The daylight revealed to them a spectacle sad enough to fill the bravest heart with discouragement. Boats had drifted into the forest, and as far as the eye could reach the level ground was one broad lake, out of which arose the dark stems of the trees like an endless succession of columns. In nine hours the water rose eight feet, totally obliterating the shores of Dead River.

But the provisions were getting lower and lower, and Arnold could not wait for the river to subside. The army was, therefore, pushed on, slowly stemming the flood; but, seven boats, carrying provisions, were caught in the whirling, angry waters, and upset, and all their contents destroyed.

The boldest now paused in dismay, for only twelve days' provisions remained, while thirty miles across the mountain were to be traversed before they could reach the head waters of the Chaudière, that flowed into the St. Lawrence. A council of war was called to decide what should be done in this crisis of affairs. They had now been a month away from civilization, the sick were increasing, while famine was staring them in the face. It was determined at length to leave the sick there, and despatch orders to Colonels Green and Knox, in the rear, to hasten up, and take them back to Cambridge.

Here was an opportunity for the young chaplain to abandon the expedition, and yet apparently be in the path of duty. He had had enough, one would think, of toil, exposure and suffering, not to wish to face still greater hardships, and perhaps death itself, by famine in the wilderness, he following its fortunes. But he believed the welfare of his country was deeply involved in its fate, and he determined, come what would, to share its vicissitudes, hazards and destiny. Having, therefore, prayed with the sick, encouraged the desponding with the promise that relief would soon come, and pointed those, whom he believed dying, to the Saviour of men, and commended all to the care and mercy of God, he bade them farewell, and moved forward with the advancing column.

The cold, autumnal rains had now turned into snow, which sifting down through the leafless tree-tops, covered the weary, wan and straggling column with a winding-sheet, that seemed to be wrapping it for the tomb. After they left the sick in the wilderness they passed seventeen falls, before they reached the head-waters of Dead River. It was still four miles across to the Chaudière, down which they were to float to the St. Lawrence.

Here, on the summit of the hills on which the waters divide, one part flowing south and the other north, Arnold distributed the last provisions to the separate companies, and taking only thirteen men, pushed on for the Chaudière. He told those left behind, in parting, that he would obtain provisions for them in advance, if human efforts could procure them; but directed them to follow after as fast as they could, for, he added, their only safety lay in advancing. Spring remained behind with the army, to share its privations and its fate, whatever that might be. The gallant fellows gave their indomitable leader three parting cheers, and then began to heave their heavy boats from the water. Hoisting them upon their shoulders, while others were loaded down with baggage and ammunition, and others still dragged the few pieces of artillery along like cattle, they staggered on through the forest. The scanty provisions that were left them, though eked out with the greatest parsimony, grew rapidly less, and finally failed entirely. Under the low rations and severe labor combined, the men had gradually grown weaker and weaker, and now, pale and emaciated, looked on each other in mute inquiry. A council of war was called, and it was determined to kill the dogs they had with them, and push on till this loathsome supply was exhausted. These faithful animals, hitherto the companions of their toils, were slain and divided among the different companies. After the bodies were devoured, their legs and even claws were boiled for soup.

It was a sad sight to see the groups of half famished soldiers seated together around a fire, watching with eager looks the pot containing this refuse of the dogs, and gazing with strange meaning into each other's eyes. The chaplain fared like the rest, and famine and incessant toil and exposure were telling on him as well as on the soldiers. The tall frame grew less erect, and the wan face showed that starvation was eating away his life. Trusting however in God, whom he served, he endured all cheerfully, and bore that famished multitude on his heart to the throne of heavenly grace. The soldiers, in all their sufferings, thought of him with the deepest sympathy, and could not but feel encouraged when they saw his serene, though emaciated countenance, and listened to his expressions of calm confidence in God, that he would yet deliver them. He often walked through the woods to look at the various groups, and see where he could be of most service. His heart bled at the destitution he witnessed on every side. One day he came upon a company gathered around a fire, boiling some dog's claws they had preserved to make soup with. As he paused to look at them, they rose, and, in true kindness of heart, urged him to share their meager, disgusting broth. It was a novel, but touching evidence of the deep affection they bore their young chaplain, and told in language stronger than words, what an example of patient endurance he had shown, and how kind and faithful had been his labors among them.

At last the dogs gave out, and then the soldiers tore off their moose skin moccasins, and boiled them to extract a little nourishment. The feet could stand the November frosts better than their stomachs endure the gnawings of famine. They reached at length the banks of the Chaudière, and launched their boats. The current however was swollen and rapid—now boiling amid the rocks, and now shooting like an arrow around a jutting precipice. On such a turbulent flood the boats soon became unmanageable, and one after another was stranded or shivered into fragments, till nearly all were destroyed.

They were still thirty miles from the French settlements, and now were compelled to shoulder their burdens, and advance on foot, in straggling parties, through the forest. During all these perils and sufferings scarce a Sabbath passed in which Spring did not mount his pulpit of knapsacks, and preach to the troops, while every morning, before the march began, his earnest prayer arose to God for help.

The last miserable substitute for food was at length exhausted, and with empty stomachs and bowed forms they slowly, despairingly toiled onward, while all along their track, the snow was stained with blood. As they were now approaching the French settlements, severe discipline was enforced. They needed no fires to cook their food, for they had none to cook; but none was allowed them to warm themselves by, and strict orders were given not to discharge a gun for any purpose. While the weary column was thus staggering silently on, suddenly the report of a musket was heard far in advance, then another, and another, till twenty echoed through the forest. They ceased, and then a long shout rolled back through the solitude, producing the wildest excitement. Mr. Spring never forgot that thrilling scene, and long after, in speaking of it, said: "The army was starving, but moving on. The pioneers, who were ahead to clear the way, roused suddenly a noble moose. It was the first that had been seen. The temptation was too strong to be resisted. One man fired—he missed. Twenty guns were leveled at him. He fell—they forgot all discipline in their extremity, and shouted. It was a noble moose, weighing not less than a thousand pounds. A halt was ordered—camp kettles taken out, *fires kindled, meat, blood, entrails, hoofs and horns chopped up, and soup made of all for the army.*"

Revived by this unexpected supply, the troops pushed on. The next day they met a company of men with provisions, sent back by Arnold to relieve them. A loud shout arose from the whole army, and a general feast was ordered. Several of the soldiers, unable to restrain their appetites, eat so voraciously that they sickened and died. They had braved the wilderness, and withstood the ravages of famine, to fall victims to unrestrained indulgence. It was with profound sadness the young chaplain performed the last religious rites over their rude graves in the northern wilderness.

The French settlements were soon reached, and exultation and joyful anticipation took the place of gloomy forebodings and despair. The weary march, the supperless bivouacs and unparalleled hardships were now all forgotten in the enterprise before them, and on every side arose the sound of preparation. On Sunday, the 12th of November, they reached Point Levi, opposite Quebec. They were to cross the next morning, and hence the sabbath was given up to active toil, and Spring saw how the Lord's day is sometimes passed in camp.

It is not necessary to dwell here on Arnold's failure to surprise Quebec, nor the state of affairs that compelled him to wait the arrival of Montgomery from Montreal, before attempting to take the place by storm. He retreated between twenty and thirty miles to Point aux Trembles, and pitched his camp.

There was a beautiful catholic chapel here, which Arnold turned into a hospital for the sick. On Sundays it was used by Spring as a church, in which he preached regularly to officers and men. On these occasions the richly decorated chapel presented a singular spectacle. In the elegant recesses and rooms adjoining, costly hangings drooped amid elaborate carvings and gilt work, while all around lay the sick Americans, to whom these luxuries seemed a dream after the hardships of the wilderness. The walls and ceilings were lavishly adorned, and the whole interior presented a strange contrast to a New England Meeting-house. Yet here the sons of the Puritans assembled, and reverently listened to their chaplain, who preached a gospel that had never before been heard there.

Montgomery at length arrived, and preparations were set on foot for an assault on Quebec, and Sunday, the last day of December, was selected for its execution. On this morning, before daylight, the two generals advanced, cautiously and silently, against the two points which had been designated for the attack. A furious snow-storm was raging at the time, while snow two feet deep obstructed the way. This was not to be a Sabbath of worship, and Spring, anxious for the result of the contest, would not stay in camp, but advanced with the troops to the walls of the city.

How Montgomery fell, sword in hand, at the head of his troops, is a matter of history. Arnold, gallantly leading his men up a narrow street, swept by the enemy's fire, received a musket-ball in his leg, which brought him to the ground. Struggling up from the snow, he attempted again to move on, but was compelled to fall back, and yield the command to Morgan, who fought like a lion amid the storm and darkness. Every soldier was needed to press the assault, and Arnold would allow none to help him, but taking the arm of Ogden, the surgeon, and Spring, his chaplain, who had rushed forward to his succor, limped slowly out of the fire. They supported him for more than a mile to the hospital in the rear, while he, though pale and faint, urged every soldier he encountered on the way to hasten forward to the assault. At last, driven back at every point, the American army retired.

The rest of the winter it remained in camp, unmolested by the enemy. Spring preached regularly to the troops on Sundays, and devoted his remaining time to the sick and wounded. It was a severe winter.

With the opening of spring, offensive operations were recommenced, but they resulted in nothing. In the mean time, troops arrived from England—small pox broke out in the American camp, and one misfortune succeeded another, till at length the invading army was driven out of Canada. Spring bore his part in all these hardships and disasters with unshaken fortitude.

After this, the portion of the army which had been assigned for the invasion of Canada, was broken up, and a reorganization took place. He, therefore, resigned his commission, and accepted a call from the people of Newburyport, who had listened the year before to his eloquent discourse on the departure of the expedition from that town. He remained pastor of this church for forty years, or until his death, in 1819. Of his after career of usefulness; his influence in establishing Andover Theological Seminary, or his other labors, it is not my province to speak.

When an old man, he was once on a visit to his son, the present venerable Dr. Spring, of New York, and expressed a wish to have an interview with Aaron Burr. The son attempted to dissuade him from it, remarking that such was Mr. Burr's present character and reputation, that he thought an interview would not be agreeable. But the venerable man recalled to mind the time when he was chaplain in the army under Arnold—the terrible assault before daylight on Quebec—and the fact of young Burr carrying the dying Montgomery on his back out of the fight, and still said he wanted to see him. So Dr. Spring invited him to his house, and the two met; but the conversation soon passing from memories of the past to more general topics, Burr gave utterance to opinions and sentiments, so repulsive to the man of God, that, when the door closed on the visitor, he remarked to his son that he never wished to see him again.

He died on the 4th of March, 1819, seventy-three years of age. His closing hours were peaceful, and full of calm confidence in his Saviour, and almost the last words, that broke from his aged lips, were, "*Oh, let me be gone—do let me be gone—I long to be home.*" While, as one of the leaders in Israel, he occupies a prominent position in the history of the American Church, he also, as a true patriot, stands linked with one of the most arduous, perilous expeditions in the annals of the Revolution.

CHAPTER IX.

EBENEZER PRIME.

His Patriotism.—Driven from his Church.—His Library destroyed.—His Death.—Insult to his Grave.

Ebenezer Prime was born in the year 1700, and hence was seventy-five years old when open hostilities between the Colonies and mother country commenced. Though past his threescore and ten, and already tottering on the confines of the grave—when the trumpet of war pealed over the land; his aged ear caught the sound, and the last failing energies of life were devoted to his country. He had apparently done with earth, and the scenes of eternity were opening on his vision, yet he deemed himself doing God's service in urging his people to fight for their liberties. His voice coming back as it were from the borders of the unseen world, invested the cause he advocated with peculiar solemnity, and gave it the high sanction of heaven. To one who had no future in this world, nothing but a solemn sense of duty to his God and his country could have aroused him to enlist in a struggle, the end of which he never expected to see.

Having graduated at Yale College, in 1718, he began at the early age of nineteen his ministerial labors at Huntington, Long Island, where he remained till the close of his long and useful life.

After the disastrous battle of Long Island his parish was invaded by the enemy, and he and his son were compelled to flee for safety. The latter, with his family, left the island, while the aged pastor found shelter in a remote, secluded part of his parish. The firm stand he had taken on the side of liberty was well known to the enemy, and his name was never mentioned by them except with curses. His parishioners, sharing his patriotism, shared with him also the suffering caused by the outrages of the invaders. Their property was destroyed, and they themselves compelled to flee for their lives. The church, in which he had so long preached, and where prayers for his oppressed country had so often arisen, was converted into a military depot, and desecrated by the licentious soldiery. They littered his stables, in which they housed their horses, with unthreshed sheaves of grain, mutilated his library by tearing to pieces his most valuable books, and consigning them to the flames. The old patriarch looked on this desolation of his home with sorrow, but without one regret for the stand he had taken for a just and noble cause. Though his voice could no longer proclaim from the pulpit the doctrine of civil and religious freedom, it could send up the fervent prayer, that God would deliver his suffering country from the hands of the oppressor. There would drift to his aged ear, in his seclusion, the news of defeat and of victory, that by turns depressed and animated the struggling patriots, but he never lived to be gladdened by the triumphant shout of victory that proclaimed a nation free forever. He closed his eyes on his country, torn and bleeding, but unshaken in her determination never to abandon the struggle till she was free. He died August 2d, 1779, and was buried in the grave-yard hard by the dilapidated church from which he had been driven. Afterwards, the notorious Col. Thompson, of Massachusetts, who subsequently became Count Rumford, quartered his troops in the town, and pulled down the church, and used the timbers and boards to construct barracks and block houses for their accommodation. To insult and outrage the feelings of the inhabitants still more, these were put up in the center of the burying ground, and the graves leveled so that the consecrated spot became a hard-trodden common. The grave-stones were pulled up, and used as stones to build their ovens with. From these the bread would often be taken with the inverted inscriptions stamped on the crust. The Colonel, to show his malignity, pitched his marquée at the head of Mr. Prime's grave, so that, to use his own language, "he might *tread on the old rebel every time he went out or in.*"

But the venerable patriot was beyond the reach of his insults and his rage, safe with the God whom he had served, and to whose protection he had in life committed without wavering his suffering country. The Rev. Dr. Prime, present able editor of the New York Observer, is his grandson, who has furnished for Dr. Sprague's American Pulpit an extended sketch of his ministerial life.

CHAPTER X.

SAMUEL EATON.

Is settled in Harpsburg, Maine.—Practices three Professions.—Attends a Political Meeting.—His stirring Address.—Narrow Escape of an Officer of the King.—Recruiting Officer seeks his Aid.—Eaton addresses the People on Sabbath Evening.—Thrilling Scene.—Soldiers obtained.—His Death.

Rev. Samuel Eaton was born in Braintree, Mass., and graduated at Harvard in 1763. Though a native of Massachusetts, he spent the greater part of his life in Maine. Endowed with a strong intellect, amiable yet fearless and independent, of strict integrity and warm piety, he exerted a powerful influence throughout the Colony. Possessed of considerable knowledge of medicine, he acted as physician in ordinary cases of sickness, while his character as peace-maker, and his knowledge of common legal documents were so well known and highly prized, that his people were seldom obliged to consult a lawyer. Acting thus in a threefold capacity his influence was felt far and wide. When the contest between the Colonies and the mother country commenced, he threw this influence on the side of the former; and, both in and out of the pulpit, strove to arouse the people to active resistance. He frequently took his texts in reference to the coming struggle, and spoke of it as a religious one, and directed his hearers to look to the Lord of Hosts for aid in carrying it forward. He declared that the people of New

England were a chosen generation, and it was God's purpose, if they depended on him, and obeyed his laws, to make them successful in securing the freedom they had made such sacrifices to establish in this new hemisphere.

After the battles of Lexington and Concord a meeting was called of all those capable of bearing arms in the towns of Harpswell and Brunswick. From far and near the yeomanry gathered to the meeting-house —the common place of *rendezvous* in those times—to consult on the course they should pursue in the impending crisis.

Mr. Eaton was present simply as one of the audience; and while the business was being transacted, listened in silence to the conflicting opinions that were presented. Some were doubtful and hesitating, and advocated mild measures that would leave them uncommitted; others openly opposed anything that looked like revolution. Although he said nothing while the debate was proceeding, he was observed to be moving amid the crowd, conversing with the disaffected, and endeavoring to convince them of the right and duty of resistance. The business at length being accomplished, the chairman, a zealous patriot, who had kept his eye on the pastor, arose, and requested him him to speak to the people. He consented; and, mounting the pulpit, addressed them with an eloquence and pathos that bore down all opposition, and made each heart leap as to a trumpet call. Flashing eyes and compressed lips on every side told that doubt and indecision were over. The patriots became excited almost to frenzy, and the chairman at length, no longer able to control himself, arose, and rushing to the leader of the opposition, who held a commission under the king, seized him by the collar, and demanded, with a loud voice, that he should at once, and on the spot, renounce king and Parliament. The officer refused to do so, and, scoffing at his threats, denounced him as a rebel. Stung to madness by the insulting epithet, the chairman cried out, " Away with him to the grave-yard—let us bury him alive !" The proposition was received with loud shouts, and the people, rising *en masse*, rushed on their terrified victim, and hurried him away.

They were in earnest ; and would soon have had the trembling wretch under ground ; but the counsels of a few of the more temperate, backed by the urgent solicitations of the pastor, calmed their passions, and they released him. Humbled and terrified, the trembling official turned and fled, escaping from an opposition he saw he was not only unable to stem, but which threatened to bear him away in its fury. The parson was found to be more powerful than the king in Harpsburg.

Some two months after, Falmouth, now Portland, was burned by the enemy. The country was at once aroused, and messengers were dispatched in every direction to summon the people to arms. A recruiting officer was sent to Harpswell to raise volunteers, but, to his surprise, found the people backward in responding to his call. Discouraged and sad he, as a last resort, repaired on Sunday morning to Mr. Eaton, to beg him to use his influence in his behalf. Meeting him on his way to church, he laid his case before him, and besought him to speak to the people, and urge them to come to the rescue. "Sir," said the pastor, "it is my communion Sabbath, and I must not introduce secular subjects during the day. I will think of the matter, and see what I can do. Perhaps I will invite the people to assemble in front of the meeting-house at the going down of the sun." So, after service, he told the congregation that he wished to see them after sunset on the church green. He then dismissed them to their homes, and retired to his study.

It was a warm August evening, and as the sun stooped behind the western hills, closing the New England Sabbath, and while his beams still lingered on the glittering spire, men singly and in groups were seen bending their steps towards the meeting-house. Some, surprised at the strange invitation, were wondering what it meant, while others, knowing their pastor's patriotism, more than suspected its object. When the crowd had all assembled, and early twilight was gathering over the landscape, Mr. Eaton left his study, and proceeded thoughtfully to the meeting-house. The crowd gave way respectfully as he approached, and passing through it he mounted the horse block standing near the door. Pausing a moment, and casting his eye over the crowd, he said: "Let us look to God in prayer." It was a strangely solemn scene — that venerated pastor in the gray twilight, with head uncovered, lifting his voice to the heavens, while the assembly, with bowed heads and motionless forms, stood and reverently listened. When he had closed, he stood for a minute as if lost in thought, and then burst forth, "*Cursed be he that keepeth back his sword from blood!*"—Jeremiah, xlvi. 10.

A sudden thunder peal breaking from the clear heavens would not have startled those quiet farmers more than the unexpected deliverance of this fearful anathema. Coming from the minister of God, and uttered there under the shadow of the sanctuary, on the evening of the solemn Sabbath, it carried with it a strange, resistless power. A silence profound as that which rested on the neighboring grave-yard followed. He then went on to describe briefly the circumstances under which it was pronounced—drew a parallel between them and the present oppressed and perilous state of God's people in the Colony, and making a direct application of the subject to those present, closed with a powerful appeal to them as men, as patriots, to gird on the sword without delay, and strike for God and liberty.

The minister effected what the recruiting officer failed to accomplish, and that night forty men enrolled their names as volunteers.

After the termination of the war, his life moved on in the even tenor of its way to its close in 1822. Courtly in his manners, faithful in his duties, never failing to warn, rebuke, and instruct the highest as well as the lowest whenever a proper occasion presented itself, he lived to the good old age of eighty-five, and, like a shock of corn fully ripe, was gathered to his fathers in peace.

CHAPTER XI.

WILLIAM TENNENT.

His Birth and Education.—Settled at Norwalk, Conn.—Removes to Charleston, S. C.—His personal Appearance.—His Eloquence.—His Boldness and Zeal in the Cause of the Colonies.—Makes Patriotic Appeals on the Sabbath.—Is elected Member of the Provincial Congress of South Carolina.—Sent with Henry Drayton to the back Settlements to baffle the Tories.—His Letters to Henry Laurens and the Congress.—Again sent to Congress.—His Character and Death.

The 'Tennents seemed to be of the Aaronic line, and William was a favorite name in the various branches of the family. There were three William Tennents who early devoted themselves to the cause of their Master, and when the Revolution broke out made the cause of their country one with it. The clergyman, whose name stands at the head of this sketch, is sometimes called William Tennent (Third), to distinguish him from the other celebrated William Tennents, and was born in Freehold, N. J., in 1740. Gifted with a fine intellect, he made such rapid progress in his early studies that he graduated at Princeton when but eighteen years of age. He was licensed to preach in 1761, and labored as an itinerant for six months under the direction of Hanover presbytery of Virginia. In 1765 he was settled at Norwalk, Conn., where he remained a little over six years. At the end of that period, he received a call from an independent church in Charleston, S. C., and though for a time the church at Norwalk refused to part with him, they finally gave a reluctant consent, and he was installed pastor of the former church. He was laboring here when the storm of the Revolution broke over the land.

The contest at once enlisted his whole heart, and he threw himself into it with a boldness and zeal that astonished and troubled some of even his best friends. He was of a manly presence, vivid imagination, great beauty of person, and lofty genius. Consciousness of his great powers made him bold and enterprising, and he became a great favorite with the people. Said one who knew him well, over his dead body: "His honest, disinterested, yet glowing zeal for his country's good demands from us a tribute of respect. Impressed with a sense of the justness, greatness, and vast importance of the American cause, he engaged in it with an ardor and resolution that would have done honor to an ancient Roman. For this he was indeed censured, and perhaps too liberally, by his friends. Early in the contest he magnanimously stepped forth as an advocate for this continent. Here was a field suited to his great abilities, and here his abilities shone with increasing lustre. He first endeavored to rouse his fellow-citizens to a just sense of their inestimable rights and a willingness to contend for them, and to his spirited exertions, among others, may in a great measure be attributed that noble, patriotic zeal which soon blazed forth to the immortal honor of this State."

Being at the center of influence in the province, his

eloquent appeals reached those who controlled its destinies. He rarely preached political sermons; but so holy did he feel the struggle to be, in which the Colonies were engaged, that often, after the services of the Sabbath were over, he would repair to the court-house, and address the people on their duty to their country. He did not regard this as any desecration of the Sabbath, for though he felt that the services of the sanctuary were consecrated to divine worship, he yet believed that the Sabbath was made for man, not man for the Sabbath.

His pen was also devoted to the cause of his country, and he left no measure untried to reach the ear and heart of the inhabitants of South Carolina. His enthusiastic patriotism and his great talents made him so prominent that the people, contrary to established usage, elected him member of the Provincial Congress. In 1775, the tories in the back settlements began to assume such an attitude of decided hostility towards the friends of the Revolution that serious consequences were apprehended. To counteract their influence, the Council of Safety appointed Mr. Tennent and Wm. Henry Drayton* a deputation to visit different portions of the State. They at once set out on their mission, and traveling through the back settlements, had private interviews with the people, and held public meetings at which Tennent addressed them in such burning eloquence that the adherents of the royal government trembled for their influence. Public meetings, private conferences, the formation of volunteer companies,

* President of Provincial Congress.

and unceasing efforts to bring in the wavering, and overawe the openly hostile, occupied all his time and energies.

The following extracts from his letters while on this mission will give a slight idea of his labors. In one of them, to Henry Laurens, dated "Bullock's Creek, Aug. 20th, 1774," he says, after speaking of what others, in conjunction with himself, were doing, "I turned my course into the new acquisition, where I am to have a meeting, from day to day, in Col. Neil's regiment. *I think I shall fix this district in the right cause.* I discovered on my way a scheme to surprise Fort Charlotte, took an affidavit of it, and sent it express to Mr. Drayton—so hope it will be prevented. * * * I have formed one, and am forming, in this district, another troop of volunteer horse rangers, who are good as sworn to the Council of Safety, when they enlist. We are hemming in the dissidents on all sides as much as possible, but their leaders seem determined, if possible, to bring the people to draw blood before they have time to be enlightened. I have forsook my chaise, and ride on horseback, from day to day meeting the people."

In another letter, dated "Long Cane, Sept. 1st," addressed to the Committee of Safety, he says, "I thought it necessary to visit the settlements on this side of Saluda. Met a large congregation yesterday, and found the people divided in their sentiments. Spoke at least two hours to them with good effect. The prevailing party here is for American measures, but they need confirmation. I have, therefore, appointed three meetings, at which I expect to see a great number of the disaffected. I shall then cross over into Fletchell's regiment once more, to be at an election appointed at Ford's, on the Emoree, where we expect great opposition, if not violence, from Cunningham's party. Brown will bring them to blood if he can, but I still hope it may be prevented. I consider myself as running great risks, but think it my duty * * * *." He then speaks of the want of ammunition, and adds, "I shall visit Charlotte before I return, and hope to let you hear more particularly on this subject next week."

In executing this mission he not only swayed the people by his eloquence, but by his shrewdness and sagacity broke up many dangerous plots and combinations.

Returning to Charleston, he again took his seat in Congress, to which he was successively elected. Says the Rev. Mr. Alison, who preached his funeral sermon: "Both in the Provincial Congress and General Assembly he displayed great erudition, strength of argument, generosity of sentiment, and a most unbounded eloquence. He continued his fervent endeavors to the last, resolutely regardless of the attacks of envy and calumny he met with."

In 1777, his aged father died at Freehold, and the next summer he came north to take his widowed mother to his own home, that he might cheer and solace her declining years. On his return, when about ninety miles from Charleston, on the high hills of Santee, he was seized with a violent nervous fever which carried him rapidly to the grave. Just as the spirit was leaving the body, he remarked to the clergyman beside him, that his mind was calm and easy, and he was willing to be gone.

Thus passed away, as it were on the very threshold of the great struggle in which his heart was so deeply interested, this young, eloquent, gifted divine and ardent patriot. Had he lived to the good old age of Dr. Wetherspoon, he would, like him, have been not only one of the leading patriots, but one of the great intellectual lights of the country. It is rare that great personal beauty, impressive bearing, genius, eloquence, and piety are united in one man as they were in him. He was one of the few on whom nature seems to delight to lavish her choicest gifts. These were all sanctified and consecrated to God and his country.

CHAPTER XII.

PETER GABRIEL MUHLENBURG.

Fighting Clergymen.—Muhlenburg's Birth and Education.—Goes to England.—Settles in Virginia.—Takes a prominent Part in Political Movements.—Becomes Member of the House of Burgesses.—Raises a Regiment, of which he is chosen Colonel.—Preaches His Farewell Sermon.—Orders the Drum to beat for Recruits at the Church-door.—Marches to Charleston.—Camps at Valley Forge.—Fights bravely at Brandywine.—At Monmouth.—Commands the Reserve at Stony Point.—Makes a desperate Assault at Yorktown.—Is made Major-General.—His Political Career after the War.—Defence of his Course in Abandoning his Profession.

THERE was a class of clergymen in the Revolution who regarded the struggle so sacred that they felt it to be their duty to fight sometimes as well as pray. They did not, however, consider it necessary to abandon their profession to do so. That duty depended on the emergency of the case. In a perilous crisis, when one idle arm might turn the scale against the patriots, they had no hesitation in stepping into the ranks, and fighting like a common soldier. They saw nothing incongruous in this course, and hence seldom condescended to make an apology for it. Nor did it interfere with their professional duties—for, when the smoke of battle had cleared away, they were found praying with the wounded who had been struck by their side, or offering thanksgivings in front of the battalions for a victory won.

The subject of the following sketch, however, abandoned entirely his profession, and became a distinguished military man.

John Peter Gabriel Muhlenburg was born in the village of Trapp, Montgomery Co., Pa., on the first of October, 1746. Educated partly in this country and partly in Europe, he received ordination in 1768, and commenced his labors in Western New Jersey. In 1772 he went to London to receive ordination from an English bishop, that he might take charge of a church in Virginia, to which he had been called. Returning to America, he settled at Woodstock, and entered on the duties of a country pastor.

His ministerial profession, however, did not prevent him from feeling a deep interest in the quarrel between the Colonies and the mother country—on the contrary, he took the lead in every measure of hostility to her oppressive acts.

In 1774, when the people of his county assembled to choose a committee of safety, he was unanimously elected its chairman. He was the head and soul of the opposition in that whole region, and so much did he possess the confidence of the people that they sent him to the House of Burgesses of the state. Ardent, fearless and patriotic he became so absorbed in the approaching struggle, that, when the news of the battle of Bunker Hill reached him, he resolved at once to throw up his profession, and enter the army. Having talked and preached for freedom, he determined now to *strike* for it. He immediately commenced to organize a Virginia regiment, and laying aside his ministerial character, became its colonel.

FAREWELL SERMON. 123

He took leave of his people in a farewell sermon, which glowed throughout with the most devoted patriotism. At the close he told them of the resolution he had taken to fight, and if need be, die for his country on the battle-field. It was a strange announcement from the pulpit, but there were few to criticize his abandonment of his profession, for he had breathed his own fervid spirit into his congregation, and the kindling eye and speaking countenance told him that his course had their hearty approval. Said he, in conclusion, "The Bible tells us 'there is a time for all things,' and there is a time to preach, and a time to pray, but the time for me to preach has passed away;" then, raising his voice, till it rung like the blast of a trumpet through the church, he exclaimed, "*and there is a time to fight, and that time has now come.*"

Closing the services he stepped into the vestry-room, and laying aside his gown, put on his colonel's uniform, and stood before his astonished congregation in full regimentals. This sudden apparition of a Virginia colonel, in full uniform, walking down the broad aisle, in the place of their pastor, took every one by surprise. Turning neither to the right hand nor to the left, he strode sternly on to the door, and ordered the drum to beat for recruits.

The silence that had reigned, while this extraordinary scene was passing, was suddenly broken by the loud and rapid roll of the drum. The congregation rose simultaneously to their feet, and the men gathered in a mass around their former pastor—scarcely one capable of bearing arms remaining behind. The calm quiet of the Sabbath day was now changed into a scene of bustle and excitement. The drum was kept beating, and those who were not in the church came rushing towards it, to learn what strange event had happened. The sight of the pastor in uniform, standing at the door and calling for recruits, kindled the most unbounded enthusiasm, and before night nearly three hundred men had joined his standard. He immediately marched south, and was present with his regiment at the battle of Charleston.

The next year he was promoted by Congress to the rank of brigadier-general, and ordered to take charge of all the Continental troops in Virginia. The next May he joined Washington at Middebrook, New Jersey, and marched with his brigade to the desolate encampment of Valley Forge. Among the devoted leaders who closed with unflinching resolution and courage around their great chieftain, during the trials of this terrible winter, none took a firmer and nobler stand than Muhlenburg. At the battle of Brandywine his brigade formed a part of the division of Greene, which at the close of that disastrous day was ordered up from the rear, where he had been stationed, to cover the retreat. For three quarters of an hour these noble troops withstood the onset of the entire British army, and then steadily and in good order withdrew. At Germantown he was in the thickest of the fight, and at Monmouth, on that scorching Sabbath day, led his troops over the burning sands as steadily as if on parade. Known for his coolness, courage, and determined resolution, he was selected by

Wayne to command the reserve at the assault on Stony Point. He was afterwards stationed in Virginia, and aided in the operations that finally shut up Cornwallis in Yorktown. His brigade was actively employed during the siege of that place. On one occasion he led a storming party against a redoubt, and with such desperate and deadly resolution did he carry it through the fire, that not a man returned unwounded.

At the close of the war he was elevated to the rank of major-general. Removing to Pennsylvania, he was made chairman of the executive council of the State, and afterwards was sent to Congress. In 1801 he was elected United States Senator, and in the same year received the appointment of supervisor of the internal revenue of Pennsylvania. The next year he was made collector of the port of Philadelphia, which office he held till his death, in October 1807. He was buried close by the village church where he was baptized, and the following true epitaph placed above his grave: "He was brave in the field, faithful in the cabinet, honorable in all his transactions, a sincere friend, and an honest man."

It is but just to the memory of this unflinching patriot to let him be heard in his own defence for his course in abandoning the pulpit for the army. In a letter to his brother Frederick, a clergyman also, who had written to another brother condemning his (Peter's) course for laying aside the ministerial profession for that of arms, he says: "Thus far I had written when I received brother Henry's letter from you to him, wherein you make observations on my conduct in the present alarming crisis. You say, as a clergyman nothing can excuse my conduct. I am a clergyman, it is true, but I am a member of society as well as the poorest layman, and my liberty is as dear to me as to any man. Shall I then sit still, and enjoy myself at home, when the best blood of the continent is spilling? Heaven forbid it! You make a comparison with Struensee. The comparison is odious. Did he die in defence of his country? Far from it. He suffered for crimes, and his life was justly forfeited to the law.

But even if you was on the opposite side of the question, you must allow that in this last step I have acted for the best. You know that from the beginning of these troubles I have been compelled to have a hand in public affairs. I have been chairman to the committee of delegates from this county from the first. *Do you think, if America should be conquered, I should be safe? Far from it. And would you not sooner fight like a man than die like a dog?* I am called by my country to its defence. The cause is just and noble. Were I a bishop, even a Lutheran one, I should obey without hesitation, and so far am I from thinking that I am wrong, I am convinced it is my duty so to do, a duty I owe to my God and to my country."

This same Frederick, notwithstanding his condemnation of his brother, two or three years later, under the pressure of the Revolution, left the church for the state, and entered Congress under the Federal Constitution.

CHAPTER XIII.

THOMAS ALLEN.

His Birth and Education.—Settles in Pittsfield.—Takes decided Part with the Colonies.—Is made Chairman of the Committee of Safety and Correspondence.—His Labors.—His Interest in the Conquest of Ticonderoga.—New and interesting Letter to Gen. Seth Pomeroy.—Helps to furnish Knox with an Ox-train to carry Cannon to Boston.—Joins the Army as Chaplain.—His Diary at the Battle of White Plains.—Goes to Ticonderoga.—His Address to the Soldiers, when momentarily expecting an Attack from Burgoyne.—Leaves the Army in Disgust at the Retreat.—Rallies the Militia to the Aid of Stark, at Bennington.—His Interview with him.—Summons the Enemy to surrender, and is fired at.—Fights in the Ranks.—First over the Breast-work.—His Care for the Wounded.—Returns to his Parish.—Dialogue with a Parishioner.—"Puts out the Flash."—Goes to Georgia after his Brother's Widow.—Voyage to England after an Infant Grandchild.—Prays with and addresses the Crew in Expectation of an Attack.—His Conduct in the Shay's Rebellion.—His Statesmanship.—His Death.

Some of the clergy who were deeply engaged in the Revolution kept a record of the stirring scenes through which they passed, and left letters and documents that are still preserved with religious care by their descendants, and which have a priceless value in the eyes of the historian. The pleasure of perusing them, however, is sadly diminished by the regret they awaken, that so much similar material has been lost, through accident, want of proper care, or appreciation of its true worth.

The descendants of the subject of the following sketch are among the fortunate few who possess such documents and memoranda saved from the wreck of the past.

Among the patriotic clergymen of New England none occupies a higher rank than Thomas Allen, of Pittsfield, who was born in Northampton, January 17th, 1743. An uncle, whose name he bore, having bequeathed to him a sum sufficient to provide for his education, he commenced his studies early in life, and at nineteen graduated with high honor at Cambridge. He was only twenty-one when he was ordained pastor of Pittsfield, then a frontier town on the western borders of Massachusetts. He was the first minister ever settled in the place, which was then a rude collection of log huts, with the exception perhaps of half a dozen framed houses.

In 1768 he married the daughter of Rev. Jonathan Lee, of Salisbury, Conn., by whom he had twelve children, many of whose descendants at this day shed lustre on the State that gave them birth. He was of middle height and slender frame, yet strong and active, and capable of great endurance. His frank, open countenance was lit up by a keen and piercing eye. Ardent in his feelings, hating wrong, and scorning oppression, he became deeply enlisted in the cause of the Colonies, from the commencement of the struggle for redress of grievances, while his zeal and ability made him the leader in all the measures taken to resist the encroachments of the mother country. Hence, in June 1774, when the selectmen of the town called a town meeting, and seven men were appointed a standing committee of safety and correspondence, he was chosen chairman. This position brought him into correspondence with the leading patriots of the State, and in the commencement of the Revolution was one calling for great activity and labor. Though earnest and eloquent in his appeals, he was a man of deeds rather than words, and gave his time and energies to the carrying out of practical measures.

When the expedition against Ticonderoga was being organized, he took a deep interest in it, and wrote letters to Seth Pomeroy, at Cambridge, not only keeping him informed of what was going on in the western part of the State, but suggesting plans of future action. He helped to unravel plots against the patriots, caused some to be sent to jail, and drove others with "hue and cry" out of the region. He traveled over into New York, bringing back the disaffected, and stirring up rebellion on every side.

The conquest of Canada, at this time, seemed to occupy the attention of military leaders almost as much as the defence of our sea coast; and Ticonderoga and Crown Point being regarded as the key to it, their capture became of vital importance. It was necessary, however, that any expedition against them should be conducted with great secrecy, or reënforcements from Canada would be hastened down to garrison them more effectually. Mr. Allen thus refers to the expedition that was finally set on foot:

"PITTSFIELD, May 4th, 1775.

"GENERAL POMEROY:

"SIR—I have the pleasure to acquaint you that a

number of gentlemen from Connecticut went from this place last Thursday morning, having been joined by Col. Easton, Capt. Dickinson, and Mr. Brown, with forty soldiers, on an expedition against Ticonderoga and Crown Point, expecting to be reënforced by men from the grants above here, a post having previously taken his departure to inform Col. Ethan Allen of the design, and desiring him to hold his Green Mountain boys in actual readiness. The expedition has been carried on with the utmost secrecy, as they are in hopes of taking the forts by surprise. He expects they will reach those forts by Saturday next, or Lord's day at the farthest. The plan was concocted at Hartford, last Saturday, by the Governor and Council, Col. Hancock, Mr. Adams, and others from our Province being present. Three hundred pounds were drawn immediately out of the treasury for the aforesaid purpose, and committed to those gentlemen who were here. We earnestly pray for success in this important expedition, as the taking of those places would afford us a key to all Canada. There is, if the accounts are to be depended upon, not more than twenty soldiers at each fort. There are a large number of cannon, and I hear four as excellent brass cannon as we could wish. Should success attend the expedition, we expect a strong reënforcement will be sent from the western part of Connecticut, to keep those forts, and to repair and fortify them well.

We have had much work here of late with the tories. A dark plot has been discovered of sending names down to Gen. Gage, in consequence of which, and the critical situation of the times, we have been compelled to act with vigor, and have sent Mr. Jones and Graves to Northampton goal, where they now lie in close confinement, and have sent a hue and cry after Maj. Stoddard and Mr. Little, who have fled to New York for shelter. We hope it will not be long before they are taken into custody, and committed to close confinement.

"Our tories are the worst in the Province—all the effect the late and present operations have had upon them is, they are *mute* and *pensive*, and secretly *wish* for more *prosperous days to toryism*. As to your important operations, sir, you have the fervent prayers of all good men that success may attend them. I hope God will inspire you with wisdom from above in all your deliberations, and your soldiers with courage and fortitude, and that Boston will speedily be delivered into your hands—the General thereof, and all the king's troops—that that *den of thieves, that nest of robbers, that asylum for traitors and murderers*, may be *broken up*, and never another red coat from England *set foot on these shores*.

"I have been concerned, lest General Gage should spread the small pox in your army. May heaven protect your army from his wicked wiles. May you be shielded, sir, in the day of battle, and obtain a complete victory over those enemies of God and mankind. I have but one observation to make, which I have often made, upon the histories I have read, and then I must put an end to this tedious epistle—it is this: seldom or never do the greatest generals improve a victory when it is obtained.

"I am, with great respect,
"Your humble, obedient servant,
"THOMAS ALLEN."

The young divine, chairman of the committee of safety and correspondence, is closely watched, and his name sent down to Gen. Gage as the most dangerous character to the king's cause in the western part of the Colony. He is a marked man; and his clerical profession will not save his neck from the halter, if he once falls into the hands of the enemy; but, instead of being alarmed by these secret efforts to accomplish his destruction, he marks the conspirators, puts some of them in chains, and drives others over the border in affright. Though by profession a man of peace, in this great struggle he is a man of blood. Active and keen, his knowledge extends everywhere, and his blow falls quick and sudden as a bolt from heaven. Plotting tories are struck in the midst of their conspiracies, and while they are sending his name to Gen. Gage for future reference, he sends them to prison.

The closing sentence of this letter is significant. He is afraid of temporizing measures—that victory would be followed by delays, in hopes of adjusting matters without farther bloodshed. His theory is the one Bonaparte carried out triumphantly—follow up a successful blow with strokes so rapid that the staggered enemy will not have time to recover. It is a delicate hint, and well worth attending to. This letter reveals a characteristic that belonged to all the patriotic clergy of that day—belief that faith and works must go together. While leaving no stone unturned to secure the ends he has in view, he yet looks upward for the blessing of heaven, without which all his labors he knows will be in vain.

Five days after this he writes again to Gen. Pomeroy, evidently in answer to a letter he has received from him, asking for information. This correspondence shows that Mr. Allen was looked upon as the leading patriot in the part of Massachusetts where he resided, and that in addition to the duties of the parish, he had on his shoulders the charge of the political movements of the county.

The second letter to Gen. Pomeroy is dated:

"PITTSFIELD, May 9th, 1775.

"GEN. POMEROY:

"SIR—I shall esteem it a great happiness if I can communicate any intelligence to you that shall be of any service to my country. In my last I wrote to you of the northern expedition. Before this week ends we are in raised hopes here of hearing that Ticonderoga and Crown Point are in other hands. Whether the expedition fails or succeeds, I will send you the most early intelligence, as I look on it as an affair of great importance.

"Solomons, the Indian king at Stockbridge, was lately at Col. Easton's, of this town, and said that the Mohawks had not only given liberty to the Stockbridge Indians to join us, but had sent them a belt, denoting that they would hold in readiness five hundred men to join us immediately on the first notice, and that the said Solomons holds an Indian post in actual readiness to run with the news as soon as they shall be wanted. Should the council of war judge it necessary to send to them, after being better informed of the matter by Capt. Goodrich, now in the service, if you should issue out your orders to Col. Easton, I make no doubt that he would bring them down soon. These Indians might be of great service, should the king's troops march out of Boston, as some think they undoubtedly will upon the arrival of their recruits, and give us battle.

"Our militia this way are vigorously preparing for actual service — adjacent towns and this town are bringing arms and ammunition. There is plenty of arms to be sold at Albany as yet, but we hear, by order of the major, no powder is to be sold for the present there. *The spirit of liberty* runs high there, as you have doubtless heard by their post to our headquarters. I have exerted myself to disseminate the same spirit in King's district, which has of late taken surprising effect. The poor tories at Kinderhook are mortified and grieved, and are wheeling about, and begin to take the quick step. New York government *begins to be alive in the glorious cause, and to act with vigor.* Some this way say that the king's troops will carry off all the plate, merchandise, and plunder from the town of Boston, to pay them for their ignominious expedition, which, in my opinion, would not be at all inconsistent with the shameful principles of those who sent them on so inglorious an expedition.

"I fervently pray, sir, that our Council of War may be inspired with wisdom from above, to direct the warlike enterprise with prudence, discretion, and vigor. O, may your councils of deliberation be under the guidance and blessing of heaven. Since I began to write, an intelligent person, who left Ticonderoga Saturday before last, informs me that, having went through there and Crown Point about three weeks ago, all were secure, but on his return he found they were alarmed with our expedition, and would not admit him into the fort—that there were twelve soldiers at Crown Point, and he judged near two hundred at Ticonderoga—that those forts were out of repair and much in ruins—that it was his opinion that our men would undoubtedly be able to take them, and that he met our men last Thursday, who were well furnished with cattle and wagons laden with provisions and in good spirits, who he supposed would arrive there last Sabbath day, and he doubted not that this week they would be in possession of those forts. He informed them where they might find plenty of ball, and there are cannon enough at Crown Point which they can not secure from us. That he saw the old *Sow*,* from Cape Breton, and a number of good brass cannon, at Ticonderoga. Should the expedition succeed, and should the Council of War send up their order for the people this way, to transport by land twenty or thirty of the

---

* Taken at the siege of Louisburg.

best of the cannon to head quarters, I doubt not but the people in this country would do it with expedition. We could easily collect a thousand yoke of cattle for the business.

"Since I wrote the last paragraph, an express has arrived from Benedict Arnold, commander of the forces against Ticonderoga for recruits, in consequence of which orders are issued out for a detachment of eighteen men of each company in this regiment to march immediately, who will be on their way this day.

"I am with great respect, sir,
"Your humble servant,
"THOMAS ALLEN."

This letter shows how complicated and extensive was the business devolving on Mr. Allen. He ascertains the state of things at Ticonderoga and Crown Point—finds where ammunition can be obtained, corresponds with New York, goes over in person to the "King's District," and gives the "glorious cause" there a fresh impulse—furnishes important information respecting the attitude of the Indians, anticipates the need there will be at Boston for the cannon in Ticonderoga, and offers to collect a thousand yoke of cattle to transport them thither; and while in the midst of all this, he is arrested by the arrival of an express from Arnold demanding recruits, and stops long enough to add that eighteen men from each company are detailed for the service.

The next day, Ticonderoga surrendered to Ethan Allen, creating great exultation throughout the New

JOINS THE ARMY AS CHAPLAIN.

England Colonies. Thomas Allen sent off his posts in every direction, speeding the glad news.

Throughout the summer that followed, Washington laid close siege to Boston. He was, however, very much crippled in his operations for want of cannon, and next winter Knox volunteered to go to Ticonderoga, and transport some of those in the fort across the country. Had Allen's proposition been accepted in May, they would have been at Boston as soon as Washington was.

Knox took no means of transportation from the army, relying entirely on the inhabitants of the western frontier to furnish them. Allen was foremost in responding to his call, and soon a train of forty-two sleds, laden with over fifty guns and two thousand pounds of lead, was seen slowly traversing the wilderness towards Boston. In a short time they were frowning from Dorchester Heights, and under their stern and threatening aspect the British fleet dropped down the bay, and the city became untenable.

After the battle of Long Island and the fall of New York, which sent much discouragement throughout the land, Allen could no longer remain at home an idle spectator of the conflict, and set out for the army at Kingsbridge, and offered his services as chaplain.

In the movements and battles that followed after the army broke up its position at Harlaem Heights, until it commenced its sad retreat through New Jersey, he bore a conspicuous part. Like Gano and others, he did not consider his duty limited to preaching to the soldiers and praying with them, but felt called upon to furnish an example of courage in danger, and endurance under privations.

A part of a journal kept by him at this time has been preserved by one of his descendants, now residing in Pittsfield, in which we get transient gleams of his life in camp. Among others we find such entries as the following, evidently made in a great hurry, and jotted down perhaps on the head of a drum or the crown of his hat.

"*October 23d, at White Plains.*—I saw our men bringing in a Hessian on a sort of bier, who was wounded in the leg. There had been an action just before, between a party of our men and the enemy—we killed between ten and twenty of the enemy, and took two prisoners, whom I saw. The Hessian's leg was broken—as he was brought in the multitude behaved badly. The Hessian behaved well, took off his hat to the crowd. He was a rifleman, dressed in green faced with white—was very dark, owing to his long voyage of twenty weeks, had arrived only three weeks before."

Oct. 24.—At night struck our tents—moved off four miles towards White Plains—this night encamped without a tent upon the ground."

Oct. 25.—All day under arms, in continual expectation of an attack from the enemy, who appeared, paraded in sight, marching and countermarching—a great battle expected to be at the door. Night after this day lay also on the ground under a brush shelter."

BATTLE OF WHITE PLAINS.

Saturday, Oct. 26.—Sun rose clear, the enemy near—a great battle drawing on."

The latter part of October, with its frosty nights, was not a good time for a young clergyman to begin sleeping on the ground, in the open air. Yet to one in whose bosom the fire of patriotism burned with such a fervent glow as in his, these privations and exposures were unthought of, and do not receive a passing notice. He says:—

"Yesterday forgot to dine. This day made an excellent dinner on bread and butter only,—being in a continual expectation of a cannonade from the enemy, who now lay in plain sight at the distance of little more than half a mile."

He is not a mile or two from camp, in the hospital with the surgeons, but in full view of the enemy, snatching his dinner of bread and butter, with his eye watching the gleaming lines and the long rows of cannon within point blank shot, and whose thunders may at any moment bring his frugal repast to a close.

"Kindled up our fires after dark, and began our retreat, with General Bell's brigade in the most excellent order—keeping out our flank guards, etc."

"*Lord's-day, Oct. 27.*—Arrived at break of day at White Plains, having performed a march of above twelve miles in the night. Lay down after daylight for sleep on the ground."

They had not lain long before the sharp rattle of

musketry roused them from their repose, and the march recommenced. The balls flew thick around the chaplain, but the only remark he makes about it is—"Encamped on White Plains in our tent, having been *marvellously preserved in our retreat.*" "Dr. Wright, of New Marlborough, was buried this day—such a confused Sabbath I never saw."

The retreat under fire—the booming of cannon at intervals—shouts and orders of officers—the pealing bugle and the fierce roll of the drum—giving way at last to the almost equally great tumult of pitching the camp, might well make a Sabbath day long to be remembered. The whistling of bullets near him had more than once reminded him from what a scene of confusion he might, in a moment, be called away to the still land, where the tread of armies is never heard, and the sound of battle never comes.

In the battle of the 28th he occupied a position where he could see distinctly every movement of the hostile line, and towards the close of it, when the militia under Gen. McDougal fled, he, in his eagerness to help save the army from defeat, hurried forward to offer his services as a volunteer.

One sees occasionally in Mr. Allen's letters and journal that, in his earlier days, he had read military history with more than ordinary care. This is evident from the following short entry in his diary, in which he unconsciously reminds us that, amid the terrific cannonade and rattle of small arms, and smoke and confusion of the conflict, he forgot every thing in the manœuvering of the two armies—looking to *that* more than to the effect of the cannonade, as indicative of the final result :—

"*Oct.* 28.—About 9 o'clock, A. M., the enemy and our out parties were engaged ; about 10, they appeared in plain sight, falling off towards our right wing. A strong cannonade ensued from both armies. A great part of the enemy's strength seemed bent towards our right wing, but no *additional force of ours was as yet directed that way.*

"At length the enemy came up with our right wing, and a most furious engagement ensued by cannonnade and small arms, which lasted towards two hours. Our wing was situated on a hill,* and consisted of, perhaps, something more than a brigade of Maryland forces. The cannonades and small arms played most furiously without cessation—I judge more than twenty-three cannon in a minute.

"At length a reënforcement of Gen. Bell's brigade was ordered from an adjacent hill, where I was. I had an inclination to go with them to the hill, that I might more distinctly see the battle, and perhaps *contribute my mite to our success.* Just as we began to ascend the hill, we found our men had given way, and were moving off the hill in some confusion, at which some elevated shots from the enemy came into the valley where we were very thick—one of which took off the fore part of a man's foot in about three rods of me. I saw the ball strike, and the man fall ; as none appeared for his help, I desired five or six of those who

---

* Chatterton's Hill.—EDITOR.

had been in battle to carry him off. Others I saw carrying off wounded in different directions. With the rest I retreated to the main body. Our men fought with great bravery; they were sore galled by the enemy's field-pieces."

The whole British force now drew up before the fortified heights, on which Washington lay, but dared not attempt to carry them until the arrival of reënforcements on the 30th, when it was resolved to move *en masse* on the position. But that night a terrific storm of wind and rain set in, and when it cleared away, Washington quietly withdrew with his army to North Castle. The wind roared fiercely through the Highlands, fanning into greater fury the flames of the burning village, which lighted their pathway over the hills.

How long he remained with the main army after this is not known, but it is evident that the formidable movements on our northern frontier soon called him thither; for, when the news of Burgoyne's invasion was spreading consternation over the country, we find him at Ticonderoga, where St. Clair was posted to arrest the progress of the invader. Believing in his courageous soul, that Burgoyne's powerful expedition would be broken in pieces against this strong fortress, he looked forward in high spirits to the day of its arrival before it. He animated the men by his patriotic appeals, and promised them that he would fight and fall by their side. He would not only pray with them, but die with them. He saw the deep design of the British in this formidable movement, and felt that its success would be a death blow to the Colonies. He believed it, therefore, to be the duty of every man, to die in his place rather than to suffer the enemy to pass this barrier, the only one of importance that crossed his march to the heart of New York State. He for one was willing then and there to offer himself up a sacrifice to his country, and he called on all to follow his example. They might be overborne, but even in their death inflict, like Sampson, a mortal blow on the enemy.

His feelings and determination at this fearful crisis in our history, as they are exhibited in an address he made to the soldiers, when the enemy was drawn up in battle array before them, and an attack was momentarily expected, challenge our highest admiration. The American outposts towards Lake George, after a mere show of resistance, had been driven in. The enemy had covered Mount Hope with artillery that completely commanded the road in that direction, while artillery, and ammunition, and stores were being hurried rapidly forward. The "Thunderer," with the battery train, had come up, and anchored in full view, while, to complete their dismay, the sun, as it rose on the morning of the 5th over the eastern hills, lit up the summit of Mount Defiance glowing in scarlet uniforms, while between, a long row of heavy brass cannon flashed in the early light, and looked threateningly down into the uncovered works. This fearful apparition had come in the night time, and as the officers gazed on it, they were filled with consternation, and St. Clair immediately called a council of war,—for an attack was momentarily expected. Mr. Allen, too, gazed on the alarming spectacle, but while the council of war was discussing the best plan of retreat, he mounted the platform of a gun, and turning to the soldiers drawn up in battle array, strove to arouse them to meet the coming shock like men. Every eye was turned on that frowning eminence, expecting each instant to see the white puffs of smoke herald the iron storm that should send death amid their ranks. In this fearful moment, when the fate of the Colonies, as he believed, rested on their conduct in the next few hours, he thus addressed them:

"Valiant soldiers! Yonder" (pointing to the enemy that lay in sight) "are the enemies of your country, who have come to lay waste, and destroy, and spread havoc and devastation through this pleasant land. They are enemies hired to do the work of death, and have no motive to animate them in their undertaking. You have every consideration to induce you to play the man, and act the part of valiant soldiers. Your country looks up to you for its defence. You are contending for your wives, whether you or they shall enjoy them. You are fighting for your children, whether they shall be yours or theirs — your houses and lands—for your flocks and herds, for your freedom, for future generations, for *every thing* that is great and noble, on account of which only life itself is worth a fig. You must, you *will* abide the day of trial. You can not give back, whilst animated by these considerations.

"Suffer me, therefore, on this occasion to recommend to you, without delay, to break off your sins by righteousness, and your iniquity by turning unto the Lord. Turn ye, turn ye, ungodly sinners; for why will ye die? Repent, lest the Lord come and smite you with a curse. Our camp is filled with blasphemers, and resounds with the language of the infernal regions. Oh! that officers and men might fear to take the holy and tremendous name of God in vain. Oh! that you would now return to the Lord, lest destruction should come upon you, lest vengeance overtake you. Oh! that you were wise, that you understood this your latter end.

"I must recommend to you the strictest attention to your duty, and the most punctual obedience to your officers. Discipline, order and regularity are the strength of an army.

"VALIANT SOLDIERS! should our enemy attack us, I exhort and conjure you to play the man. Let no danger appear too great—let no suffering appear too severe for you to encounter for your bleeding country. God's grace assisting me, I am *determined to fight and die by your side, rather than flee before our enemies, or resign myself to them.*

"Prefer death to captivity. Ever remember your unhappy brethren, made prisoners at Fort Washington, whose blood now crieth to heaven for vengeance, and shakes the pillars of the world, saying, 'How long, O Lord holy and true, dost thou not charge our blood on them that dwell on the earth.'

"Rather than quit this ground *with infamy and*

disgrace, I should prefer leaving *this body of mine a corpse on the spot.*

"I must finally recommend it to you, and urge it on you again and again, in time of action to keep silence. Let all be hushed and calm, serene and tranquil, that the word of command may be distinctly heard, and resolutely obeyed, and may the God of heaven take us all under his protection, and cover our heads in the day of battle, and grant unto us his salvation."

Noble and brave heart! how little he thought that at that very moment, when he was pouring his own heroic spirit into the troops, and nerving them to the high resolution to stand or die at their posts, saying that he would stand and die with them, it had been resolved in a council of war to abandon those strong works, the key of the north, and retreat through the wilderness.

The announcement of this decision fell like a thunderbolt upon him. It is difficult to say whether despair or scorn predominated in his bosom, when he saw the army defile out of the works—leaving all the artillery, ammunition and baggage behind, the prey of the enemy—and take up its precipitate, disorderly flight southward. A catastrophe, so sudden and unexpected, overwhelmed him. It seemed a dream that those strong defences, so gallantly won at the beginning of the revolution by a handful of brave men, and hitherto so firmly held, could be abandoned without one blow being struck for their preservation; and arms and stores, gathered with such expense and care, abandoned to the proud and exultant foe. It had never occurred to him that the commanding officers would be found wanting in this terrible crisis; hence, all his efforts had been with the men, to make them, who were unaccustomed to the sight of carnage and the shock of arms, firm and steadfast. And when the infamous deed was done, he did not stop to consider what rules of the martinet had influenced the officers in their action. It was enough for him that the guns, shotted and primed, slept dumb in their places, and were not allowed to speak for freedom.

He was one of those men who did not look upon defeat as the most direful calamity that could happen. A great example was next in value to a great victory to a country struggling to be free. A fierce-fought battle, though disastrous, made heroes, while a disgraceful, hasty retreat made cowards. Thermopylæ did as much for Greece as Platæa; and Leonidas made more heroes than Pausanias. He had told Gen. Pomeroy that "in his reading of history he had noticed that great generals seldom if ever made proper use of victory," he had also seen that without conflicts troops are never made brave.

He did not retreat with the army to Saratoga, and though it does not appear at what point, or how he left it, it is evident he took his departure with feelings of the deepest disgust. He would not stay with an army, whose commanding officers he considered poltroons, and more worthy of court martial than of positions of trust. He returned home discouraged and indignant. He felt that had he commanded at Ticonderoga, its ramparts, though carried at last by the overwhelming foe, would first have been baptised in blood.

That these feelings were not an ebullition of the moment, but the result of calm and sober reflection, is evident from the following note, appended to the above address, and written several weeks after, and subsequent to the battle of Bennington.

"In about five hours afterwards," he scornfully writes, "the garrison was evacuated, and our vast army fleeing before their enemies with the utmost precipitation and irregularity, leaving behind, for the use of the enemy, an immense amount of baggage, artillery, ammunition, provisions, and every warlike necessary. 'How are the mighty fallen, and the weapons of war perished!' A short time will decide the fate of America. It must depend on the *treatment of those five general officers who gave up Ticonderoga,* and and those one hundred and seventy-five tory traitors, taken in the militia battle near Bennington. *If these can not be brought to justice, then am I ready to pronounce what is, in my opinion, the sad doom of these states—*the end is come. 'Your end is come, your destruction draweth nigh.'

"Justice is one of the pillars of civil government, without which it can not exist and last amongst them."

These views did not spring from a naturally fierce and warlike spirit, for he was distinguished for the kindliness of his nature, and the warmth and tenderness of his feelings, but from his judgment; for, like the clergy generally of New England, he was thoroughly versed in the history of nations, and was governed by views, more comprehensive and statesmanlike, than those whose knowledge was confined to technical military rules.

Though Mr. Allen returned home, disgusted with St. Clair, the moment he received the call of Stark, asking the Berkshire militia to rally to the defence of Bennington, against which Col. Baum with his band of Hessians was advancing, all his old energy returned. He knew Stark, and that wherever he commanded there would be fierce fighting, whatever the result might be. This gallant officer, though smarting under the insulting conduct of Congress, that did not hesitate to appoint and promote inferior officers, and neglect good ones, still loved his country. He would not serve under a Congress that he despised, but he would keep his own state from the foot of the invader.

Allen took an active part in rallying the Berkshire militia to his aid, and accompanied them in their rapid march to his camp, which they reached on the morning of the 16th of August, just before daylight. They arrived in a pouring thunder-shower, and though drenched to the skin, Mr. Allen immediately sought an interview with Stark. Still smarting under the disgrace of Ticonderoga, the brave divine this time determined not to waste his efforts on the soldiers, but to tell the commander beforehand, that they had not obeyed his call, and marched thither to join in an ignominious retreat, but to *fight*. He therefore said to him, plainly and bluntly, "Gen. Stark, the Berkshire militia have often been summoned to the field, without being allowed to fight; now, if you don't give them a chance this time, they will never turn out again." Stark, a hero himself, loved to hear the ring of the true metal, and was amused instead of offended at the gallant bearing and outspoken fearlessness of the young clergyman, and smiling, replied: "Do you wish to march now, while it is dark and raining?" "No; not just at this moment." "Well then," said the former, "if the Lord will give us sunshine to-morrow, and I do not give you fighting enough, I will never ask you to come out again." The Lord did give them sunshine, and the morning-drum roused up the soldier to as beautiful a day as ever blessed the world. A brisk west wind shook the rain drops in a shower of pearls from the surrounding forest—the blue sky bent tranquilly above the gentle stream, on whose banks they stood in martial array—and all was bright and peaceful.

During the forenoon, while the several columns were marching to the various positions assigned them, one of the militia remarked to Mr. Allen, "We will do our own fighting to-day." "Yes," said he, "we shall have a good time at the enemy, but we are not quite ready yet, we must first join in prayer;" and there, under the August sky, he lifted up his earnest prayer, that God would give them the victory. He had no intention, however, of doing the praying, and letting his congregation do all the fighting. He meant to *fight* himself, and if the example of their pastor could make them brave, he resolved there should be no cowards among the Berkshire men that day. When they came in sight of the Hessians, and just before the attack commenced, he advanced alone in front, in his clerical gown, and, mounting a stump, called out in a voice distinctly heard by them, to surrender, and save the effusion of blood, promising them generous treatment if they would. The only reply to his summons was a volley of musketry. As the bullets whistled around his ears, one passing through his hat, he descended from his stump, and returned to the ranks. When the battle commenced, he did as he had resolved to do at Ticonderoga, if the commander had given him a chance—fought in the ranks with the soldiers. Some of his parishioners stood around him, and among them a brother. Seeing that he was a better marksman than his brother, he said to him in the midst of the battle, "Joe, you load, and I'll fire," and so they fought side by side God's own battle on that warm August day. At the final charge he led the militia, and was among the first over the breastworks, and heard with an exultant, overflowing heart the shout of victory go up from the blood-stained heights.

No sooner was the battle over than he devoted himself, with his accustomed tenderness and energy, to the wounded. Amid the Hessian steeds straying over the heights without masters, he came across a surgeon's horse loaded with panniers of wine. While the others were roaming the field in search of plunder, he seized on these, and immediately distributed them to the wounded and weary, and moved like an angel of mercy among friends and foes alike. Two large square crystal bottles he carried home with him as trophies of the fight, which were long preserved in his family as choice relics, and in which the health of the gallant old patriot was often drunk in the juice of the currant.

The night succeeding the battle, and the following day, he ministered to the disabled and dying, and on the third day, Saturday, mounted his horse, and making a long journey, reached his parish that night, and preached next day. It is a pity that the sermon and services of that Sabbath have not been preserved. They would doubtless remind one of the song of Miriam that rose so sublimely from the shores of the Red Sea, strewn with the wreck of Pharaoh's host.

This great battle and victory were the theme of every tongue, and the part Mr. Allen bore in it a subject of general comment. One of his parishioners, hearing that he had fought like a common soldier, came to him, and inquired if it was so. "Yes," he said, "I did, it was a very hot, close battle, and it became every patriot to do his duty." "Well, but," said the parishioner, "Mr. Allen, did you *kill* any body?" "No," he replied. "I don't *know* that I killed any body; but I happened to notice a frequent flash from behind a certain bush, and every time I saw that flash one of our men fell. I took aim at the bush, and fired. I don't know that I *killed* any body, *but I put out that flash.*"—Ah! but for the clergy of New England it is doubtful, if the flash of the enemy's guns in the Revolution would ever have been put out!

At the close of the next year, his brother Moses, of

Georgia, also a chaplain in the army, and one of the most influential, uncompromising patriots in the State, and fearless like himself, was taken prisoner in the battle before Savannah, where he exposed himself to the hottest of the fire, and with unheard of brutality put on board a prison ship. Here he suffered every indignity that could be conceived for weeks, and then threw himself overboard, and attempted to swim ashore. Unequal to the task he was drowned, leaving a young wife and infant son in that new country, with her home burned to the ground, and the congregation, amid which she had lived, scattered in every direction by the merciless foe. Thomas, unwilling to leave her thus unprotected and alone, determined to bring her to his own home. This was not so easy a task, but with his accustomed energy, that never would permit obstacles, however formidable, to deter him from a purpose once formed, he set out to make the long journey on horseback. In those early times it would have been sufficiently arduous, had the country been at peace, and the most public thoroughfares open to him. But, with the country distracted by war—all the cities of the sea board in the hands of the enemy, forcing him to skirt the dangerous frontiers—it was one full of peril. Of the hardships he underwent, and dangers he escaped in this journey, there remains no record—we only know it took him eleven days to reach Baltimore. They were sufficient, it seems, to prevent him from returning the same way, and he chose the nearly equally dangerous one of returning by water. Protected by heaven, however, he escaped the enemy's ships, and at length had the gratification of seeing the widow and son under his own roof in Pittsfield.

During the famous "Shay's rebellion," which reached to his own county, he took prompt and decided ground on the side of government. His powerful influence, which the insurgents could not make head against, so exasperated them that they openly threatened to seize him, and carry him as a hostage to New York State. This threat, however, was easier made than executed. A man, who had stood unmoved amid the carnage of battle, and carried his life in his hand through the long struggle of the Revolution, was not one likely to yield tamely to a lawless rabble. He openly defied them, and slept with loaded arms in his bed room, ready to shoot down the first miscreant that dared attempt to lay hands upon him. None were found willing to make the hazardous experiment. They thought in this case discretion to be the better part of valor, and let him alone.

In 1799, his eldest daughter, who had married Mr. Wm. P. White, a merchant of Boston, died in London, leaving an infant behind, without a relative in the kingdom to care for it—her husband being in the East Indies on business. His heart, great as his courage, was moved by the friendless condition of this infant grandchild, and he resolved at once to go for it. His affections were strong as his will, and when impelled by either, it was no common obstacle that could arrest him. Bidding his congregation an affectionate farewell, he embarked on board the ship Argo for London. On the way they were pursued by a large vessel which they took to be a French ship of war. The captain was alarmed, and assembled all on board, to deliberate on the course to be pursued. After a short consultation, it was resolved to fight, however unequal the contest might be: for a French prison could only be their fate if conquered, while they were certain to be thrown into one if they surrendered. In this extremity Mr. Allen requested the captain to let him pray with the men, and make a speech to them, to encourage them to fight bravely. He gave his consent, and the voice, that twenty years before had nerved American patriots to battle, now thrilled the hearts of that little crew on the broad Atlantic. The frigate continued to approach, but at length, to their great joy, she ran up the British ensign. Mr. Allen then assembled passengers and crew, and offered up fervent thanksgiving to God for their escape.

In England he formed the acquaintance of John Newton, Rowland Hill, and others, through whom his warmest sympathies became enlisted in the subject of foreign missions, which he showed by his earnest advocacy of them on his return home. He was absent from his congregation on this voyage nearly six months — his tempestuous return passage alone occupying three months lacking five days.

In those times of high political excitement between federalists and democrats, Mr. Allen was one of the few New England divines that sympathised with the latter.

At the present day, the patriotic clergy of the Revolution are often looked upon as good, zealous men, and nothing more—while in fact they were the soundest statesmen of the time. This was the case with Mr. Allen, and the jealous eye with which he watched every step of the civil government during the war, showed how keenly he felt the danger of illegal authority springing up in the midst of revolution, whose decisions would lead to after-trouble. Thus, in 1779, a session of the Superior Court was appointed in Great Barrington. He immediately drew up an able remonstrance against it, on the ground that it was a dangerous precedent to consent to the operation of law until a constitution, or form of government, or bill of rights had been adopted. This paper is still preserved in the family, and shows a clear head and a far-reaching political wisdom, not commonly found in turbulent times.

It does not come within the plan of this work to write his biography as a clergyman to its close. He was an impressive preacher, and on occasions, that called forth the tenderer feelings, such as the sacrament of the Lord's Supper, would drown his audience in tears. He preached forty-six years, faithful to his high calling as he was to his country. When prostrated by his final sickness, he approached the grave serene and tranquil. No cloud darkened its portals, no doubt dimmed the clear vision of his faith. Resting not on his own merits, but on his crucified Lord, in whom he trusted without wavering, he murmured in sweet peace, "Come, Lord Jesus, come quickly!" Just before his death, one of his children urged him to take some nourishment, saying that it would be impossible for him to live if he did not.

"*Live!*" exclaimed the dying patriot and saint, "*I am going to live forever.*"

Thus, Feb. 11th, 1810, in the sixty-eighth year of his age, passed away this great and good man. Noble by nature, an earnest Christian, a faithful minister of the Gospel, a brave patriot—his name should be inscribed high on the monument that commemorates his country's independence.

CHAPTER XIV.

JOHN ROSSBURGH.

An Irishman by Birth.—His Education.—Is settled at the "Forks of the Delaware."—His Patriotism.—Joins a Company formed in his own Parish as a Soldier.—His painful Parting with his Wife.—Makes his Will.—Chaplain of a Regiment.—Marches against the Enemy.—Is taken Prisoner, and murdered while praying for his Enemies.—The mutilated Corpse stealthily buried.—His Letters to his Wife just before a Skirmish.—His Character.

It was hardly possible, in a war in which clergymen often exposed themselves like the meanest soldier, and rendered themselves so obnoxious to the enemy by the leading part they took in the rebellion, that some should not have fallen on the battle-field, or otherwise suffered a violent death from the hands of their foes. The Revolution would have been less sacred, if their blood had not mingled in the costly sacrifice that was laid on the altar of freedom.

John Rossburgh was one of these, giving his life to the cause to which he had already given his heart. He was an Irishman by birth, though he came to this country when a lad of eighteen years of age. The death of his wife and infant son early in life caused him to turn his thoughts to the ministry. He had already learned a trade, but at once abandoned it, and though compelled to rely almost entirely on his own resources, prepared himself for college, and graduated at Princeton in 1761. He was licensed to preach in

1763, and soon after settled at the "Forks of the Delaware," in New Jersey. At the outbreak of the Revolution his feelings at once became deeply enlisted in the struggle, and in his prayers and sermons he showed with what absorbing interest he watched its progress.

The fall of New York and the subsequent disasters that overtook the army so wrought upon his patriotism that, when he saw that dispirited and diminished army fleeing through the State before their haughty and insolent foes, he could remain an idle spectator no longer. Calling together his congregation, he besought them as patriots, as Christians, to fly to the help of Washington and his despairing troops. They responded to his appeal, and organized a company in which he, to show a noble example, was the first to enroll himself as a private soldier: and pastor and people rallied under one standard.

The evening before he was to take his departure for camp was a solemn one, for at break of day he expected to leave his wife and children, perhaps never to see them again on earth. He felt all the perils of the step he had taken, but he had no misgivings. It was the more solemn to him because he had a presentiment, that his parting with his family in the morning was to be a final one. So after they had retired to rest, he communed for a while with himself and his maker—thought over the dependent position in which his death would leave those he had loved better than his life, and then calmly drew up his will.

The following extract from it shows that it was no sudden impulse that drove him to the field of battle, but a well considered purpose, and one with which he had gone with a devout heart and a clear conscience to the throne of God. "Having," he writes, "received many singular blessings from Almighty God in this land of my pilgrimage; more especially a loving wife and five promising children, I do leave and bequeathe them all to the protection, mercy and grace of God from whom I received them. Being encouraged thereto by God's gracious direction and faithful promise, Jeremiah, xlix. 11 : 'Leave thy fatherless children, I will preserve them alive, and let thy widows trust in me.'"

Those whom he thus committed to the care of his heavenly Father, were quietly slumbering near him, and tears would rise, and emotions he could not control bear him to the earth, as he thought it was perhaps the last time the same roof should cover them— but his resolution never faltered. He trusted serenely in God; for not the shadow of a doubt crossed his mind, that it was His cause for which he was about to offer up his life.

At early dawn he shouldered his musket, and bidding his family an affectionate, tender farewell, turned to depart. But when the last moment came, his wife could not let him go. Clinging to his neck with a painful tenacity, she declared she never would part with him, while tears and sobs choked her utterance. Finding himself unable by a gentle effort to untwine her closely locked arms, and feeling his own fortitude rapidly giving way before her passionate grief, he was compelled almost to use violence to disengage himself, when hurrying out of the house, he mounted his horse, and galloped off to join his company. The drum was already beating for parade, and they soon took up the line of march for Philadelphia. Having arrived there, the company was incorporated into a regiment of which he was appointed chaplain.

The troops immediately hurried forward, and joined the retreating army. Being fresh they were sent to the rear, to check the enemy, and hence were soon engaged in a severe skirmish with his advance guard. Mr. Rossburgh was a fine-looking, portly man, and consequently was conspicuous in every part of the field, and by his cool courage and resolute bearing furnished a noble example to his parishioners. The encounter took place near the banks of the Trenton, and in the melée he lost his horse. Going towards the river in search of him, he suddenly came upon a company of Hessians, under the command of a British officer. Being right upon them, before he discovered their presence, he saw at once that escape was hopeless, and surrendered himself as prisoner, requesting them at the same time, for the sake of his wife and children, to spare his life. An insulting epithet was the only reply deigned him, and he immediately discovered by their movements that his death was determined upon. Knowing that entreaty would be of no avail with the barbarous, bloodthirsty wretches, he turned away, and kneeling down, calmly committed his wife and children, and his own soul about to take its flight from earth, into the hands of his Maker. He then, in the spirit of his divine Master, prayed aloud, that he would forgive his murderers, and not lay his blood to their charge. His inhuman captors could hardly wait till his prayer was ended, and before the petition for their pardon had died on his lips, drove a bayonet through his body, when he fell forward in the agonies of death. They then snatched away his watch and part of his clothing, and mutilating left him weltering in his blood. The man, or rather fiend, who had acted the part of executioner, immediately after entered one of the hotels of Trenton, and told the woman who kept it, that he had killed a rebel minister, and showed the watch as proof of what he had done, but added, in a frenzied manner, that it was too bad he should have been praying for them while they were killing him. "Oh!" said she, "you have made bad work for his poor family." With a frightful oath he retorted, "If you say another word, I will run you through." He then seized his sword, and ran off like one possessed with a devil, and told some British officers what he had done, who, instead of condemning the dastardly deed, commended it.

A young soldier, named Hayes, one of his congregation, who had often sat under his preaching, took the mangled corpse, and concealed it, and the next day buried it in an out of the way spot near Trenton. Rev. Mr. Duffield, another chaplain, hearing of it, went and had the body disinterred, and buried with proper services in the grave-yard of an adjoining church. The widow, accompanied by her brother, a member of the Provincial Congress, came on to see the corpse, but his murderers had so disfigured it, that it was with difficulty she could recognize it. Two short weeks before, her arms had entwined that noble form, and now it lay a mutilated mass before her.

She received three letters from him, after he bade her farewell, full of affection, and glowing with patriotism. The following extract from one shows the spirit that animated him : " My dear, I am still yours. I have but a minute to tell you that the company are all well. We are going over to attack the enemy. You would think it strange to see your husband, an old man, with a French fusee slung at his back. This *may be* the last you shall ever receive from your husband. I have committed myself, you, and the dear pledges of our mutual love to God. As I am out of doors, I can write no more. I send my compliments to you, my dear, and to the children. Friends, pray for us. I am your loving husband."

Let the scrupulous Christian of to-day condemn, if he can, this noble divine for fighting in defence of his country. *He* had no doubts of the righteousness of his conduct, when passing with prayer on his lips into the presence of his God.

Amiable, kind, and distinguished as a peace-maker, he had to overcome all his natural tendencies to war, to take up arms ; but having settled it to be his duty, he had no after-misgivings.

In the turbulent scenes that followed his death, his grave was left unmarked, and no one, at this day, can tell where the sainted patriot sleeps.

CHAPTER XV.

ABNER BENEDICT.

His Birth and Education.—Settled at Middletown.—Becomes Chaplain in the Army at New York.—Description of a terrific Thunder-storm.—The Battle of Long Island.—His Feelings.—The Last to leave the Shore in the Retreat.—Inventions in Submarine Navigation.—Manufactures Saltpetre for Powder.—Elected Professor in Yale College.—His Character and Death.

ABNER BENEDICT was born at North Salem, N. Y., Nov. 9th, 1740. A classmate of Timothy Dwight, he graduated at Yale College, in 1769, and studied theology with the celebrated Dr. Bellamy, of Bethlehem, Conn. He married Lois Northrup, of New Milford, Conn., in 1771, and the next year was ordained and settled in Middlefield, Middletown, of the same state. He retained his connection with this church fourteen years, though, like his classmate Dwight, he was absent a part of the time as volunteer chaplain in the army. An ardent patriot, his sympathies drew him away to the field where his countrymen were battling for their rights, but when the tide of war rolled southward, he returned to his parish.

He was with the army in New York, and being deeply interested in the efforts put forth to destroy the enemy's ships by torpedos, made some inventions in submarine navigation, which were looked upon with great favor by those to whom they were submitted.

He often spoke of the excitement which the news of the landing of the British on Long Island created in the army, and of its effect on the inhabitants, who saw that the final struggle for New York was at hand. The day, around which clustered such momentous destinies, closed with what seemed an awful omen of good or ill to the American cause. Mr. Benedict was in the ranks on Brooklyn Heights at the time, from the ramparts of which he could look out on the rolling country, dotted with troops, hurrying in every direction. The most intense excitement prevailed throughout the city, and reënforcements had been pushed rapidly forward all day to meet the coming shock.

But crowded as the day had been with anxious fears and gloomy forebodings, the coming on of evening brought new terrors. In the west slowly rose a thunder-cloud, the glittering, coruscated edges of which seemed solid as marble, so that when the sun passed behind it, it was like a total eclipse, and sudden darkness fell on sea and land.

Mr. Benedict's description of the appearance and passage of this thunder-cloud was appalling.* As it continued to rise higher and higher, he observed that it was surcharged with electricity, for the lightning was constantly searching it from limit to limit, and the deep reverberations that rolled along the heavens without

---

* Mr. Benedict was my grandfather, and I can remember, when a mere child, the effect this description had on me; but, as I can recall only disconnected portions of it, I have chosen to put the whole account in my own language.—ED.

intermission, sounded more like successive billows bursting on the shore, than the irregular discharges of a thunder-cloud.

At length, at seven o'clock, it began to rain. All before had been the skirmishing that precedes the battle, but now like some huge monster that cloud suddenly gaped and shot forth flame. Then followed a crash louder than a thousand cannon discharged at once. It was appalling. The soldiers involuntarily cowered before it. In a few moments the entire heavens became black as ink, and from horizon to horizon the whole empyrean was ablaze with lightning, while the thunder that followed did not come in successive peals, but in one long continuous crash, as if the very framework of the skies was falling to pieces, accompanied with a confused sound, as though the fragments were tumbling into a profound abyss. The lightning fell in masses and sheets of fire to the earth, and seemed to be striking incessantly and on every side. There was an apparent recklessness and wildness about the unloosed strength of the elements that was absolutely terrifying. The power that was abroad seemed sufficient to crush the earth into a thousand fragments. The fort was silent as the grave, for the strongest heart bent before this exhibition of God's terrible majesty. It did not pass away like an ordinary shower, for the cloud appeared to stand still, and swing round and round like a horizontal wheel over the devoted city. It clung to it with a tenacity that was frightful. For three hours, or from seven to ten, the deafening uproar continued without cessation or abatement.

EFFECTS OF THE STORM. 167

When it finally took its sullen tumultuous departure, every heart felt relieved.

The morning dawned mild and peaceful, as if nothing unusual had happened, but soon reports began to come in of the devastation and death the storm had spread around. There was no end of the accounts of almost miraculous escapes of the inmates of houses that were struck. In others the inhabitants were more or less injured. A soldier, passing through one of the streets, without receiving apparently any external injury, was struck deaf, dumb and blind. A captain and two lieutenants belonging to McDougal's regiment, were killed by one thunderbolt; the points of their swords melted off, and the coin melted in their pockets. Their bodies appeared as if they had been roasted, so black and crisped was the skin. Ten men encamped outside of the fort near the river, and occupying one tent, were killed by a single flash. When the tent, that had fallen upon them, was lifted, they lay scattered around on the ground, presenting a most melancholy appearance. They belonged to one of the Connecticut regiments, and were buried in one grave. The service performed by the chaplain was very solemn and impressive. Familiar as we become with death in the midst of war, it somehow affects us very differently when sent, apparently, direct from the hand of God. In battle we hear the roar of the guns, and after the smoke and tumult have passed away, we expect to see bleeding and mangled forms scattered around. But there seems a hidden meaning, some secret purpose, when the bolt is launched by an invisible arm, and from the mysterious depths of space.

From every side came in reports of soldiers more or less injured, and the excitement could hardly have been greater, and the returns caused more surprise, if there had been a night-attack on the camp.

Mr. Benedict said he could not account for the cloud remaining so long stationary, unless the vast amount of arms collected in and about the city held it by attraction, and drew from it such a fearful amount of electricity.*

At regimental prayers, next morning, he felt peculiarly solemn. The great battle so near at hand, to be perhaps a decisive one for his country, filled him with sad forebodings.

Scarcely were the religious services finished, when strains of martial music were heard near the ferry, and not long after column after column came winding up the heights towards the fort. They were six battalions sent over by Washington, accompanied by General Putnam, who was to take chief command. The General was received with loud cheers, and his presence inspired universal confidence.

In a short time the whole country, to the front and right, as far as the eye could reach, was covered with the smoke of battle, and shook to the thunder of cannon. When the tumult ceased, the fields alive with fugitives from the American army, told how disastrous the day had been. Mr. Benedict's heart was filled with the most poignant sorrow, for not only had the

---

* This explanation was in accordance with the theory of thunderstorms at that time.—ED.

Americans lost the battle, but the whole army was now threatened with total destruction. The silence of the evening that followed was more oppressive than the uproar and carnage of the day, for "*what now can save the army?*" trembled on every lip. No one believed the fort could be defended, as all the approaches to it were in the enemy's power; while the first movement to retreat across to the city would bring the ships of war lying just below into their midst.

In this fearful dilemma fervent prayers went up to Him who alone could deliver. As if in answer to those prayers, when night deepened, a dense fog came rolling in, and settled on land and water. At the same time, with the turn of the tide, a strong east wind arose, that sent the water with the force of a torrent into the bay, effectually preventing for the time the ships, if they had desired it, from entering the river. Under cover of this fog and the night, Washington silently withdrew his entire army across to New York. Mr. Benedict, who watched the progress of this movement with an anxiety that mocked expression, remained behind, while boat load after boat load drifted away in the darkness. When the army was all over, he then consented to go also, and stepping into a boat, was one of the last who left that disastrous shore. He retreated with the army to Harlaem Heights, and was present in the skirmishes that followed, and witnessed the battle of White Plains. In the disruption of the army that succeeded the fall of Fort Washington, he returned to his parish.

He continued an ardent patriot throughout the war, rendering his country every service within his power. When it was in distress, on account of the scarcity of powder, he made various experiments in the manufacture of saltpetre from materials never before used, in which he was entirely successful. He hailed with unbounded delight the return of peace, and a daughter being born to him on the day of its declaration, he named her "Irene," the Greek word for peace.

He dissolved his connection with the parish in Middletown in 1785, and was afterwards settled over various parishes in succession. The last field of his labors was Roxbury, New Jersey, where he died in 1818, aged seventy-eight years. At one time he was elected professor in Yale College, but declined to accept the appointment.

A man of thorough education, of a deeply philosophical mind, and a distinguished mathematician, he left behind him several pamphlets on various subjects, and among others one on tides and winds, and another on submarine navigation and attack. Of noble sympathies, warm and generous affections, and ardent piety, he was known and loved far and wide, and his memory is still fondly cherished in the places where he labored.

CHAPTER XVI.

WILLIAM WHITE, D.D.

His Birth and early Studies.—Goes to England.—Friend of Goldsmith and Johnson.—Settled in Philadelphia.—Takes the Oath of Allegiance.—Noble Determination.—Elected Chaplain of Congress.—His Conduct after the Revolution.—Is made Bishop.—His Character and Death.

Among the few Episcopal clergymen, who took part with the Colonists in their struggle for liberty, Bishop White stands preëminent. He was born in Philadelphia, April 4th, 1748. He gave evidences of piety in early life, and when a mere child showed the strong bent of his mind towards the ministry. Having graduated at the age of sixteen he early commenced his preparations for holy orders and when he was twenty-two sailed for England to obtain ordination.

While in London, he was for a while a neighbor of Goldsmith, with whom he became acquainted. He was also intimate with Dr. Johnson, of whom he spoke warmly, and related the following as the only instance in which the learned lexicographer showed that harshness of manner, of which so many complained. They were conversing on the Stamp Act, which had caused such dissatisfaction in the Colonies, when the doctor remarked, "Had I been prime minister, I would have sent a ship-of-war, and leveled one of your principal cities to the ground."

Having been ordained as deacon and priest, he returned to Philadelphia in 1772, and was chosen assistant minister of Christ and St. Peter's churches.

Though he took no active part in the opening scenes of the Revolution, his sympathies were all with the Colonies. He continued, however, to pray for the king until the Declaration of Independence was given to the world, and then he came forward and took the oath of allegiance. While it was being administered to him, an acquaintance, standing near, made a significant gesture by putting his hands to his throat. After the ceremony was finished Mr. White remarked to him, " I perceived by your gesture, that you thought I was exposing myself to great danger by the step I have taken. But I have not taken it without full deliberation. I know my danger, and that it is the greater on account of being a clergyman of the Church of England. But I trust in Providence. The cause is a just one, and I trust will be protected." Noble words, that do him far more honor than even the exalted position he afterwards attained.

In September, 1777, he was elected chaplain of Congress. The circumstances attending the reception of this appointment, and its acceptance, he often related afterwards to his friends. He said that "he had removed with his family to Maryland, and being on a journey, stopped at a small village between Harford County and Philadelphia, at which he was met by a courier from Yorktown, informing him of his being appointed by Congress as their chaplain, and requesting his immediate attendance; that he thought of it a short time; it was in one of the gloomiest periods of the American affairs, when General Burgoyne was marching without having yet received a serious check, so far as was then known, through the northern parts of New York; and, after a short consideration, instead of proceeding on his journey, he turned his horse's head, and traveled immediately to Yorktown, and entered on the duties of his appointment."

In this brief account it leaks out accidentally that the main motive, which induced his acceptance, was the gloomy prospect of the American cause. He felt that *that* was the time, if ever, when the minister of God should give his prayers and efforts to sustain the sinking courage of those who stood at the head of power. It was because the post was fraught with so much danger, and was connected with such high responsibilities, that he accepted it. His faith never wavered, for it passed beyond the strong battalions to the Source of all power.

When the British evacuated Philadelphia, every clergyman of the Episcopal denomination left the state but himself. Solitary and alone, he remained at his post, and, like Abdiel, faithful to the last, cast his lot in with his suffering country.

As soon as peace was restored, he devoted himself to the reörganization of the Episcopal Church in the state, and at the first regular convention was elected bishop.

Of his after-labors in the church, his transcendent virtues, his elevated character, and his influence, I shall say nothing. His memory is embalmed in the hearts of the good of all denominations. When the yellow fever ravaged Philadelphia, he remained at his post, exhibiting to the last that noble devotion to duty, regardless of consequences, which characterised him as the friend of Washington and of his country.

For the last forty years of his life, he was Senior, and consequently Presiding, Bishop of the United States. He died on the morning of the 17th of July, 1836, at the advanced age of eighty-eight.

CHAPTER XVII.

TIMOTHY DWIGHT.

PATRIOTISM OF OUR COLLEGES.—DWIGHT'S BIRTH.—HIS EARLY LIFE.—TUTOR OF YALE COLLEGE.—IS LICENSED TO PREACH.—HIS PATRIOTISM.—BECOMES CHAPLAIN.—ADVOCATES COMPLETE INDEPENDENCE.—HIS DESCRIPTION OF THE DESOLATE APPEARANCE OF WESTCHESTER COUNTY.—HIS SERMONS TO THE SOLDIERS.—ELOQUENT SERMON AFTER THE VICTORY AT SARATOGA.—ANECDOTE OF PUTNAM.—COMPOSES THE ODE TO COLUMBIA.—DEDICATES A POEM TO WASHINGTON.—SHARES THE SUFFERINGS OF THE SOLDIERS AT WEST POINT IN THE WINTER OF 1778.— HIS FAITH.— HIS DESCRIPTION OF SCENE FROM SUGAR LOAF MOUNTAIN.— ALSO OF THE DEAD UNBURIED AT FORT MONTGOMERY.— DEATH OF HIS FATHER.— LEAVES THE ARMY.— SETTLES AT NORTHAMPTON.— GOES TO THE LEGISLATURE.—PUBLISHES SEVERAL POEMS.—ELECTED PRESIDENT OF YALE COLLEGE.—A FEDERALIST IN 1812.—HIS EMINENCE AS A THEOLOGIAN.—HIS DEATH.

THE lover of education will always point with pleasure and pride to the bold and patriotic stand taken by our colleges in the Revolution. Warmly espousing the cause of the Colonies, they not only shared the common suffering, but yielded their full proportion of active patriots to the struggle. Presidents and students alike, made common cause with the people, and the eloquent voice pleaded, and the strong arm struck for liberty. Hence our institutions of learning were peculiarly obnoxious to the British, who regarded them only as so many hot beds in which young rebels were reared.

Timothy Dwight was born in Northampton, May 14th, 1752, and hence was only twenty-three when the war broke out. But though young in years, he possessed a remarkably mature intellect. When a mere child he learned his alphabet in a single lesson. He could read the Bible at four years of age, and at six commenced the study of Latin by himself. Entering Yale College at the early age of thirteen, he was thrown into all the temptations of a college life, and for a time suffered from their influence. The two first years were very much wasted, and he spent much time in gambling, though not for money. But the faithful, kind remonstrances of his friend and tutor, Stephen Mix Mitchell, who saw with pain the growing waywardness of his gifted pupil, brought him to serious reflection, and he immediately shook off his habits of indolence and folly, and commenced a studious, earnest life. Fourteen hours out of the twenty-four were devoted to his books. This close application brought on weakness of the eyes, which was increased afterwards by using them too soon after an attack of small pox, and from which he suffered great deprivation to the end of his life. He was only seventeen when he graduated. He then became engaged as a teacher in New Haven, and at the same time continued his studies. At nineteen he was chosen tutor in the college. During this year his attention was seriously turned to the subject of religion, and he soon made a public profession of his faith, and was admitted to the communion of the church in the College. His mind at first had been inclined to the profession of the law, and his studies were pursued to that end. He however changed his plans, and without a lengthy preparation for the duties of the profession, offered himself as a candidate for the ministry, and was licensed in 1777.

He had not however been an indifferent observer of the struggle going on between the Colonies and the mother country, but warmly espoused the cause of the former. Ardent and imaginative, hating wrong, and loving liberty, he threw himself heart and soul into the contest. Though chained to his duties in college, his eloquent tongue was never weary in defending his country, and in kindling the patriotism of the students. Hence, when in May, 1777, in consequence of the convulsed state of the country, and the danger that threatened our entire sea coast, the college was disbanded, he immediately offered his services as chaplain to the army. Had his engagements been thus summarily dissolved previous to his entering the ministry, it is impossible to say what his career would have been. Very probably the same ardent patriotism which made him volunteer as chaplain would have impelled him to join the rebel army as a soldier; and he who afterwards rose to such eminence in theology, might have formed one of that brilliant military group that cluster around the name and memory of Washington—the sharers of his greatness and his immortality. As he was situated, however, he felt that he could not take up arms, and so he did the most patriotic thing in his power—enrolled himself professionally in the American army.

This course might be expected from the views and feelings which he entertained. What these were, and had been for a long time, he has given us in his own words. He says: "I urged in conversation with several gentlemen of great respectability, firm Whigs, and my intimate friends, the importance, and even the necessity, of a declaration of independence on the part of the Colonies, and alleged for this measure the very same arguments which afterwards were generally considered as decisive, but found them disposed to give me and my arguments a hostile and contemptuous, instead of a cordial reception. Yet at this time all the resentment and enthusiasm, awakened by the odious measures of Parliament, by the peculiarly obnoxious conduct of the British agents in this country, and by the recent battles of Lexington and Breed's Hill, were at the highest pitch. These gentlemen may be considered as representatives of the great body of thinking men in this country. A few, perhaps, may be excepted, but none of these durst at that time openly declare their opinions to the public. *For myself, I regarded the die as cast*, and the hope of reconciliation as vanished, and believed that the Colonists would never be able to defend themselves, unless they renounced their dependence on Great Britain."

The time selected by him for joining the army, September 1777, shows his fearless spirit and lofty patriotism. The summer had been marked by disasters. The battles of Brandywine and Germantown had been followed by the fall of Philadelphia, while the northern horizon was dark as night with the gathering storm. Burgoyne was on his victorious march, and in the beginning of this month the heads of his menacing columns were almost in striking distance of Albany. Forts Schuyler, Edward, Ticonderoga, those keys of the north, had already fallen, and but one more successful blow seemed necessary to finish the struggle. A profound solemnity rested on the nation, for all knew that, if Clinton from the south formed a junction with Burgoyne, a cordon of posts would be established from Canada to New York, and the Eastern and Middle Colonies be hopelessly separated. All eyes were turned on that veteran host with its splendid train of artillery, as, treading down every thing in its passage, it emerged from the northern wilderness. Washington rapidly concentrated the eastern troops around the Highlands, while the farmers from Western Massachusetts and Vermont left their harvest fields unreaped, and descended to the greater harvest of men at Bennington and Saratoga.

While events were thus drawing to a crisis, Dwight joined the army. Parson's brigade, to which he was attached, was soon ordered to the Hudson, and placed under General Putnam. At this time, rumors of projected expeditions by Clinton from New York, and counter movements on the part of Putnam, and various plans for annoying the enemy, and breaking up his outlying posts, kept the camp in a state of constant excitement. Between his duties as chaplain, Dwight had much leisure time, a part of which he spent in riding over the deserted and silent country. The British lines were at Kingsbridge, extending across to the East River. The Americans were in the region of Peekskill, touching Long Island Sound at Byram river. The people between were exposed to the depredations of both, and Dwight, as he traveled along the deserted roads that intersected this dangerous interval, was struck with the somber and suspicious character of the inhabitants. Constantly exposed to marauding parties from both armies, and plundered without mercy at the slightest suspicion of being Tories, by the Americans, or of being patriots, by the British, they lived in constant trepidation. Dwight said: "To every question they gave such an answer as would please the inquirer, or, if they despaired of pleasing, such an one as would not provoke him." His heart was pained at the stone-like apathy into which men and women had fallen—all animation and feeling had left their countenances, and a fixed, stolid expression showed to what a depth of despair they had been forced by the evils of war. The houses, he said, were scenes of desolation, and the neglected fields were "covered with rank growth of weeds and wild grass," while the great road leading from Boston to New York, on which the eye usually met a constant succession of horses and carriages, presented a melancholy, deserted aspect. "Not a single solitary traveler," he writes, "was visible from week to week, or from month to month. The world was motionless and silent, except when one of those unhappy people ventured upon a rare and lonely excursion to the house of a neighbor no less unhappy, or a scouting party traversing the country in quest of enemies alarmed the inhabitants with the expectations of new injuries and sufferings. The very tracks of the carriages were grown over and obliterated, and where they were discernible resembled the faint impressions of chariot wheels said to be left on the pavements of Herculaneum."

But notwithstanding these scenes of gloom, so oppressive and disheartening to the beholder, and the disastrous news that almost every wind brought from the commander-in-chief, the faith of the young chaplain, in the ultimate triumph of his country, never shook, and his eloquent voice never faltered in uttering words of encouragement and hope, when preaching or praying to and with the army. He commonly spoke extempore, and his sermons were always listened to with profound attention. His form was finely proportioned, stately and majestic, and his eye black and piercing, while his voice, rich, full and melodious, fell like the softened strains of a bugle on the ear. When he gave wings to his brilliant imagination, and passed beyond the gloom and darkness of the present, and painted the glories of the future—the country reposing in peace and independence, the asylum of the oppressed, and the hope of mankind—he soared into the highest regions of oratory. He became a great favorite in the army, and especially with General Putnam. At this time, although the Highlands swarmed with troops, and every effort was made to prevent Sir Henry Clinton from advancing up the river, and all felt the vital importance of maintaining this formidable pass, yet the eye of the nation was fixed on Saratoga. The first battle of Bemis' Heights had taken place, and both armies were preparing for a second and final struggle.

At length, on the 7th of October, it came, and notwithstanding the pusillanimity of Gates, was won by the fiery valor and desperate daring of Arnold. It is impossible, at this day, to imagine the effect of this victory on the nation. The terrible load of anxiety was lifted from its heart, and one long, triumphant shout rolled over the land.

The effect on Putnam's army was electrical. Forts Clinton and Montgomery had just fallen, and the British fleet, breaking through the boom above West Point, had ascended to Kingston, and burned it to the ground. The next breeze from the north might bring the disastrous intelligence of the overthrow of Gates, and the junction of the British forces. What lay beyond this catastrophe, no prophet could tell, and each one held his breath in dread. While the army at Peekskill was in this state of intense excitement, catching eagerly at every rumor that the tide of the Hudson floated southward, there suddenly burst along the bosom of the lordly river the triumphant shout of victory. Glad tears rained from patriotic eyes,—many hearts were too full of thanksgiving for utterance, from others shouts and huzzas arose in deafening clamor, while the granite gateway of the Highlands shook to the thunder of jubilant cannon.

The news of the surrender reached camp on Saturday. Next day Dwight preached at head-quarters. Putnam and his principal officers were present, and never before did the young chaplain seem so inspired. His patriotic heart, like that of the meanest soldier, had been thrown into ecstacy at the glorious tidings, and it was now too full and too eager for utterance, to require any preparation. Rising before his attentive, brilliant auditory, he took for his text, Joel, ii. 20: *"I will remove far off from you the northern army."* The effect of its enunciation was astonishing, and seemed like a voice from heaven reminding them of the promise of deliverance so often uttered by the chaplain.

The whole chapter from which the text was taken had a peculiar significance. It commences: " Blow ye the trumpet in Zion, and sound an alarm in my holy mountain : let all the inhabitants of the land tremble, for the day of the Lord cometh, for it is nigh at hand, a day of darkness and gloominess, a day of clouds and thick darkness, as the morning spread upon the mountains, a great people and a strong; there hath not ever been the like. * * A fire devoureth before them, and behind them a flame burneth; the land is as the garden of Eden before them, and behind them a desolate wilderness." So the verses immediately preceding the text had a solemn power in them, that the most indifferent could not fail to feel: " Let the priests, the ministers of the Lord, weep between the porch and the altar, and let them say, Spare thy people, O Lord, and give not thine inheritance to reproach, that the heathen should rule over them. Wherefore should they say among the people, Where is their God ? Then will the Lord be jealous for his land, and pity his people. Yea, the Lord will answer, and say unto his people, Behold, I will send you corn, and wine, and oil, and ye shall be satisfied therewith: and I will no more make you a reproach among the heathen, but *I will remove far off from you the northern army.* * * * Fear not, O Land, be glad and rejoice, for the Lord will do great things." The language applied with wonderful force to the invasion and overthrow of Burgoyne. The "day of darkness and gloominess, the day of clouds and thick darkness" had in reality come upon them. Before the resistless legions of Burgoyne the inhabitants of the land had fled in terror, and desolation marked their progress. It was a time for "the ministers of the Lord to weep between the porch and the altar," and cry, " Spare thy people, O Lord." Their prayer had been answered, and God had " removed the northern army" forever, and they could now shout aloud, "Fear not, O land, be glad and rejoice !" The theme was one peculiarly adapted to Dwight's glowing imagination and enthusiastic patriotism. He painted in vivid colors the terror and dismay this northern invasion had spread through the land, described the victory and exultation of the people, giving God all the glory, and declared that he saw in it the bright assurance of final triumph.

The officers and soldiers were carried away by his eloquence, and Putnam was especially delighted, and did not attempt to conceal his pleasure, but nodded and smiled in delighted approval throughout the discourse, though he did not for a moment suppose the text was in the Bible, but rather an inference which Dwight had drawn from the preceding passages. After service was over, he was loud in his expressions of admiration of the sermon and the preacher, but remarked at the same time to some of the officers, that of course there was no such text in the Bible, and that it was made up by Dwight for the occasion—still, he said, the sermon was just as good for all that. The officers smiled in reply, saying that Dwight had taken no such liberty with the sacred volume, for the text was really in it. Putnam, however, stoutly denied it, and refused to yield the point, till one of them brought a Bible, and pointed it out to him. He could at first hardly believe his own eyes, yet there it was, beyond all cavil. He read it over carefully, and then exclaimed: "*Well, there is every thing in that book, and Dwight knows just where to lay his finger on it.*"

The forest-clad Highlands had put on their most gorgeous apparel, as if on purpose to celebrate this great victory, and all the glories of an American autumn were spread upon the mountains. The dreary atmosphere resting like a gentle haze upon the sleeping river—wild fowl sweeping in clouds far over head, seeking the sea—the falling leaf: all disposed the poetic mind of Dwight to musing, and he spent many of his leisure hours strolling through the forest and cedar groves near the encampment. His country ever lay uppermost in his heart, and the victory at Saratoga had filled his mind with the brightest anticipations of her future glory, and he here composed the well-known ode, commencing:—

> "Columbia! Columbia! to glory arise,
> Thou queen of the world, and child of the skies."

The last verse beautifully describes the circumstances connected with its composition, and one familiar with the cedar-clad shores of this region can easily picture the quiet rambles of the young poet. He says :—

> "Thus, as down a lone valley with cedars o'erspread,
> From war's dread confusion I pensively strayed,
> The gloom from the face of fair heaven retired—
> The winds ceased to murmur, the thunder expired—
> Perfumes as of Eden flowed sweetly along,
> And a voice as of angels enchantingly sung:
> 'Columbia! Columbia! to glory arise,
> The queen of the world, and child of the skies.'"

I give below the entire ode,* that it may be read

---

* Columbia! Columbia! to glory arise,
  The queen of the world, and child of the skies!
  Thy genius commands thee; with rapture behold
  While ages on ages thy splendor unfold.
  Thy reign is the last and the noblest of time,
  Most fruitful thy soil, most inviting thy clime;
  Let the crimes of the east ne'er encrimson thy name,
  Be freedom, and science, and virtue thy fame.

  To conquest and slaughter let Europe aspire,
  Whelm nations in blood, and wrap cities in fire;
  Thy heroes the rights of mankind shall defend,
  And triumph pursue them, and glory attend.
  A world is thy realm—for a world be thy laws,
  Enlarged as thine empire, and just as thy cause;
  On freedom's broad basis that empire shall rise,
  Extend with the main, and dissolve with the skies.

  Fair science her gates to thy sons shall unbar,
  And the east see thy morn hide the beams of her star.
  New bards and new sages unrivalled shall soar
  To fame, unextinguished when time is no more;
  To thee, the last refuge of virtue designed,
  Shall fly from all nations the best of mankind;
  Here, grateful to heaven, with transport shall bring
  Their incense, more fragrant than odors of spring.

in the light of these interesting facts. Written only one year after the struggle commenced, it exhibits a wonderful faith in the final triumph of the Colonies, and its inspiring prophecies read to-day like descriptions of past events. The young divine and poet certainly saw farther than most men, and the glowing future spread out before him in entrancing grandeur and beauty.

Mr. Dwight did not content himself with composing this national ode, but, with Barlow, Trumbull and others, wrote several patriotic songs, which became great favorites not only in the army, but throughout the land. He felt the full force of the celebrated say-

> Nor less shall thy fair ones to glory ascend,
> And genius and beauty in harmony blend;
> The graces of form shall awake pure desire,
> And the charms of the soul ever cherish the fire.
> Their sweetness unmingled, their manners refined,
> And virtue's bright image enstamped on the mind,
> With peace and soft rapture shall teach life to glow,
> And light up a smile in the aspect of woe.
>
> Thy fleets to all regions thy power shall display,
> The nations admire, and the oceans obey;
> Each shore to thy glory its tribute unfold,
> And the east and the south yield their spices and gold.
> As the day spring unbounded thy splendor shall flow,
> And earth's little kingdoms before thee shall bow,
> While the ensigns of union in triumph unfurled,
> Hush the tumult of war, and give peace to the world.
>
> Thus, as down a lone valley with cedars o'erspread,
> From war's dread confusion I pensively strayed—
> The gloom from the face of fair heaven retired—
> The winds ceased to murmur, the thunder expired—
> Perfumes as of Eden flowed sweetly along,
> And a voice as of angels enchantingly sung:
> Columbia! Columbia! to glory arise,
> The queen of the world, and child of the skies!

ing—"Let me write the songs of a nation, and you may make its laws."—He was aware that the heart of the people was moved far more by them than by harangues, and that they reached every class.

At this time he finished another poem entitled, "The Conquest of Canaan," and dedicated it to "George Washington, Esq., commander-in-chief of the American armies—the savior of his country—the supporter of freedom, and the benefactor of mankind."

Unacquainted with Washington personally, he was averse to apply to him directly for the privilege of dedicating it to him, and asked General Parsons to be the medium through which he could make his request known. The general, proud of his young chaplain, cheerfully consented.*

---

* General Parsons to General Washington :—

"Camp West Point, March 7th, 1778.

"Dear General—The writer of the letter, herewith transmitted you, is a chaplain of the brigade under my command. He is a person of extensive literature, an amiable private character, and has happily united that virtue and piety, which ought ever to form the character of a clergyman, with the liberal, generous sentiments and agreeable manners of a gentleman.

"The merits of the performance he mentions I am not a competent judge of; many gentlemen, of learning and taste for poetical writings, who have examined it with care and attention, esteem this work in the class of the best writings of the kind. He will be particularly obliged by your Excellency's consent that this work should make its public appearance under your patronage. * * *

"I am, with great esteem,
 "Your Excellency's obedient, humble servant,
  "Samuel H. Parsons.

"To Geo. Washington."

But though such streams of glory irradiated the departing footsteps of autumn, dark clouds and a threatening sky heralded the coming on of winter.

The following is the enclosed letter to which he refers:—

"*May it please your Excellency:*

"The application, which is the subject of this letter, is, I believe, not common in these American regions, yet I can not but hope it will not on that account be deemed impertinent or presumptuous. For several years I have been employed in writing a poem on the *Conquest of Canaan by Joshua*. This poem, upon the first knowledge of your Excellency's character, I determined with leave to inscribe to *you*. If it will not be too great a favor, it will certainly be remembered with gratitude.

"I am not insensible that the subject of this request is delicate; as consent on the part of your Excellency can not possibly add to your reputation, it may be followed by consequences of a disagreeable nature. Of the merit or demerit of the work your Excellency can not form a guess, but from the character of the writer, with which you will be made acquainted by General Parsons, who does me the honor to enclose this in one from himself. All that I can say upon the subject (and I hope I may assert it with propriety) is that I am so independent a republican, and so honest a man, as to be incapable of a wish to palm myself upon the world under the patronage of another; as to be remote from any sinister will in this application, and to disdain making the proffer, slight as it be, to the most splendid personage for whose character I have not a particular esteem.

"I am, with great respect,
"Your Excellency's most obedient and most humble servant,
"Timothy Dwight, Jr.
"*March 8th*, 1778."

To this dignified and manly letter Washington made the following reply:—

"Head-Quarters, Valley Forge, 18th March, 1778.

"Dear Sir—I yesterday received your favor of the 8th inst., accompanied by so warm a recommendation from General Parsons, that

The army under Washington, after committing itself with solemn religious ceremonies to the God of liberty, took up its painful, suffering march for Valley Forge. The same severe winter that wrought such misery and desolation in that encampment of naked, starving men, closed round the Highlands with a silent gloom that made those within its fastnesses forget the joy and exultation of the autumn that had past.

The recent successful attempt of Clinton to force the Highlands, and the narrow escape the Colonies had made, showed the imperative necessity of taking more efficient measures to fortify them. Engineers were therefore dispatched to select a site for a fortification less assailable than Forts Clinton and Montgomery had proved to be, and West Point was finally chosen as possessing the greatest natural advantages. The Hudson being locked by ice in winter, it was impossible for the British vessels below to annoy the workmen at that season, and so, notwithstanding the intensity of the cold, and the frozen state of the ground, it was resolved to commence the works at

---

I can not but form favorable presages of the merit of the work you propose to honor me with the dedication of. Nothing can give me more pleasure than to patronize the essays of genius, and a laudable cultivation of the arts and sciences, which had begun to flourish in so eminent a degree before the hand of oppression was stretched over our devoted country; and I shall esteem myself happy if a poem, which has employed the labor of years, will derive any advantage, or bear more weight in the world, by making its appearance under a dedication to me.

"I am, very respectfully, your, etc.
"G. WASHINGTON.

once. General Parsons, therefore, in the latter part of January, though the snow was two feet deep on the level, started with his brigade for the scene of operations. While the unpaid, naked, and starving soldiers were crouching and shivering in their miserable huts at Valley Forge, Parsons' troops, almost as poorly sheltered, were toiling in the snow, under the gigantic precipices of the Highlands. And as the chaplains shared the privations and sufferings of the former in their gloomy encampment, so did Dwight cheer by his presence and words of encouragement the latter in their painful, exhausting labor. Though half fed, half clothed, and not half paid, the men worked with such vigor and determination that soon formidable defences appeared on the banks; and by the time navigation should be opened, it was evident that an effectual barrier would be placed to the enemy's ships. The sufferings of the troops during this winter in the region of the Highlands may be partially imagined from the following statement of Putnam. After remarking that part of Meigs' regiment was down with the small pox, he says: "*Dubois' regiment is unfit to be ordered on duty, there being not one blanket in the regiment. Very few have either a shoe or a shirt, and most of them have neither stockings, breeches, nor overalls. Several companies of enlisted artificers are in the same situation, and unable to work in the field. Several hundred men are rendered useless merely for want of necessary apparel, as no clothing is permitted to be stopped at this post.*"

To such soldiers Dwight had to preach words of

comfort, and utter promises of God's blessing on their labors. From the depths of such a night he had to promise a bright and glorious morning. He never desponded, and though moved by the suffering he could not alleviate, felt a serene confidence in ultimate success. The faith of the clergy amid all the vicissitudes of fortune seemed at times almost presumptuous, but in the hour of deepest discouragement, when to human eye there seemed no way of deliverance, they pledged without hesitation the strength of Israel's God to the cause. Though circumstances were at times so disheartening that they seemed to ask in mockery, "Where now is thy God?" these men unhesitatingly, confidently replied: "Our God is in the heavens, and will assuredly in his own good time make bare his arm for our deliverance."

At length the long and dreary winter melted away into spring, the ice slowly yielded to the sun and rain, and soon the river, which for so long a time had presented a white and silent surface, was turbulent with the heaving, grinding masses that came driving down on the tide. Dwight lodged a part of the time with Parsons, and a part of the time with Putnam, in the house of Beverly Johnson, which was afterwards occupied by Arnold.

The following little episode in the duties of his office exhibit his keen appreciation of natural scenery, and at the same time presents a graphic picture of the country surrounding West Point in early spring. One Sunday, in the middle of March, after having performed religious services, he found his quarters such a scene of confusion from the constant arrival of officers and others, who came to report or receive orders, that to escape it, he, with Major Humphrey, resolved to ascend Sugar Loaf Mountain. This was a laborious and difficult task, for the sides of the mountain were not only very steep, but covered with huge boulders and fragments of rock, that gave way to the foot as they struggled upward. At length, however, the dreary top was reached, and a strangely wild and sublime scene lay spread out before them. Around them, in awe-inspiring proximity, arose the naked, savage forms of the group of mountains that compose the Highlands, completely locking them in, except at the north where stretched away the turbulent Hudson. The landscape was grand and desolate, with not a single cheerful object to relieve its savage aspect. "Every thing," he said, "which we beheld was majestic, solemn, wild, and melancholy. The grandeur of the scene defies description." West Point, dotted with white tents, lay beneath the barren mountains, which stood like sentinels around them, while far as the eye could reach, northward, moved vast fields of floating ice, now crashing against the shore, sending deep muffled groans up the far heights, or echoing in sullen thunder through the gorges. At intervals came loud explosions, caused by the rending masses, and sounding like distant cannon. "Cottages were thinly sprinkled over the mountainous regions in the east, in size resembling a dove cage, surrounded by little fields covered with snow, and spotting with white the vast expansion of the forest with which the mountains are overspread. Each seemed of itself to have dropped from the clouds, in places to which the rest of the world would never have access, and out of which they would never find a way into the world. It is difficult to conceive of any thing more solemn or more wild than the appearance of these mountains. An immense forest covered them to their summits. Its color was a deep brown—its aspect that of a universal death. The sun had far declined in the west, clouds of a singular, misty appearance overcast his splendor, and arraying his face with a melancholy sadness, imparted a kind of funereal aspect to every object." Mill streams, swollen with melted snows, roar like the ocean, mingled in with the sound of crashing ice below. Far away to the southward were the ruins of Fort Montgomery, where "more than one hundred of our countrymen became victims, a few months since, to the unprincipled claims of avarice and ambition. These, and countless millions more, will at the final judgment rise up as terrible witnesses against the pride, rapacity, and cruelty of those who have been the ultimate cause of their destruction." There, too, was West Point, where "the same scenes of slaughter may not improbably be soon enacted over again."

"The day was warm and spring-like. The campaign was about to open, a campaign in which a thousand unnecessary miseries will be suffered. Parents will be made childless, wives will be made widows, and children will be made orphans. Many a house, where peace, cheerfulness, and delight would love to dwell, will probably be reduced to ashes, and many a family to want and despair."

"The ruins of Fort Montgomery," which he describes as arresting his attention, were soon after visited by some officers, and he accompanied them. Floating leisurely down the river, they moored their boats beneath the ruins, and began their explorations. "The first thing," says Dwight, "that met our eyes, after we left our barge, was the remains of a fire kindled by the cottagers of this solitude, for the purpose of consuming the bones of some of the Americans who had fallen at this place, and had been left unburied. Some of these bones were lying partially consumed round the spot where the fire had been kindled, and some had evidently been converted into ashes. As we went onward, we were distressed by the fœtor of decayed human bodies. To me this was a novelty, and more overwhelming and dispiriting than I am able to describe. As we were attempting to discover the source from which it proceeded, we found at a small distance from the fort a pond of moderate size, in which we saw the bodies of several men who had been killed in the assault upon the fort. They were thrown into this pond the preceding autumn by the British, when probably the water was sufficiently deep to cover them. Some of them were covered at this time, but at a depth so small as to leave them distinctly visible. Others had an arm, a leg, and a part of the body above the surface. The clothes they wore when they were killed were still on them, and proved that they were militia, being the ordinary dress of farmers.

Their faces were bloated and monstrous, and their postures were uncouth and distorted, and in the highest degree afflictive. My companions had been accustomed to the horrors of war, and sustained the prospect with some degree of firmness. To me, a novice in scenes of this nature, it was overwhelming. I surveyed it a moment, and hastened away. From this combination of painful objects we proceeded to Fort Clinton, built on a rising ground, a little farther down the river. The ruins of the fortress were a mere counterpart of those of Fort Montgomery. Every thing which remained was a melancholy piece of destruction. We went from this to find the grave of Count Grabourkil, a Polish nobleman, who was killed in the assault. The grave was pointed out by Col. Livingston, who saw him fall."

With the advance of spring, formidable preparations for the summer campaign were set on foot, to which, on the last of April, a mighty impetus was given by the arrival of the news, that France had joined our cause, and declared war with England. The battle of Saratoga had fixed her wavering policy, and now not only ships and men, but money and clothing were promised. Universal confidence was restored, and strong aggressive movements against the enemy were planned in every part of the Colonies.

In the meantime a sad calamity overtook the family of Dwight, which changed all his plans. The year before, his father, with two of his sons, went to the southwestern part of Mississippi, to provide for a permanent settlement on a tract of land which he and his brother-in-law, General Lyman, had received as a grant from the crown. While carrying out his plans, he was taken sick at Natchez, and died during the winter that his son Timothy was serving as chaplain in the Highlands. Owing to the unsettled state of the country, and uncertain modes of communication with that then remote portion of the country, the latter did not receive the news of his father's death for several months. The support and comfort of his widowed mother seemed now to him his first duty, and he immediately resigned his office as chaplain, and went to Northampton where she resided, and for the next five years devoted himself to her welfare. The history of his after career does not come within the design of this sketch. From 1778 to 1781 he supplied successively vacant congregations in Westfield, Muddy Brook, Deerfield, and South Hadley. In November of the latter year he preached an eloquent sermon on the capture of Cornwallis. At this time he was prevailed on to give his services to his country temporarily in political life, and represented Northampton in 1781-2 in the General Court of Massachusetts. In 1783 he was settled over the church in Greenfield, Conn. In 1785 he published a poem in eleven books, entitled "The Conquest of Canaan." Besides this he published two other poems, called "The Triumph of Infidelity," and "Greenfield Hill." In 1795 he was elected president of Yale College. From this time he became one of the acknowledged theological leaders in this country, and his works were well known in Europe. Partaking of the prejudices of New England, he was bitterly opposed to the war of 1812, and imbibing the same erroneous views that characterized the old federalists respecting the struggle of Revolutionary France and the character of Napoleon, he opposed both with a warmth, one might say bitterness, of spirit that always accompanies views founded on prejudice, and not on fact. His fame as a theologian, his eloquence as a preacher, his success as president of Yale College, and his excellence as a man and Christian are known throughout the land. A devoted patriot and faithful preacher, his brilliant talents and best feelings were given to his country and his God, and he rested from his labors in 1816, at the age of sixty-four.

CHAPTER XVIII.

NAPHTALI DAGGET.

Professor of Divinity in Yale College.—The College broken up.—Invasion of Tryon.—Terror of the Inhabitants.—A Company of a Hundred Young Men raised to resist him.—Dr. Dagget and his black Mare.—Advances alone to reconnoiter.—The Fight.—The Retreat.—Dr. Dagget refuses to run.—Interview with the British Officer.—Forced to guide the Column.—Brutal Treatment.—Rescued by a Tory.—His Sickness.—Death.

Naphthali Dagget, D. D., professor of divinity, and for a time President of Yale College, was another distinguished clergyman, who was as illustrious for his patriotism as for his theological learning. He instructed the students in the duty of resistance to Great Britain as earnestly as he did in that of obedience to God; indeed, he regarded them as one and the same duty.

In 1779, the college had recovered from the panic that had scattered the students into various towns in the interior, and was in a prosperous condition. But, in the midst of its tranquillity, a rumor reached New Haven that General Tryon was preparing to make a descent upon it. The place was immediately thrown into great alarm, and a meeting was called to deliberate on what was to be done. Counsels were various as to the best course to pursue, but Dr. Dagget declared that whatever else was determined upon, one thing was clear, *the citizens must fight*.

At length the dreaded calamity came, and swift riders galloped into town, bringing the startling news that the British, twenty-five hundred strong, had landed about five miles distant at West Haven. At once all was confusion and terror. The college was hurriedly broken up, and, as all regarded it useless to attempt to resist so large a body of regular troops, it was determined that early in the morning the inhabitants and students should take their flight into the interior, and leave the place to the mercy of the marauders. To give the former as much time as possible to remove their goods, a volunteer company of a hundred young men was formed, to retard the march of the British, by beating back their advance guards. Accordingly they assembled on the green, with such arms as they could lay their hands on, and paraded in front of the deserted college. The streets were filled with the terrified fugitives, as in wagons, on horseback, and on foot, they streamed towards the country. It was a scene of wild confusion, and contrasted strangely with that courageous little detachment preparing to go forth against such an overwhelming force.

At length every thing being ready, drum and fife struck up a lively strain, and taking up its line of march, the band passed out of the city. It had not proceeded far, when the clatter of horse's hoofs was heard along the road, and the next moment the reverend professor of divinity galloped up on his old black mare, with a long fowling-piece in his hand. He had not contented himself with giving good patriotic advice, but had resolved to set an example. To their surprise, however, he did not stop to join them, but pushed straight on towards the enemy. The little band gave him a loud cheer as he passed, but the old man never turned to the right or left, but dashed resolutely onward, and, ascending a hill, halted in a grove, and commenced reconnoitering the enemy.

The detachment, turning a little to the south, swept round the base of the hill, and kept on till they came in sight of the advance guard of the British; when, throwing themselves behind a fence, they poured in a destructive volley. The guard halted, and returned the fire. But as volley succeeded volley, each more deadly than the last, they turned and fled. The young volunteers then broke cover, and leaping the fence, pursued them, firing and shouting as they went. Driving them from fence to fence, and across field after field, they kept courageously on, till they suddenly found themselves face to face with the whole hostile army. As far as the eye could reach on either side, the green fields were red with scarlet uniforms— the extended wings ready, at the word of command, to enfold them, and cut off every avenue of escape. Suddenly halting, and taking in the full extent of their danger, they without waiting for orders, turned, and ran for their lives.

As they fled along the base of the hill, on the top of which Dr. Dagget had taken his station, they saw the venerable man quietly watching the advancing enemy. As the noise and confusion of the flying detachment reached his ears he turned a quiet glance below, then leveling his fowling-piece at the foe, blazed away. As the British pressed after the fugitives, they were surprised at the solitary report of a gun every few minutes from the grove of trees on that hill. At first they paid but little attention to it, but the bullets finding their way steadily into the ranks, they were compelled to notice it, and an officer sent a detachment up to see what it meant. The professor saw them coming, but never moved from his position. His black mare stood near him, and he could any moment have mounted and fled, but this seemed never to have entered his head. He was thinking only of the enemy, and loaded and fired as fast as he could.

When the detachment reached the spot where he stood, the commanding officer, to his surprise, saw only a venerable man in black before him, quietly loading his gun to have another shot. Pausing a moment at the extraordinary spectacle of a single man thus coolly fighting a whole army, he exclaimed, "What are you doing there, you old fool, firing on His Majesty's troops?" The staunch old patriot looked up in the most unconcerned manner, and replied, "*Exercising the rights of war.*" The whole affair seemed to strike the officer comically; and, rather amused than offended at the audacity of the proceeding, he said, "If I let you go this time, you old rascal, will you ever fire again on the troops of His Majesty?" "*Nothing more likely,*" was the imperturbable reply. This was too much for the good temper of the Briton, and he ordered his men to seize him. They did so; and dragged him roughly down the hill to the head of the column.

The Americans, in their retreat, had torn down the bridge over the river, after crossing it, thus compelling the British to march two miles farther north to another bridge. The latter immediately placed Dr. Dagget, on foot, at the head of the column as a guide, and pressed rapidly forward.

It was the 5th of July, and one of the hottest days of the year. Under the burning rays of the noonday sun, and the driving pace they were kept at, even the hardened soldiers wilted; while Dr. Dagget, unused to such exposure, soon became completely exhausted. But the moment he showed signs of faltering, the soldiers pricked him on with their bayonets, at the same time showering curses and insults upon his head. Before the five miles' march was completed, the brave old man was ready to sink to the earth. But every time he paused and reeled as if about to fall, they caught him on the points of their bayonets, and forced him to rally, while the blood flowed in streams down his dress. As they entered the streets of the town, they commenced shooting down the peaceable citizens who had remained behind, whenever they appeared in sight, and Dr. Dagget expected every moment to share their fate. At length they reached the green, when a tory, who had come out to welcome the enemy, recognised Dr. Dagget, as he lay covered with blood and dust, and requested the officer to release him. He did so, and the wounded patriot was carried into a house near by, more dead than alive.

His utter exhaustion and brutal wounds combined brought him to the very gates of death, and his life for some time was despaired of. He however rallied, and was able a part of the next year to preach in the chapel, but his constitution had received a shock from which it could not fully recover, and in sixteen months he was borne to the grave, one more added to the list of noble souls who felt that the offer of their lives to their country was a small sacrifice.

CHAPTER XIX.

EZRA STILES.

His Prophecy respecting the Colonies, in 1760.—President of Yale College.— Chancellor Kent's Eulogy of him.— His Patriotism.— Keeps a Diary of Revolutionary Events.—His Death.

Ezra Stiles, who succeeded Dr. Dagget as President of Yale College, forms a third in the illustrious trio of patriotic Presidents that Yale can boast. His far-reaching mind as early as 1760 seemed to foresee the struggle which would eventually take place between the colonies and England. In a sermon delivered at that time on the reduction of Canada by the English he used the following language: "It is probable that in time there will be formed a provincial Confederacy, and a Common Council standing on free provincial suffrage, and this may in time terminate in an Imperial Diet, when the imperial dominion will subvert *as it ought in election.*" He lived to see this prophecy fulfilled in the Continental Congress. The late Chancellor Kent, one of his pupils, thus speaks of his patriotism: "President Stiles' zeal for civil and religious liberty was kindled at the altar of the English and New England Puritans, and it was animating and vivid. A more constant and devoted friend to the revolution and independence of the country never existed. He had anticipated it as early as 1760, and his whole soul was enlisted in every measure which led on gradually to the formation and establishment of the American Union. The frequent appeals which he was accustomed to make to the heads and hearts of his pupils concerning the slippery paths of youth, the grave duties of life, the responsibilities of men, and the perils and hopes and honors and destiny of our country, will never be forgotten by those who heard them, and especially when he came to touch, as he often did with a master's hand and prophet's fire, on the bright vision of the future prosperity and splendor of the United States." Ezra Stiles was born at North Haven, Connecticut, December 10th, 1727, and died in 1795, and hence had nearly reached his threescore and ten. He kept a voluminous diary during the Revolution, which is still preserved in manuscript in the library of Yale College, and contains many useful and interesting facts connected with those times.

CHAPTER XX.

JOEL BARLOW.

His Birth and Early Education.—A Friend of Dwight.—His Poem, "The Prospect of Peace."—Joins the Army in Vacations.—Becomes Chaplain.—Writes Patriotic Ballads.—"Hymns for Yankee Rebels."—The Burning of Charlestown."—Occupation in the Army.—Friend of Washington.—Sermon on Arnold's Treason.—Becomes Lawyer and Editor at Hartford, Connecticut.—Revises Watt's Psalms and Hymns.—Agent of Scioto Land Company.—Visits England, France.—Becomes enlisted in the French Revolution.—His Occupations in Europe.—Consul at Algiers.—Makes a Fortune in France.—Returns to America.—Remarkable Prophecies in his Columbiad.—Minister to France.—His Death.—Charge of Religious Apostacy.

Mr. Barlow occupied so prominent a place before the public *after* the Revolution that but little has been written of his career as a patriot. Indeed, there is a great dearth of details respecting his early life in the army, for his own papers are silent on the subject. He was the youngest son of ten children, and was born in Reading, Connecticut, in 1755. He entered Dartmouth College in 1774, but before he finished his course removed to Yale, where he became acquainted with Dwight, who was tutor there, and a warm friendship sprung up between the two young patriots and poets. Entering with all the ardor of a youthful and impulsive nature into the revolutionary struggle, he spent his vacations in the army, fighting in the ranks like a common soldier. At Whiteplains he distinguished himself by his bravery. He graduated in 1778, and on commencement day delivered a poem, entitled "The Prospect of Peace," which was published. His early poems breathe the spirit of true patriotism, and exhibit an unbounded faith in the triumph of liberty, not only in this country but throughout the world. Of America he sang:

> "On this broad theatre unbounded spread
> In different scenes what countless throngs must tread,
> Soon on the new formed empire rising fair,
> Calms her brave sons now breathing from the war,
> Unfolds her harbors, spreads the genial soil,
> And welcomes freemen to the cheerful toil."

After he left college Barlow commenced the study of law; but the Massachusetts line being in great need of chaplains, he abandoned it for theology, and after six weeks' study was licensed to preach, and entered the army as chaplain. At the outset he and Dwight and Trumbull and Humphreys and others frequently wrote patriotic songs for the soldiers and people, which were sung everywhere, and had a powerful effect in animating the spirits of both. Barlow had great faith in popular ballads; and when he entered the army, said, "I do not know whether I shall do more for the cause in the capacity of chaplain than I could in that of poet. I have great faith in the influence of songs, and I shall continue while fulfilling the duties of my appointment to write one now and then to encourage the taste of them which I find in the camp. One good song is worth a dozen addresses or proclamations." He carried out his resolution, and during the intervals of his arduous campaigns and on the fatiguing march composed many a stirring ode, which cheered and animated the soldiers. Writing not for fame, but to kindle patriotic feeling, he took no pains to let their authorship be known, and hence the most of his revolutionary ballads have passed into oblivion, or exist as anonymous effusions. Those written by New England patriots were stigmatized as "psalms and hymns adapted to the taste of Yankee rebels." Among these we find one written by Barlow, entitled

THE BURNING OF CHARLESTOWN.

After enlarging on the atrocity of the act at some length, he closes with the following prophetic denunciation:—

"Nor shall the blood of heroes, on the plain,
   Who fell that day in freedom's cause,
Lie unrevenged, though with thy thousands slain,
   Whilst there's a king who fears nor minds thy laws.

Shall Cain, who madly spilt his brother's blood
   Receive such curses from the God of all?
Is not that Sovereign still as just and good
   To hear the cries of children when they call?

Yes, there's a God, whose laws are still the same,
   Whose years are endless, and whose power is great:
He is our God: Jehovah is his name:
   With him we trust our sore oppressed State.

When He shall rise, (Oh! Britain, dread the day,
   Nor can I stretch the period of thy fate;)
What heart of steel, what tyrant then shall sway
   A throne that's sinking by oppression's weight

> Thy crimes, Oh *North*, shall then like specters stand,
>   Nor *Charlestown* hindmost in the *ghastly roll*,
> And faithless *Gage*, who gave the dread command,
>   Shall find dire torments gnaw upon his soul.
>
> Yea, in this world we trust those ills so dread,
>   That fill the nation with such matchless woes,
> Shall fall with double vengeance on thy head,
>   Nor 'scape those minions which thy court compose."

Barlow's whole soul was so enlisted in the struggle that he seemed to have lost sight of his individual prospects, in the future of his country. Although serving as chaplain in the army, he evidently had no design of following the clerical profession for life. He pursued it from a sense of duty in the existing emergencies—as the best way he could serve the cause of liberty. Had he remained a clergyman after the close of the war, the personal incidents connected with his career as chaplain would doubtless have been preserved with greater care, but his subsequent public life ran in such an entirely opposite channel, with which these seemed to have no connection, that they were mostly overlooked, and the papers containing them perhaps destroyed by himself.

Only now and then we get glimpses of him—always at his post—always confident and courageous, and endeavoring to infuse his spirit into others. We see the young poet and preacher looking sadly but approvingly on the execution of Andre, and as the body of the brave, but ill-fated officer, swings in mid-air, saying to those around him, it is heaven's own justice. Soon after he preached at West Point a sermon on the treason of Arnold, in which the vengeance of God was proclaimed against all those who dared to lift a traitorous hand against their oppressed country. The exalted, fearless patriotic spirit of the chaplain won the heart of Washington, and he invited him to dinner, placing him on his right hand, while Stirling occupied the left. On another occasion we find him on the anniversary of the battle of Saratoga reciting an ode of his own composition with great eclat, and giving a patriotic toast. Barlow's time, however, during the war was not wholly occupied in the discharge of his duties as chaplain, nor in composing patriotic songs for the camp and field. He also completed the plan of an elaborate poem, entitled "The Vision of Columbus," though it was not published till 1787.

At the close of the war he laid aside his clerical profession, and returned to the study of the law, settling at Hartford, Conn. At the same time he edited a weekly newspaper, called "*The American Mercury.*" He was admitted to the bar in 1785, and the same year was employed by the "General Association of Connecticut" to correct and prepare Watt's Psalms for the use of the churches under its charge. The work was satisfactorily performed, and adopted in all the churches. Dwight's collection subsequently took its place.

"The Babylonian captivity," (version of the one hundred and thirty-eigthth Psalm, so much admired), was one of these, beginning:

> "Along the banks where Babel's current flows,
>   Our captive bands in deep despondence strayed;
>   While Zion's fall in sad remembrance rose
>   Her friends, her children, mingled with the dead."

The profession of the law, however, did not suit the bent of his mind, and in 1788 he accepted the agency of the "Scioto Land Company," and went to England to dispose of the property. But while engaged in negotiations he discovered that the title to the land was stolen, and the company a pack of swindlers, and he resigned his position. Having now nothing to occupy him, his attention was naturally directed to France, at that time fully launched on the sea of revolution, and he crossed over to Paris. His sympathies immediately became deeply enlisted for the noble Girondins, and his love of liberty being as extensive as the human race, his whole soul was absorbed in this great, yet wild struggle of man for his rights. Returning to England in 1791, he published the first part of his "*Advice to the Privileged Orders*," and in the February following, a poem on "*The Conspiracy of Kings*," or the unholy alliance against France. Both of these productions are written in the vigorous style and bold, daring spirit which characterized him. The same year he translated Volney's "*Ruins and Reflections on the Revolutions of Empires*," which was published in London. The next year he was delegated by the "Constitutional Society" in England, of which he was a member, to carry an address to the French Convention, to which he had already written a letter. For the performance of this duty the honor of French citizenship was conferred upon him. Soon after the execution of Louis XVI. he wrote the following ode, a parody on "God save the King."

> Fame, let thy trumpet sound,
> Tell all the world around—
> How Capet fell;
> And when great George's poll
> Shall in the basket roll,
> Let mercy then control
> The Guillotine.
>
> When all the sceptered crew
> Have paid their homage to
> The Guillotine;
> Let freedom's flag advance,
> Till all the world like France
> O'er tyrant's grave shall dance,
> And peace begin."

The next year he was made one of a deputation sent to organize the territory of Savoy. While here he addressed a letter "*to the people of Piedmont on the advantages of the French revolution, and the necessity of adopting its principles in Italy.*" At the same time he wrote a poem, entitled "*The Hasty Pudding,*" with a dedicatory letter to Mrs. Washington. His brain seemed to be in a state of fusion, throwing off letters, addresses, poems, with astonishing rapidity, while outward occupation was as necessary to him as air. In 1795 he was appointed legal and commercial agent to the north of Europe, but was soon transferred to a field more congenial to his tastes. Washington appointed him consul to Algiers, to negotiate a treaty with the Barbary States, which he successfully executed, exhibiting all the daring and energy of his nature in behalf of the American prisoners there. Returning to Paris he made a fortune in some commercial speculations, and purchased the hotel of the Count Clermont de Tonnerre, in which he lived in the style of a prince. In 1805 he returned to America and built a fine mansion in the District of Columbia, which he called "Kalorama."

Two years after his great work, the Columbiad, appeared, dedicated to Fulton. In this poem, which is an enlargement of the vision of Columbus, occur some of the most remarkable prophecies or anticipations found in uninspired writings. As an example, take the following prediction of the construction of the Erie canal:

> "From fair Albania, tow'rd the falling sun,
> Back thro' the midland, lengthening channels run,
> Meet the far lakes, their beauteous towns that lave,
> And Hudson join to broad Ohio's wave."

This extraordinary description of the great internal work of New York State was written in 1787, when almost the entire country west of Albany to Niagara was an unbroken wilderness. American literature furnishes no parallel to this. Still more remarkable is the following prophecy of telegraphic communication:

> "Ah, speed thy labors, sage of unknown name,
> Rise into light and seize thy promised fame;
> For thee the chemic powers their bounds expand,
> *The imprisoned lightning waits thy guardian hand,*
> Unnumbered messages in viewless flight
> Shall bear thy mandates with the speed of light."

To one who read these productions in the beginning of this century they must have appeared the incoherent utterances of a diseased imagination, and the last one been pronounced unintelligible nonsense—now they are accurate descriptions of accomplished events. If the name of Erie canal had been inserted in the former, and that of Morse in the latter they would scarcely have been more definite and complete. In language almost as clear and emphatic he foretells Wilkes' discovery of a southern continent.

Always planning some new work the moment one was finished, Barlow now meditated a history of the United States, but was cut short in his labors by being appointed minister to France under Monroe. In October, 1812, when Bonaparte was returning from his disastrous Russian campaign, he received an invitation to meet him at Wilna, and immediately set off in great haste. The fatigues and exposure of this journey brought on inflamation of lungs, and on his return to Paris he died, December 22d, at Zarnawicka, a little village near Cracow. While lying sick here he dictated, at midnight, a poem to his Secretary, entitled, "*Advice to a raven in Russia*," a bitter denunciation of Bonaparte.

Charges were made against Barlow that he became an infidel, though they were never proved. They arose from several causes. In the first place, Barlow foresaw the changes in religious tolerance and theological teachings which have since taken place in New England almost as clearly as he did those in material improvements. In uttering or intimating these he would inevitably be accused of infidelity, just as he was of incoherent raving in predicting the latter. He was too far in advance of his age to be tolerated by it.

In the second place, no man could be transplanted

from the heart of Puritan New England into the midst of the moral, social and religious chaos of the French Revolution without having his views on many points materially modified. But France was infidel, and hence all changes effected by a sojourn on her soil were set down at once as the result of infidelity. An argument short but incontrovertible to the Puritan mind at that time.

In the third place, his adoption of some scientific phrases and words used by the neologists was equally convincing proof.

In the fourth place, he was a friend of the French Revolution, which the Federalists of New England considered second only in atrocity and wickedness to the apostacy of the angels.

In the last place, and chiefly, he was a bitter antifederalist—a thorough, earnest Jeffersonian. This, though not infidelity itself, was its natural product, and as "by their fruits ye shall know them" is sound doctrine, the conclusion that Barlow was a skeptic was a logical conclusion. That his views underwent great changes is evident—it could not be otherwise; but we have nowhere seen the charge of having apostatized from the faith of his fathers sustained by proof sufficient even to justify its being made.

CHAPTER XXI.

JAMES CALDWELL.

His Birth and Ancestry.—Personal Appearance.—Power of his Voice.—His Character.—His Congregation at Elizabethtown.—Made Chaplain.—His Toast on the Reception of the Declaration of Independence.—His Activity.—Rewards offered for his Capture.—Removes to Connecticut Farms.—Goes Armed.—His Services.—Letter to Lee.—Assistant Commissary General.—Last Interview with his Wife.—Her Murder.—Fight at Springfield.—" Give em Watts."—Murder of Caldwell.—His Funeral.—His Children.—Monument to Him.

No man is more deserving of a prominent place in the history of the Revolution than Rev. James Caldwell. He was born in a settlement of Charlotte county, Virginia, called "Cub Creek," and was the youngest of seven children. He graduated at Princeton College in 1759, was licensed to preach in 1760, and the next year receiving ordination was settled over the parish of Elizabethtown, New Jersey. His ancestors were Huegenots, who were driven from France to England by religious persecution, from thence to Scotland, and at last to Ireland, from which his father emigrated to this country. He thus inherited a spirit of independence and of resistance to tyranny which made him from the outset of our troubles enlist heart and soul in the cause of American independence. Though of middle height, he was powerfully made and capable of great endurance. His countenance in repose had a tranquil and somewhat pensive expression, but when roused with heroic daring there was stamped on every lineament the most dauntless, unconquerable resolution. His voice exhibited the same striking contrasts. On ordinary occasions it was low, sweet and musical, captivating the hearer by its winning tones; but when he stood in front of a regiment, haranguing the soldiers, it rose clear and distinct over the roll of the drum and piercing notes of the fife. Of refined feelings, warm and generous sympathies, and possessing true genius, he won all hearts, and fastened himself so deeply in the affections of his people that to this day his memory is tenderly cherished among the inhabitants of Elizabethtown.

In the exciting scenes that immediately preceded the Revolution he bore a prominent and leading part. His congregation upheld him almost to a man, and when we remember that such patriots as Elias Boudinot, William Livingston, Francis Barber, the Daytons and Ogdens composed it, we can not wonder that both pastor and people were looked upon as head rebels of the province, and became peculiarly obnoxious to the loyalists. In intelligence, valor and patriotism, they had no superiors, and formed a band of noble men, of which New Jersey is justly proud.

At the first call to arms the State offered its brigade for the common defence, and Mr. Caldwell was elected its chaplain—Col. Dayton, his parishioner, being the commander. Col. Ebenezer Elmer, commanding one of the regiments, gives the following account of the manner the declaration of independence was received by the brigade. The courier bearing the news arrived at head quarters on the 15th of July, 1776, causing the most intense excitement and enthusiasm. "At twelve o'clock," says the Colonel, "assembly was beat that the men might parade in order to receive a treat, and drink the State's health. When having made a barrel of gròg, the declaration was read, and the following toast was given by parson Caldwell:—'Harmony, honor, and all prosperity to the free and independent United States of America : wise legislators, brave and victorious armies, both by sea and land, to the United States of America.' When three hearty cheers were given, and the grog flew round a-main." Mr. Caldwell's activity and energy would not allow him to confine himself to the duties of chaplain. The timid were to be encouraged, the hesitating brought over to the side of liberty, and the tories met and baffled at every point. Hence, he would be on the Sabbath with his parish, the next day. in the army, and then traversing the country to collect important information, or set on foot measures to advance the common cause. His immense popularity gave him an influence that filled the tories with rage, and made his name common as a household word among the British troops. He at length became such an object of hate and dread that large rewards were offered for his capture. Consequently, when the enemy obtained possession of New York and Staten Island his position became one of extreme peril, for his residence was as well known to them as the head quarters of the army. He, therefore, took the advice of his friends and removed his family to Connecticut Farms, a small place a few miles from Elizabethtown. As an additional precaution, he went armed, and it was well known that no two or four men would take him alive. Often when preaching in the "old red store," as it was called, he would walk up to the table, and unbuckling a brace of pistols lay them before him, and then commence the services of the Sabbath. Strange as such a proceeding may seem at the present day, this good man at the time did not deem it to demand a passing explanation. He was engaged in what he firmly believed to be the cause of God, and that cause he did not consider would be advanced by yielding himself unresistingly into the hands of a skulking tory to be dragged to the scaffold. His country needed his services, not his death in this manner, though his life he held cheap enough whenever liberty should call for the sacrifice.

The retreat of Washington through New Jersey, hotly pursued by Cornwallis, coming as it did on the heels of the fall of New York and Forts Washington and Lee, paralyzed the inhabitants with terror. At the very outset they saw their State overrun with hostile troops, and the struggle that had opened so auspiciously at Bunker Hill, seemed about to close in sudden night. Mr. Caldwell, however, did not share in the general despondency produced by this gloomy state of affairs. The darker the prospects became, the higher rose his resolution, and the more complicated and disheartening the condition of the army grew, the more persevering were his efforts, and the more tireless his unsleeping activity. He seemed ubiquitous, for scarcely would he be reported in one place when his presence was announced in another, and nothing seemed to escape his keen, penetrating scrutiny. His spies were everywhere, and the enemy could not make a movement that eluded his watchful eye. The aid he furnished at this time to the American army in keeping it advised of every step taken by the invading force was of incalculable service.

Washington at length crossed the Delaware and drew up his enfeebled army on its farther shore, where he waited with deep anxiety the advance of Lee from the banks of the Hudson to his assistance. This officer, ambitious of performing some brilliant achievement which should place him in enviable contrast to Washington, lingered on his way, and from one pretext and another deferred obeying the peremptory orders of his commander. Even when he reached Morristown he postponed farther advance in hopes of making an independent movement and cutting in two the extended lines of the British. In order to effect this he constantly wrote to Caldwell to keep him advised of the motions of the enemy. The latter, though he knew Lee's orders were to move forward with all possible despatch to the main army, willingly furnished him all the information in his power. Lee's last letter to him was written on the 12th of December. Caldwell immediately replied to it, telling him that the British army had moved forward, leaving nothing behind but the guards of the several posts, and then added significantly that the American militia had been moved back to Chatam, where they would be in a situation to be of more service than if farther in advance, "*until the expected army approaches for their support.*" The stern patriot, while rendering all the aid in his power to this self-conceited and ambitious leader, could not refrain from giving him this delicate but plain and palpable hint as to his duty. The next day this haughty general, who was to perform such wonderful achievements, was captured with his entire guard while stopping at a small tavern at Barkenridge.

After the brilliant victories at Trenton and Princeton, Mr. Caldwell was very little with the main army, but devoted his time and services when not engaged in his parochial duties to the cause of liberty in his own State. Such was his popularity, and so entire was the confidence of the people in his integrity, that when the army became greatly reduced, and both provisions and money were hard to be obtained, he was appointed Assistant Commissary General. He opened his office at Chatam, and the department felt at once a new impulse imparted to it. His ability, energy, popularity and well-known honesty enabled him to be of incalculable service, and provisions began to pour in, those bringing them accepting whatever guarantees he could give, and sometimes taking his simple word as security. But though he could feed the troops, he could not pay them the money which Congress owed them. In their destitute condition the soldiers suffered greatly for the want of this, and were often on the verge of open rebellion. When matters reached such a dangerous crisis he would assemble them, and by his eloquent appeals, not only allay the excitement of anger, but kindle their enthusiasm so that they would promise to fight on whatever the sufferings and hardships they might be called to undergo.

The unselfish, entire devotion of this gifted man to his country was of the Washington type—far above the reach of all external influence—a devotion in which life itself and all its outward interests were forgotten, or remembered only as an offering ever ready to be made to her welfare.

He gave up his church as a hospital for the sick and wounded soldiers, who, in making tables of the seats, often so covered them with grease and fragments of bread and provision that the congregation on the Sabbath would be compelled to stand during the whole service. When the news of an approaching enemy was received, *its* bell would ring out the note of alarm, for pastor, congregation and church were all consecrated to the same holy cause.

The appointment of any man to the post of Assistant Commissary General at a time when it was almost impossible for the ablest officer to perform its duties satisfactorily was a high compliment, but when it is remembered that Mr. Caldwell was pastor of a church, and preached to his congregation every Sabbath, the selection of him to fill it shows what an exalted estimate was put upon his ability and patriotism. It was not to be expected that a minister and people that occupied so prominent a place in the cause of the Colonies could long escape the vengeance of the British. It was well known that threats of the most malignant kind had been made against him, but they took no positive shape till in January, 1780, when a refugee fired the church. The villain, in confession of the deed afterwards, said he was sorry that the "black-coated" rebel was not burned in his own pulpit. The inhabitants were aroused by the light of the conflagration, but too late to save the edifice sacred both to freedom and to God, and it was burned to the ground.

The next summer, in June, Knyphausen made his sudden and apparently objectless inroad into New Jersey. On the night of the 24th Mr. Caldwell slept in his own house, but was wakened early in the morning by the news of the approach of the enemy. Mounting his horse in haste he started for headquarters with the information. He had proceeded but a short distance, however, when he began to have serious fears for his wife and family that he had left behind. The former, when she bade him good-bye, told him that she had no apprehensions for her own safety, for the enemy, she said, would not harm her and her little children. He had often left them in a similar way before and always found them safe on his return, but now he was oppressed with unusual anxiety, and after striving in vain to shake it off turned his horse and galloped back. As he rode up to the door his wife came out to inquire what he wanted. He told her that he wished her and the children to accompany him to camp, for he felt very uneasy about leaving them behind. But she knowing they would encumber his movements, smiled at his fears, saying there was no danger at all, and declined entirely to leave the house. In the mean time she went in and brought from the breakfast table a warm cup of coffee. While he sat on his horse drinking it the enemy came in sight. Handing back the cup, and flinging her a hasty farewell, and commending her to the care and mercy of the God in whom they both trusted, he struck his spurs into his horse and dashed away.

He had not been gone long before she had cause to regret that she had not yielded to his entreaties, for columns of smoke rising in the distance—the screams of terrified women and children running through the streets, told her that the enemy was on a raid, and murder and devastation were marking their passage. She saw at once that she was surrounded with deadly perils, but calm as became the wife of a hero as well as clergyman, she took her infant and retired into a private room to commit herself and children in prayer to God. Arising from her devotions she sat down upon the bed, and was pondering on her desolate condition when the maid, who had accompanied her with the other children, stepped to the window to look out. As she did so she saw a "red coat" jump over the fence into the yard. Alarmed, she turned quickly and told Mrs. Caldwell. The latter knew at once that evil was intended her, and arose from the bed either to watch the man's actions or to pass out of the room, when the villain caught a glimpse of her through the window. He knew her at a glance, and having come on purpose to kill her, he raised his musket, and fired at her through the window, when she fell amid her terrified children, pierced by two balls. In the midst of the alarm and confusion that followed the torch was applied to the house, and soon the little parsonage was wrapped in flames. It was with great difficulty that some of the neighbors whom the maid informed of the murder were enabled to drag the body out of the burning building. But having accomplished this they were compelled to flee, leaving it exposed in the hot sun in the public street, where it lay for hours with no one humane enough to throw a covering over the pale and ghastly face. At length some of her friends obtained permission from the enemy to remove it into the only house left standing near by.

Mr. Caldwell was at the "Short Hills" with the army while this murderous scene was being enacted at his quiet home. That evening passing by chance two soldiers who were talking in whispers, he heard the name of "Mrs. Caldwell" repeated two or three times. Suspecting at once that something was wrong, he asked them what they were talking about—if any thing had happened to Mrs. Caldwell. They at first hesitated to reply, unwilling to break to him the painful intelligence, but he besought them so earnestly to let him know the worst that they finally told him all. The good man staggered like a smitten ox under the sudden blow, and turned pale as death. Rallying, however, he murmured a broken prayer and turned away to weep alone. That was a painful night to the noble patriot, for not only did he mourn deeply over the tragical end of his wife, whom he loved tenderly, but he was filled with apprehension respecting his orphaned children, one of whom was an infant—now in possession of the enemy. In the morning he procured a flag of truce and went over to "Connecticut Farms." The quiet little village was a heap of smoking ruins, with only here and there a solitary building standing as monuments to mark the desolation. In one of these lay the lifeless body of his wife, and in an adjoining apartment were grouped his weeping children.

The enemy, after burning Connecticut Farms, kept on towards Springfield, with the intention of committing the same barbarous cruelties there. Mr. Caldwell, after seeing his wife buried, and his children placed in the care of one of his parishioners, hastened forward to join the army. At Springfield a sharp engagement took place between the enemy and the American troops, and though the former were compelled to beat a hasty retreat, it was not till they had burned the village to the ground. Mr. Caldwell was in the hottest of the fight, and seeing the fire of one of the companies slackening for want of wadding, he galloped to the Presbyterian meeting house near by, and rushing in, ran from pew to pew, filling his arms with hymn books. Hastening back with these into the battle, he scattered them about in every direction, saying as he pitched one here and another there, "*Now put Watts into them*, boys." With a laugh and a cheer they pulled out the leaves, and ramming home the charges did give the British Watts with a will.

The next year this patriotic, gifted man met the tragical fate of his wife, and sealed his devotion to his country with his blood.

New Jersey remained comparatively tranquil after

the raid of Knyphausen, and flags of truce were constantly passing to and fro to New York, and only soldiers enough were left in the State to act as sentinels at main points. At this time there lived in New York a family by the name of Murray, who had relatives residing in Elizabethtown, and who were much beloved by the people in the vicinity for their kindness to Jersey prisoners confined in the city. One of the family, Miss Murray, wishing to visit Elizabethtown, came to Elizabethtown Point on the 24th of November, under a flag of truce. Mr. Caldwell went down in a carriage to meet her, and accompany her to the town. The details of the events that followed, I will let Dr. Murray tell in his own language. "A sentry was kept up at that time at the Fort. Tying his horse outside the sentinel, Mr. Caldwell, proceeded to the wharf, and taking with him Miss Murray, placed her in his carriage, and then returned to the boat for a small bundle that belonged to her. Thus, he passed three times the man who was keeping guard. With a small package he was returning a second time to his carriage, when the sentinel ordered him to stop, thinking, probably, that there was something contraband in the bundle. He replied that the bundle belonged to the young lady in his carriage. The sentinel said that it must be examined. Mr. Caldwell turned quickly about to carry it back to the boat, that it might be opened there, when the fatal ball struck him. The captain of the guard hearing the report of a gun looked around, and saw Mr. Caldwell staggering before him. He ran and caught him in his arms and laid him on the ground, and without speaking a word he almost instantly expired—the ball having passed through his heart.

The man who shot him was James Morgan, belonging to the Jersey militia—an Irishman by birth, and a man of the most debased and profligate character. He was always drunk when he could be; and liquor turned him into a savage. His family resided near a well in Elizabethtown, into which a child of his fell one day and was drowned. When he returned he found his child dead, and taking it by the arms he beat the broken-hearted mother with the dead body of her own child until her cries brought some of the neighbors to her rescue."

Whether Morgan was on duty as a sentinel when he shot Caldwell is at least questionable. It is said that on his trial it was proved that he had just been relieved. Different motives are assigned for the murder. Some say that Morgan was angry because he had not received his regular wages, and inasmuch as Caldwell was commissary, supposed "he was responsible for the neglect;" others, again, say that he was bribed by the British, or tories. Whatever the motives might have been that influenced him, he was, after a fair trial, convicted of murder, and hung the next January. The body of Mr. Caldwell was placed on some straw in the bottom of a wagon, and taken up to town, and the next Tuesday buried. Dr. Murray thus describes the funeral: "The funeral was one of the most solemn this town has ever witnessed. The concourse assembled on the occasion was immense. The Rev. Dr. Mc Whorter, of Newark, preached the funeral sermon from Ecclesiastes, viii. 8, and after the service was ended, the corpse was placed on a large stone before the door of the house of Mrs. Noel, where all could take a view of the remains of their beloved pastor. When this affecting ceremony was over, and before the coffin was closed, Dr. Boudinot came forward, leading nine orphan children, and placing them around their father's bier, made an address of surpassing pathos to the multitude in their behalf. It was an hour of deep and powerful emotion, and the procession slowly moved to the grave, weeping as they went. And as they lifted their streaming eyes to Heaven, they besought the blessing of God upon the orphan group, and upon their own efforts to resist and vanquish their oppressors." The promise of the orphan's God was made good to them, for friends came forward who provided for them so that they all grew up respectable and useful, and some became distinguished members of society. Lafayette took the third child, John E., and he was educated in France, under the direction of the Marchioness. Another became County Judge, while another still was for many years clerk of the Supreme Court of the United States. In honor of his efforts in the cause of African colonization, a town in Liberia is called "Caldwell" at this day.

Mr Caldwell was as earnest in the pulpit as he was out of it. He seldom preached without weeping himself, and often would melt his audience to tears.

"He was a man of unwearied activity, and of wonderful powers, both of body and mental endurance. Feelings of the most glowing piety, and the most fervent patriotism occupied his bosom, at the same time without at all interfering with each other. He was one day preaching to the battalion—the next providing ways and means for their support, and the next marching with them to battle ; if defeated, assisting to conduct their retreat ; if victorious, offering their united thanksgivings to God, and the next carrying the consolations of the gospel to some afflicted or dying parishioner."

The cause of freedom, and especially the State of New Jersey, owe him a large debt, and it is gratifying to know that his noble deeds have not been left to tradition alone for preservation, but that a monument has been erected to him in the burying ground of the First Presbyterian church, which has been built upon the site of the old one that was burned in 1780. On the east side of the monument is inscribed :—" This monument is erected to the memory of the Rev. James Caldwell, the pious and fervent christian, the zealous and faithful minister, the eloquent preacher, and a prominent leader among the worthies who secured the independence of his country. His name will be cherished in the Church and in the State so long as virtue is esteemed, and patriotism honored." On the south side :—" James Caldwell, born in Charlotte Co., Virginia, April 17th, 1734 ; graduated at Princeton College, 1759 ; ordained pastor of the First Presbyterian Church, of Elizabethtown, 1762. After serving as chaplain in the army of the revolution, and acting as commissary to the troops in New Jersey, he was killed by a shot from a sentinel at Elizabethtown Point,

November 24th, 1781." On the other two sides are inscriptions to his wife. One of them is, "Hannah, wife of the Rev. James Caldwell, and daughter of Jonathan Ogden, of Newark, was killed at Connecticut Farms by a shot from a British soldier, June 25th,* 1780, cruelly sacrificed by the enemies of her husband, and of her country."

"The memory of the just is blessed."

* The date is incorrect.

CHAPTER XXII.

BENJAMIN TRUMBULL.

His Birth and Education.—Takes Sides with the Colonies.—Enters the Army as Chaplain.—Fights in the Ranks.—Curious Interview with Washington.—Fights at Whiteplains.—Anecdote.—Fights at New Haven.—Returns to his Parish.—Writes the History of Connecticut.—His Death.—His Publications.

Hebron, Connecticut, has well earned a prominence by the number of good men she gave to the Revolution, and among them none rank higher as patriots than Mr. Trumbull. Born in this parish in 1735, he early fitted for college, and graduated at Yale when twenty-four years of age. The year after he taught in Dr. Wheelock's Indian charity school at Lebanon Creek, and at the same time studied divinity. The next year he was licensed to preach, and in the following December was ordained and settled at North Haven.

At this time the New England Colonies began to be agitated with the oppressive acts of Great Britain. Of a bold spirit and sanguine temperament, a bitter hater of wrong, and a fearless, ardent, and sometimes stormy defender of the right, Trumbull at once took sides with the former. His ruddy, determined face and stout figure typified admirably his character. He had the massive energy and strength one would expect to see in a man of his vigorous frame and robust health, and at the same time the excitability of an extremely nervous, sensitive person. These characteristics were prominently displayed in his efforts in the cause of American liberty. Zealous, enthusiastic and able in argument, he brought efficient aid to the patriots, and it is much to be regretted that one who bore so important a part in the Revolution in his native State, and afterwards became so distinguished as its historian, should not have left more details and personal incidents connected with his services in the army. But aside from his general patriotism and zeal very little is known of this part of his history. It is evident, however, that but for his clerical profession he would have been found foremost in the ranks fighting for the cause which he so nobly upheld with his tongue. As it was, he, like many other good clergymen, could not at all times be content with discharging the duties of his profession, but in the ardor of his patriotism resorted to carnal weapons to defend what he believed to be the cause of God. Having battled manfully for the right so long as the contest was confined to discussion and remonstrances, the moment hostilities commenced he offered his services as chaplain in the army. In the campaigns that followed he appears only at intervals, but the transient glimpses we do get of him deepens the regret that we cannot follow him step by step in his course. We know, however, that he was engaged in most of the battles in the autumn that immediately followed the fall of New York. On a certain occasion, having learned, as he thought, that one of the divisions of the army was in danger of being cut off, he hurried to General Washington, and in his ardent, excited manner told him of it. The latter had doubtless received the information before, if it was true, and taken the necessary precautions to meet the threatened danger, and hence listened to the chaplain's account without surprise. Looking up and noticing the clerical garb of the messenger, and seeing his intense excitement and anxiety, he said very pleasantly, "Good gentleman, you seem to be very much frightened." Mr. Trumbull had evidently taken his own instead of a military view of the matter, and on his own responsibility described a state of things that did not exist, and Washington's reply was meant to intimate as much. He, however, sadly mistook the man in supposing that his excitement was caused by fear—it was produced solely by anxiety. Fear was not one of the sensations with which he was familiar. At the battle of Whiteplains, which took place soon after, he was with the division that occupied Chatterton's Hill, and aroused by the shameful flight of the militia, seized a musket, and stepping into the ranks fought like a common soldier. Although the cannon balls were crashing around him, he loaded and fired with the most imperturbable coolness. Gano standing in front of the regiment to which he was attached, exposed to the hottest of the fire, and refusing to stir lest his example might dishearten the troops unaccustomed to battle, and Mr. Trumbull fighting on foot among those with whom he had often prayed, were not the least among the remarkable incidents of the fiercely contested action of Chatterton's Hill. When the division was ordered to retreat across the Bronx and join the main army under Washington, he found himself on the shore of the stream, over which horses, artillery and men were hurrying in confusion, at a point where the depth did not promise an easy crossing. While hesitating what to do, he saw Colonel Tallmadge spur his horse into the water close beside him. The brave chaplain immediately resolved that the colonel's horse should carry him also to the farther bank, and being an active as well as strong man, he, with a vigorous leap, landed astride the crupper. The horse, astonished at the summary manner in which this new accession to his load was made, gave a sudden powerful spring and cleared himself of both colonel and chaplain, and they fell into the water together. Floundering up from their cold bath as quickly as possible, they scrambled up the farther bank, and dripping and dirty continued their flight with the retreating force.

In July, 1799, when Gov. Tryon invaded New Haven, he joined the volunteer company of one hundred, who went out to retard the advance of the enemy till the inhabitants could effect their escape with their goods. In the skirmish that followed he fought bravely, showing an example of coolness and courage that gave new life to the younger volunteers. He was mounted on a horse that was used to the sound of battle, and while others fired from behind fences and trees, he sat in full open view of the enemy, and loaded and fired from the saddle. Whenever the enemy poured in an unusual close and deadly volley he would duck his head behind his horse's neck and let the bullets whistle by, then, rising in his seat, take deliberate aim, and fire in return. Mr. Dagget, the reverend professor of divinity, with his long fowling-piece on the hill-top, and Mr. Trumbull, with his musket in the valley below, did yeomen's service on that hot July day.

When the war was over he resumed his parochial duties.

Distinguished for his fervent spirit, and plain, fearless utterance of truths, he devoted his best energies to the cause of his Divine Master.

He was as remarkable for his earnest patriotism in times of peace as he had been in war, and found leisure to write a history of Connecticut, in two volumes, which breathes the same love of country that had characterized his whole life.

He lived to see his country again victorious in the second war with England. In the winter of 1819 and 1820 he was suddenly attacked with a lung fever, which hurried him rapidly to the grave. When told that his case was hopeless, and that he could live but a short time, he said, "I have always remembered my God— I have never forgotten Him in my study, in my family, in my rural labors, and on the field of battle, and I doubt not He will support me now in old age, and in death." The last words that escaped his lips were, "Come quickly, amen. Even so come, Lord Jesus." Thus, at the advanced age of eighty-five, this good man, faithful minister, and devoted patriot, sunk to rest. Of his seven children, two died in infancy, four reached three score and ten, and one daughter ninety years, while the widow lived to be ninety-three.

Besides the two volumes of history of his native State, he published over twenty pamphlets and sermons. Among these was one on the right of Connecticut to the large tract of land known as the " Susquehannah purchase," to which Pennsylvania laid claim. His argument was so conclusive that Congress decided in favor of the claim of Connecticut. The product of the sales of this "purchase" were appropriated to a school fund, which now amounts to more than a million and a-half of dollars.

CHAPTER XXIII.

SAMUEL KIRKLAND.

HIS BIRTH AND EDUCATION.—A TEACHER IN DR. WHEELOCK'S SCHOOL.—GOES A MISSIONARY TO THE INDIANS OF NEW YORK STATE.—HIS LABORS AND PERILS.—HIS MISSION BROKEN UP BY THE REVOLUTION.—EMPLOYED BY CONGRESS TO KEEP THE INDIANS FROM JOINING THE BRITISH.—PREVENTED BY BRANDT.—A CHAPLAIN IN SULLIVAN'S BRIGADE.—ACCOMPANIES IT TO GENESEE FLATS.—HIS SERVICES REWARDED BY CONGRESS.—SETTLES AMONG THE ONEIDAS AFTER THE WAR.—FOUNDS HAMILTON COLLEGE.—IS THROWN FROM HIS HORSE.—HIS DEATH.

SAMUEL KIRKLAND is known throughout the country for his long and faithful labors among the Indians of New York State. Indeed, he is hardly ever spoken of except as a missionary among these wandering and neglected tribes—hence, his services in the revolution have never received especial notice. The latter were regarded a mere episode in his self-denying life, and though they demanded equal sacrifices, exposures, and hardships, were so strangely overlooked by the chroniclers of the times that at this late day it is impossible to give any detailed account of them.

The tenth in a family of twelve children, he was born in Norwich, Conn., on the 1st day of December, 1741. When twenty years of age, he became a student in Dr. Wheelock's celebrated school, at Lebanon, but in 1762 entered the sophomore class in Princeton College, and at once took a high position as a scholar, and a young man of intellect. Leaving college eight months before his class graduated, he went as a missionary to the Senecas, the most remote, powerful, and warlike of the Six Nations. A mere youth, only twenty-three years of age, he plunged fearlessly into the western wilderness of New York, and underwent hardships, and encountered dangers, the narrative of which at this day would read like a romance. Alone and unprotected he wandered for a year and a-half among these lawless tribes, facing what often seemed to be inevitable death, with a calm courage that filled those wild warriors with wonder. His escapes sometimes seemed almost miraculous. He returned in 1766, bringing with him a Seneca chief, who, being introduced by him to the general assembly, of Connecticut, at Hartford, was received with marked honor. In June, of this year, he was ordained at Lebanon, and receiving a general commission as Indian missionary, returned to the Oneidas, and took up his residence with them. He remained here, prosecuting his self-denying labors till the commencement of the revolution, when the threatening sound of the rising tribes along our frontier broke up his mission. He then offered his services to Congress, and endeavored to enlist the Indians of the State on the side of the Americans, or at least induce them to preserve a strict neutrality. His knowledge of their various dialects, and the influence he had acquired over them, rendered him the most fitting agent to accomplish this object. Although, in prosecuting his mission, he visited the various tribes, he was especially anxious that the Six Nations should not take up arms on the side of the British, for he knew if they did our frontiers would be drenched in blood. To prevent this, he made long journeys, attended council after council in various places, and at one time thought he should succeed in keeping those powerful confederated tribes tranquil. But the famous Mohawk warrior, Brandt, counteracted all his efforts, and the massacres of the Mohawk valley, of Wyoming, and Minisink followed, filling the State with mourning. Shut out from the field of his labors, Kirkland entered the army as a chaplain, but, as remarked before, of his valuable services in this capacity but little is left on record, or has been handed down by tradition. We find him in 1778 and 1779 among the Oneidas, collecting and transmitting to government information of the designs and movements of the enemy along Niagara and the lakes, which was of great value, and which could be obtained in no other way. His knowledge of the Indian languages, and the desire of friendly Indians to render him any service, gave him great facilities in this respect, and he kept in constant communication with those having the direction of public affairs. His long sojourn in the wilderness, and his extensive travels in that almost unknown region, gave him also a knowledge of the country which no other white man possessed. Hence, when Sullivan was sent with his brigade to chastise the hostile nations of the Susquehannah and the Genesee valleys, he was solicited to accompany him as chaplain. He did so, and saw a powerful army sweep through the forests where, so many years before, he passed alone and unattended. The contrast was a painful one. Then, with the bible in his hand, trusting alone in the protection of Heaven, he went the messenger of peace, preaching the gospel of Christ to the savages—now he came with fire and sword, to slaughter and lay waste. The drum, and bugle, and loud-mouthed cannon had taken the place of tones of kindness and friendship, and he saw with an aching heart the awful scourge move resistlessly on. The peaceful village, smiling in the summer sun, and the waving fields of corn disappeared as it passed, while the warriors, who gathered in their defence, were stretched stark and stiff amid the desolation. At last the devastating army reached the Eden of this wild region, the beautiful Genesee flats. Twenty miles long and four broad, the cultivated valley spread out before them in all its richness and beauty. The tall grass bent before the wind—corn-field on corn-field as far as the eye could reach, waved in the sunlight—orchards, that had been growing for generations, were weighed down under the profusion of fruit—cattle grazed on the banks of the river, while a hundred and twenty houses, not huts, but large, airy buildings, nestled amid fruit trees, making a scene of surpassing loveliness. Mr. Kirkland saw the army of five thousand encamp at night amid this beauty and luxuriance. Before noon the next day the smoke of burning dwellings covered the valley, and when it lifted, a wide desolation met the eye, and the army encamped at night in a desert.

The important services he rendered the country both before and during this campaign have passed into oblivion. We can only infer their value from the action of Congress subsequently. That body voted him a liberal grant of land, specifying that it was in consideration of his services as a chaplain and other "important services rendered during the war." The State of New York, the general government and Sullivan all recognized and appreciated them. Thus, in every department of the Revolution, the influence of the clergy was felt. In the provincial legislatures, in the general Congress originating and upholding important measures—in the remote parishes rousing the people to arms—in the tented field by example and precept teaching the troops heroism, self-denial and morality—in the wilderness among the savage tribes—everywhere where wisdom and knowledge were required, soldiers wanted and work was to be done, they were found performing not a subordinate but a leading part. One cannot look anywhere over the thirteen States during that struggle or along their bleeding frontiers without seeing the clergy standing as bulwarks of freedom or toiling single handed for its success. Turn which way we will we are made to feel that a history of American Independence that leaves the clergy out, or only mentions them incidentally, is not only false in fact, but what is still worse, false in one of the great lessons God designed our early history should teach.

After the war Mr. Kirkland returned to his labors among the Oneidas, which eventually were crowned with great success. In 1791 he made a census of the Six Nations, and in the winter of the same year, at the request of the Secretary of War, took forty chiefs and warriors—representatives of the Five Nations—to

Philadelphia, for the purpose of consulting in reference to the introduction of civilization among them, and of effecting a permanent treaty of peace between them and the United States. In both of these objects he was successful, and then returned to his missionary labors among the Oneidas, where he built him a log hut into which he removed his family. He soon after established an academy at Hamilton, which continued to flourish until 1810, when it was elevated to the rank of a college, that still remains a monument of his labors in the cause of education. In 1796 he was thrown from his horse and seriously injured. He never recovered entirely from the shock he received in this accident, and remained more or less an invalid till 1808, when he was struck with paralysis, which carried him off suddenly and without his being conscious apparently of his approaching end. Brought into contact with the most prominent men of the country, he was widely known and died universally lamented.

CHAPTER XXIV.

JAMES HALL.

HIS BIRTH AND EDUCATION.—SETTLED IN NORTH CAROLINA.—ROUSES HIS PEOPLE TO OPPOSE THE MOTHER COUNTRY.—IS MADE CAPTAIN OF A COMPANY OF CAVALRY.—ACTS ALSO AS CHAPLAIN.—MARCHES TO SOUTH CAROLINA.—OFFERED THE COMMISSION OF BRIGADIER GENERAL BY GREENE.—DECLINES.—HIS AFTER LIFE.

JAMES HALL was born in Carlisle, Pennsylvania, August 22d, 1744. When he was eight years of age his parents removed to North Carolina and settled in a district now known as Iredell county. At the age of twenty he made a public profession of religion, and soon after turned his attention to the ministry, but did not enter college till 1774, or in his thirty-first year. Being a fine mathematician, Dr. Witherspoon wished to retain him as tutor in the collge, but he said he had devoted himself to the ministry and did not feel at liberty to make any engagements that would divert him from it. He therefore entered immediately on his theological studies under Dr. Witherspoon, and in less than two years was licensed to preach. In 1778 he was settled over the united congregations of Fourth Creek, Concord and Bethany, and remained their pastor till 1790.

Previous to this he had become deeply enlisted in the cause of the Colonies, and declined no service, no matter how great the sacrifice it demanded, which could in any way benefit his country. He did not confine his efforts to the pulpit, but took the lead in all public meetings held to discuss the political topics of the day. He denounced toryism unsparingly, and on every occasion when he could get a hearing made eloquent and earnest appeals in behalf of freedom. The claims of one's country he declared were next to those of God, and could not be treated with neglect without sacrificing every principle of honor and of duty. He was not one of those timorous patriots who are zealous for their country when not called upon to encounter personal danger, but are silent when the thunder of cannon is near. While the conflict was raging in the northern provinces, his sympathy and interest found expression in prayers, exhortations and public addresses, but the moment the sound of battle was heard on the borders of his own State that sympathy showed itself in action. Cornwallis, in his victorious march through South Carolina, sent out detachments in various directions to scour the country, whose barbarous conduct filled every bosom with indignation. Mr. Hall at once called together his flock, and after relating some of the bloody acts that had been committed by the invaders, besought them, in the name of their distracted* country, and for the sake of their friends and neighbors who were hewn down by their merciless foes, to take up arms in their defence. Tears rolled down the cheeks of those sturdy frontiersmen at the thrilling appeal, and catching the enthusiasm of their pastor they immediately organized a body of cavalry to go to the assistance of their fellow-countrymen in South Carolina. When the inquiry was made who should be selected as captain, they declared with one voice for Parson Hall. He accepted the appointment without a moment's hesitation and with his sword buckled to his side and the Bible in his pocket put himself at their head. He had, however, no intention of sinking his profession in his military command—he believed he was equally doing God's service whether fighting or praying, and he therefore installed himself their chaplain, and fulfilled the duties of this office as faithfully as those of captain. On their way to South Carolina he prayed with them regularly, and on the Sabbath preached to them. In fact they were a part of his usual audience at home, for they were almost to a man members of one of his congregations. It reminded one of the times of Cromwell to see this man of God assemble his company of irregular cavalry, and with head uncovered solemnly commend them and their cause to God, and then ride to their head and give the order to march. To these simple minded, brave men there was nothing incongruous in this. They had received their lessons in patriotism from their pastor—been taught by him to regard resistance to the tyrannical oppressions of the mother country obedience to God, and urged by him to the present undertaking, and it seemed peculiarly fit that he should be both their leader and spiritual teacher.

He was absent in this expedition for several months, sharing the hardships and privations of his soldiers throughout, and ever retaining their confidence and love by his cool courage, Christian forbearance, and faithfulness. Subsequently, an army was sent against the Cherokees, in Georgia, and he accompanied it as chaplain. In the long and tedious march through the wilderness, which occupied two months, he found but one opportunity to preach to the troops. The sermon he delivered on this occasion, being the first ever preached in the Indian territory, the adjacent county, in honor of the event, was named after him, Hall county. His influence and abilities were so well known that after the death of Gen. Davidson, in the skirmish of Cowansford, on the Catawba, Gen. Greene, then commanding in the Carolinas, selected him to fill his place, and the commission of Brigadier-General was offered him. He declined the appointment, however, saying, that there were others who could fill that post quite as well as himself, while he preached the gospel. Leading his little flock, whom he had urged to take up arms to assist their neighbors in driving back the enemy, who were wasting them with fire and sword, he regarded a very different thing from changing his profession, and devoting himself to a military life. The former was a duty forced on him by circumstances, the latter was not, and appeared to him more a matter of choice as to what profession he should follow.

At the close of the war he found religion in his vicinity in a low condition, and with his accustomed zeal commenced to "repair the waste places of Zion." A powerful revival followed his exertions, and many were gathered into the Church. He gave himself no rest in the work so dear to his heart, and his health at length broke down under his severe labors. Unable to rally, he was after much persuasion, induced to try the effects of a sea voyage to restore it, and embarked at Charleston for Philadelphia. In 1793 he undertook a missionary tour along the western frontier under a commission of Synod, which involved great hardships. In 1800, with two others, he commenced a mission at Natchez, the first missionary effort made in the lower valley of the Mississippi. His labors in the cause of education were of incalculable benefit to the South, and many distinguished statesmen and divines were indebted to him for their literary training. He died on the 25th of July, 1826, in the eightieth year of his age.

CHAPTER XXV.

JOHN GANO.

THE BAPTISTS OF VIRGINIA.—GANO'S EARLY LIFE.—VISITS THE SOUTH AND PREACHES.—ARRAIGNED FOR IT, BUT IS ACQUITTED AND LICENSED.—ANECDOTES OF HIS COOLNESS AND COURAGE.—SETTLED IN NORTH CAROLINA.—OFFERED A CAPTAIN'S COMMISSION IN THE ARMY AGAINST THE CHEROKEES.—DECLINES.—RETURNS NORTH.—FINALLY SETTLES IN NEW YORK.—HIS CONGREGATION BROKEN UP.—JOINS THE ARMY AS CHAPLAIN.—UNDER FIRE AT WHITE PLAINS.—AT TRENTON.—CHAPLAIN UNDER CLINTON AT FORT MONTGOMERY.—HIS DESCRIPTION OF THE TAKING OF THE FORT.—WITH CLINTON'S BRIGADE AT ALBANY.—ITS CHAPLAIN IN THE EXPEDITION AGAINST THE INDIANS.—ANECDOTES OF HIM IN THIS CAMPAIGN.—SERMON ON THE FOURTH OF JULY.—HIS FAITHFULNESS.—GOES SOUTH WITH THE ARMY ADVANCING AGAINST CORNWALLIS.—RETURNS TO HIS CHURCH AT THE CLOSE OF THE WAR.—REMOVES TO KENTUCKY.—HIS DEATH.

THE Baptists, though not so imposing a denomination in numbers at the time of the revolution as now, nevertheless threw the weight of their influence, whatever it might be, on the side of the colonies. Thus, in 1775, we find them in Virginia, presenting as a body, an address to the convention, in which they say, "that however distinguished from the body of their countrymen by appellation, and sentiments of a religious nature, they, nevertheless, consider themselves as members of the same community in respect to matters of a civil nature, and embarked in the same common cause; that, alarmed at the oppression which hangs over America, they had considered what part it would be proper to take in the unhappy contest, and had determined that they ought to make a military resistance against Great Britain in her unjust invasion, tyrannical oppression, and repeated hostilities," and left their church members to enlist, and asked that four of their ministers, whom they had selected, might be allowed to preach to the troops during the campaign with the same freedom as chaplains of the established Church.

The most distinguished clergyman of this denomination who served during the revolutionary war, was Rev. John Gano, a native of Hopewell, New Jersey. Becoming religious in his early youth, he felt it at times to be his duty to study for the ministry, but so many obstacles stood in the way that he endeavored to drive the subject from his mind. But being unable to do so, he finally yielded to what he felt to be the Divine promptings, and entered on his studies. These, however, were somewhat desultory, and at the end of two or three years he took a journey to Virginia with two distinguished clergymen, who had been appointed by the Philadelphia Association to settle some difficulties existing in some feeble churches there. Traveling through a sparsely settled country, and where the gospel was seldom heard, he found himself so pressed to preach that he finally consented. For this irregular conduct he was called to account when he returned to Hopewell by the Baptist church there, of which he was a member. He however, expressed no regrets for his course, declaring "that he had no disposition to repent having sounded the gospel to perishing sinners in Virginia, whose importunities to hear it he could not resist." It ended in the Church setting him apart to preach.

Mr. Gano was a little under the medium height, with a slender, but firmly knit frame. His countenance was open and frank, and its clear outlook indicated the self-collected, fearless spirit that characterized him.

In this southern journey through a comparative wilderness he often found himself in circumstances that called for all his presence of mind and nerve. One evening he and Mr. Miller, his companion, put up at a tavern where a noisy, profane company had assembled. At his request the landlord put them in a room remote as possible from the drinking, swearing frontiersmen, and then stepped into the apartment of the latter and asked them not to disturb the travelers who had just arrived. They were just drunk enough to have this reasonable request appear to them a gross insult, and starting up in indignation they rushed in a body to the room, where young Gano and Mr. Miller were sitting, and with loud oaths demanded who they were. Gano, only twenty-seven years old, calmly replied, "We are civil travelers, who wish neither to disturb you nor be disturbed by you." The man who acted as leader immediately advanced towards him in a threatening manner, and shaking his fist in his face, exclaimed, with an oath, pointing to one of his burly comrades, "There is a man who can whip you or anybody else in the room." Young Gano turned his quiet glance on the bully thus pointed out and replied, "Very probably, sir, for he *looks* much more like a man than *you act*, and I daresay that he and the rest of his companions are ashamed of you and your conduct." The ruffian was completely cowed by the cool manner and calm superiority of the young stranger, and before he could recover his self-possession Gano turned to the landlord, who had just entered, and in that quiet tone of command which men obey without knowing why, said, "*Put that fellow out of the room!*" He did so without the others offering the least interference. Gano then turned to them and remarked in his quiet, grave manner, that their companion who had just been turned out of the room was a striking instance of the depravity of human nature. He then went on to say that God never designed us to make others unhappy, but to benefit and help each other,—making them a short but serious speech. They heard him out in silence, then shook hands with him in a friendly manner, and wished him a good journey.

On another occasion, when just as he was about entering alone and in the night time a long piece of woods, he was overtaken by a rough-looking man, who insisted on accompanying him, although he told him he did not wish his society, seeing from the fellow's bearing and manner that his intentions were evil. Finding that he could not shake him off he rode quietly on. When he entered the woods and it became so dark that he could not see his brigand companion, he urged his horse up beside him, and placing his hand on his leg so as to detect the least hostile motion, held it there till he came to a clearing. Riding up to the log hut in it he roused the inmate, who demanded as he came to the door what he wanted. Pointing to the stranger who had forced himself on his company, he exclaimed, "*Seize that man!*" The latter alarmed, immediately gave his horse the whip and disappeared in the darkness. The cool determination and self-possession of Gano evinced by his deliberately riding to the robber's side in the darkness and laying his hand upon his thigh so astounded and overawed him that he dared not make his intended attack. It was *moral* power that subdued him—a superior soul, superior in courage, resolution and in conscious resources, before which his brutal spirit quailed.

These incidents are mentioned to show the metal of the man, who, like Paul, was fitted by nature to be a great military commander, but became by grace a great leader in the Church.

Soon after his ordination he was sent back to Virginia as a missionary, and labored for several years amid the frontier settlements South. Many anecdotes are told of him while successfully prosecuting his labors here, illustrating both his natural sagacity, and elevated piety.

In 1758 he was settled over a church in North Carolina, which he afterwards left on account of the war which had broken out with the Cherokees. The Governor sent him a captain's commission in the army, but he declined to act under it, and returned to New Jersey. He afterwards went to Philadelphia, but staid only a part of the year, then settled down in New York city, where he built up a flourishing church and congregation, with whom he remained till the arrival of the British troops, which dispersed them over the country. Having removed his family to Connecticut, he returned to the city, determined to stay there till the enemy entered it. Col. Webb's regiment being at Stamford at that time, he was invited by him to become its chaplain. He declined, but accepted an invitation to come out to them and preach once every Sabbath.

The simultaneous passage of the enemy's ships up the North and East rivers after the battle of Long Island, and the retreat of Washington, gave him no time to remove his household furniture, and leaving everything behind, he mounted his horse and set out for the American camp. He was with the army in the skirmishes at Harlem—retreated with it to Kings bridge, and thence to White Plains. In the fierce conflict on Chatterton's hill he was continually under fire, and his cool and quiet courage in thus fearlessly exposing himself was afterwards commented on in the most glowing terms by the officers who stood near him. He himself in speaking of it said, "My station in time of action I *knew to be among the surgeons ; but in this battle I somehow got in front of the regiment, yet I durst not quit my place for fear of dampening the spirits of the soldiers*, or of bringing on me an imputation of cowardice. Rather than do either, I chose to risk my fate." One can not repress a smile at this naive account of himself in the front of battle. When a soldier, whose appropriate place is there, finds himself in the rear, we sometimes hear some such lame excuse as "that somehow he got there," but for one to use it for being under the enemy's fire when his appointed place is elsewhere, is both novel and amusing. If the brave, heroic chaplain had analyzed his feelings a little closer, he would have found that the reasons given for *staying* under fire were really the ones that *brought* him under it—the impulses of his noble, patriotic nature. He saw around him on every side cowardice and fear; and carried away by his own heroic impulses, he involuntarily sought the dangers that he could not bear to see his countrymen so afraid to meet. To one acquainted with the perfectly fearless and chivalrous character of the man, and at the same time familiar with the details of this battle, it is the easiest thing in the world to understand how he came into the exposed position in which he so unaccountably found himself.

McDougall, with fifteen hundred men, assisted by Alexander Hamilton, attempted to defend the hill, while the main army lay farther back behind the little stream called Bronx river. On the 29th of October Howe moved across the country with his heavy columns, and instead of assaulting Washington at once, stopped to carry Chatterton's Hill. As soon as he got his twelve or fifteen pieces of artillery within range he opened on the American lines. The heavy thunder rolling over the heights carried consternation into the ranks of the militia, and as a round shot struck one of their number, mangling him frightfully, the whole turned and fled. Colonel Hazlet tried in vain to induce them to drag forward the field pieces so as to sweep the ascending columns, but he was able to man only one, and that so poorly that he was compelled to seize the drag ropes himself. But he was denied the gratification of using even this one gun, for as it was being slowly trundled to the front a ball from the enemy's batteries struck the carriage, scattering the shot in every direction, and setting fire to a wad of tow. In an instant the piece was abandoned in terror. Only one man had the courage to remain and tread out the fire and collect the shot. Hamilton, however, with two guns in battery, coolly swept the slope carrying away whole platoons at every discharge. But after a little time McDougall found only six hundred of the fifteen hundred with which he commenced the fight, left to sustain the shock of the whole British army. This he did gallantly for a whole hour, then retreated slowly and in good order, taking all his artillery and baggage with him, and crossing the Bronx joined the main army. It was on such a sight as this the fearless chaplain gazed with a bursting heart. As he saw more than half the army fleeing from the sound of cannon—others abandoning their pieces without firing a shot, and a brave band of only six hundred manfully sustaining the whole conflict, he forgot himself, and distressed at the cowardice of his countrymen, and filled with chivalrous and patriotic sympathy for the little band that scorned to fly, he could not resist the strong desire to share their perils, and eagerly yet involuntarily pushed forward to the front. This is the true explanation of the "*somehow*" he got out of his place in the rear, and "found himself in front of the regiment," just as it is the reason that he would not retire though cannon balls were crashing around him. A truly brave man can never refrain from stepping to the side of brave men when, overpowered by numbers, they still make a gallant and desperate stand for the right.

He accompanied the army in its retreat to North Castle, where it encamped near a meeting-house, which was turned into a hospital for the sick and wounded. Supposing the army would remain here for some time he obtained a furlough for a few days to visit his family. When he returned, instead of encountering pickets and sentries and a bustling encampment, he found the place deserted and silent. Every thing had changed like a dream of the night, and he rode slowly forward towards the meeting-house, but around it there was not the sign of a living thing. Dismounting at the door he opened it and passed up the empty aisle. The groups of sufferers he had prayed with there were all gone. Pausing for a moment to contemplate the changed scene he heard a slight noise, and going in the direction from whence it proceeded found one poor wounded soldier all alone in a pew with a bottle of water by his side.

Ascertaining that the regiment to which he belonged was with General Lee, he hastened forward to join it. The orders had already been received by this officer to effect a speedy junction with the main army concentrated on the banks of the Delaware. Delaying to obey them as long as he dared, he at length set out, but was captured in Baskingbridge. Gano then accompanied the division which marched rapidly forward to join Washington. He crossed the wintry Delaware with the army when it made its fearful midnight march on

Trenton, and shared in the dangers of the battle that followed.

Soon after this engagement the time of the troops to which Gano belonged expired, but Washington urged them to remain six weeks longer, until reënforcements which he expected should arrive, offering them ten dollars bounty, though he did not know where the money was to come from. They responded to his urgent appeal, and Robert Morris, that noble patriot, on receiving a letter from Washington stating what he had done, immediately borrowed fifty thousand dollars on his own credit and forwarded it to him, telling him to call on him again when he wanted more.

At the expiration of the six weeks the troops were discharged. The officers, however, determined to raise another regiment, and having seen the value of Gano's services came to him, and asked him if he would join them as chaplain if they succeeded in their efforts. He said he would, but on his arrival at home he found a letter awaiting him from Colonel Dubosque, stationed at Fort Montgomery, just below West Point, asking him to accept the post of chaplain to his regiment. Instead of writing his refusal he determined to ride across the country and see the colonel, and deliver it in person. On his arrival, however, General James Clinton, the commander-in-chief, who had heard of him, joined his solicitations to those of Colonel Dubosque, and urged him so warmly to remain that he finally consented, and entered at once on the discharge of his duties.

The two forts, Montgomery and Clinton, situated

near West Point, were considered the key of the Hudson, yet in 1777, when Burgoyne was pushing his victorious columns on towards Albany, and it was well known that Henry Clinton at New York would make a desperate effort to effect a junction with him, they were garrisoned with only six or seven hundred men. Clinton, aware of their feebleness, determined to capture them, and embarking between three and four thousand men advanced up the Hudson, and landed at Verplanck's Point to convey the impression that his object was to attack Putnam, stationed at Peekskill. But soon as it was dark he reimbarked the troops, and concealed by a dense fog crossed the river and landing at Stony Point, at daybreak entered the defiles that led to the forts. Now hanging along the sides of the mountain and now plunging into deep ravines he toiled on all day, and, driving before him the various detachments sent out to arrest his progress, arrived two hours before sunset in front of the works.

The mountain sides, and the thick forest at their base, had all the afternoon rung with the sound of drum and bugle, and volleys of musketry marking both the lines of progress, and the rapidity of the advance of the hostile columns, and now, as they drew near, Gano, with his accustomed indifference to danger, walked the breastworks, viewing their approach till the whole open space around the Fort was red with the scarlet uniforms. The British immediately commenced a general fire, and he, finding the musket balls flying rather too thickly around him, descended into the Fort. In speaking of it afterwards he said, "I observed the enemy marching up a little hollow that they might be secured from our firing till they came within eighty yards of us. Our breast-work immediately before them was not more than waist-band high, and we had but few men. The enemy kept up a heavy firing till our men gave them a well-directed fire, which affected them very sensibly. Just at this time we had a reinforcement from a redoubt next to us, which obliged the enemy to withdraw. I walked to an eminence where I had a good prospect, and saw the enemy advancing toward our gate." It "somehow" always happened that Gano forgot in time of action "his place among the surgeons," and was where he could see how the battle was going. This "advance toward the gate" was observed by Capt. Moody in Fort Clinton, who, "seeing our desperate situation, gave the enemy a charge of grape shot, which threw them into great confusion. Moody repeated his charge, which entirely dispersed them for that time." At sunset a couple of flags were sent demanding the immediate surrender of the Fort, and threatening in case of refusal to put the garrison to the sword. The two brothers, Clintons, commanding in the two Forts, sent the same answer to the summons, viz., that they chose the latter alternative. On the return of the flags the firing recommenced, and for two hours it flamed and thundered there in the darkness, and then came the final assault. The drums beat a hurried charge, and the overwhelming mass of the enemy poured in one wild torrent over the feeble defences, and by mere weight of numbers crushed down the little handful that had stood so bravely at bay. Gano was in the midst of the melee, and with the rest, when driven back, leaped over the breast-work in the darkness and plunged down the cliffs to the river. "Many," he says, "escaped to the water's side and got on board a scow and pushed off. Before she had got twice her length we grappled one of our row galleys into which we all got, and crossed the river." The fugitives then made their toilsome way to New Windsor, where they arrived several days after. Here they were joined by others who had escaped. On looking over their returns they found, he says, that "we had lost, killed, and taken prisoners about three hundred men. The enemy, as we afterwards understood, had one thousand or eleven hundred killed, among whom were eighteen captains, and one or two field officers, besides a great number wounded.'

Obtaining a furlough for a short absence, he now returned to his family at New Fairfield, but tarried only till the birth of a daughter relieved his solicitude respecting his wife, when he again started for the army.

At the opening of the next campaign, Gen. Clinton's brigade, consisting of four regiments, had not a chaplain in it, and he earnestly urged Gano to accept the post. He consented, and soon after received his commission from Congress. During this summer the brigade was not engaged in active service, and Mr. Gano's duties assumed the quiet character of those of a pastor among his people. At the close of the campaign it was ordered to take winter quarters at Albany. A large portion of the troops encamped at Canajoharie, and they sent a request to Clinton that he would let the chaplain come and spend some time with them, and preach to them. He consented and Mr. Gano went over to the camp. On his arrival they asked him to preach a little more about politics than he commonly did. He took for his text the words of Moses to his father-in-law. "*Come go thou with us, and we will do thee good ; for he that seeketh my life seeketh thy life, but with us thou shalt be in safeguard.*" He was always peculiarly happy in the choice of his texts, selecting them in reference to the immediate occasion, while his original mode of treating them, and plain familiar way of talking, as it were, to the soldiers, never failed to give him an attentive audience. His known coolness in danger, and even complete *sang froid* when under fire of the enemy, made him a great favorite with the troops, and indeed an object of admiration as a man to the officers.

At this time the expedition against the Indians of western New York was organized, and General Sullivan placed at the head of it. He immediately issued orders for the main army to assemble at Wyoming, the seat of the massacre, from which point he determined to ascend the Susquehanna to the Indian settlements. Clinton, in the meantime, received orders to advance up the Mohawk, and crossing over to Otsego Lake, the head of the Susquehanna, form a junction with Sullivan at any point he should designate. A hundred and eight flat-bottomed boats were provided to convey his troops and provisions, and floated up the Mohawk to Canajoharie. Here they were lifted from the water and transported through the woods and swamps sixteen miles to Otsego. While a part of the army was cutting and making a road for the boats and carrying them across the country, another portion was sent to Otsego to dam the outlet and raise the water in the lake, for it was now midsummer, and Clinton had learned that the Susquehanna was so low that it would be impossible to float the loaded boats down it. The army lay here for six weeks waiting for orders to march, during which time Mr. Gano's labors as chaplain were uninterrupted. In all his intercourse with the troops he kept in view the duties of his station, and never suffered an opportunity to pass in which he could rebuke sin or put in a word of admonition. One morning, as he was going to the regimental prayers, he passed by a group of officers, one of whom not seeing him approach was swearing in an excited manner. The other officers saluted the chaplain as usual, when the profane lieutenant turning quickly round saw him, and checking himself, said, "Good morning, doctor." "Good morning," replied Gano, "I see you pray early." The abashed officer colored and stammered out, "I beg your pardon, sir." "Oh," replied the chaplain, passing on, "*I* cannot pardon you, you must carry your case to God." On another occasion he was standing near some soldiers who was disputing respecting whose duty it was to cut wood for one of the camp fires. At length one exclaimed in an angry manner, "I'll be d——d if *I* will do it." Soon after finding he must, he took up the axe to perform it. Gano immediately stepped forward, and reaching out his hand, said, "Give me the axe." "Oh no," replied the soldier, "the chaplain shan't cut the wood." "Yes, but I *must*." "Why?" said the soldier in surprise. "Because I just heard you say you would be d——d if you would cut it, and I had rather do it for you than that you should be made miserable forever." The longest homily on the guilt of profanity would not have produced half the effect on the soldiers that this indirect rebuke did.

The army lay here on the 4th of July, and General Clinton prepared to celebrate the day with appropriate ceremonies. Having in my possession the original order book of Clinton, kept during this expedition, I insert the order he issued on this occasion as a curiosity. "This day being the anniversary of the independence of America, the General is pleased to order that all the troops under his command should draw a gill of rum per man, extraordinary, in memory of that happy event.

"At one o'clock this afternoon a Fatigue party, composed of four Captains, four Subordinates, eight Sergeants, two hundred rank and file will assemble in the usual place of parade in front of the camp with hatchets or axes, to clear the ground of the brushes and other inconveniencies which are thereon, for the purpose of parading the Army for the (fue De Joye). Lieut. Col. Willett will take command of of the above party.

"The commanding officers of regiments will see that on inspection of the Ammunition in their respective regiments be made through the different companies, and if there is any spoiled cartridges, three of them will be allowed for every soldier for the fue De Joye, in lieu of which those who shall not be provided the different Quarter Masters will make a return to the conductor of Military stores to be supplied with spoiled or blank cartridges, three per man.

"The troops now in camp will parade for that purpose in front of the encampment at half past three this afternoon in one line from right to left, each battalion will take place as they are now encamped," (then follows the names of the officers). "After (fue De Joye) is finished, a sermon will be preached by the brigade chaplain on this happy event.

"And it is the General's pleasure that the troops under his command will assemble at 7 o'clock every evening while we remain in this place, upon the grand parade, for prayers. The General expects that the troops will be clean as possible, and begs that every officer will exert himself on that subject."

The parade being finished, Mr. Gano mounted a platform, and casting his eye over the glittering ranks, whose bright uniforms were thrown into strong relief by the green woods that surrounded them, exclaimed, *"This day shall be a memorial unto you throughout your generations."* Officers and men listened with the deepest attention as he spoke of the time when the day on which the declaration of independence was given to the world would be celebrated like the Jew's passover, with thanksgivings and public rejoicings, and kept as a perpetual memorial of God's deliverance of His people. In speaking of it he said, "On this occasion the soldiers behaved with the most decency that I ever knew them to during the war. Some of them usually absented themselves from worship on Lord's day, and the only punishment they were subjected to was the digging up of stumps, which in some instances had a good effect."

The long delay at this point was very vexatious, and a nightmare seemed to rest on the expedition. Gano, who saw that both officers and privates were getting very impatient, at length spoke to Clinton on the subject. "The General," he says, "informed him that he had received orders to march, and that he should move the next Monday. He requested me not to mention it till after service the next day, which was Sunday. I preached to them from these words, "*Being ready to depart on the morrow.*" The soldiers, who were accustomed to look for a deep meaning in his very texts, listened with more than common interest to the sermon that followed. As soon as the services closed, Clinton assembled the officers, and ordered that each captain should detail a certain number of men from his company to draw the boats from the lake, and string them along the Susquehannah below the dam and load them so that they might be ready to depart in the morning. The following day at sunrise the camp broke up, and though the dam had been opened several hours previous, yet the swell it had occasioned in the river served to carry the boats over the shoals and flats, which otherwise would have been impassable. There had been a long drought, and it was, therefore, a matter of profound wonder to the Indians down the river, for above a hundred miles, what could have occasioned such an astonishing freshet. The soldiers marched along both banks, excepting the invalids, who went in the boats with the baggage and provisions." Thus, the host streamed on through the forest, lining the picturesque shores of the Susquehanna with their gay uniforms, while the long fleet of boats wound like a huge serpent between. Day after day they toiled on, and at length came in sight of Sullivan's tents at Cayuga, when loud shouts from both armies made the wilderness ring. The whole army then took up its line of march for the Genesee flats.

The battle of Newtown followed, in which the Indians, though under the leadership of Butler and Brant, were completely routed. After the battle was over, and the different divisions of the army were collected, "we saw ourselves," says Gano, "surrounded by a large field of Indian corn, pumpkins, squashes, beans, &c., which was no unpleasant sight to soldiers who were hungry as we were. Here General Sullivan displayed his generalship by putting the army on half allowance, that we might more effectually secure the victory by pursuing the Indians. Our success and the exhortation of our officers induced the soldiery to a cheerful compliance, and they consequently sent up a loud huzza. An Irishman observing this, said he had been a long time in the British army, and some time in the service of America, but he never heard soldiers cry huzza for half allowance before; however, as they all had, *he would,*" and shouted lustily.

Scattering the Indians from its path, and burning their towns as it advanced, the army at last reached the point of its destination, the beautiful Genesee

Flats. Here it encamped over night, and in the morning, while Gano stood looking over the amazing fields of waving corn that spread away on every side, he heard the heavy boom of cannon sullenly swelling over the western wilderness. It was the morning gun of the English at Niagara, whither the Indians were supposed to be fled. Laying waste those vast fields ripe for the sickle—the Indians' only hope for the coming winter—the army took up its retrograde march for Easton. "But here," says Gano, "I must not forget to mention a circumstance peculiarly pleasing to me. Two or three young soldiers were under great distress of mind concerning their souls, and frequently came to see and converse with me."

As he witnessed the destruction of the grain, and imagined the despair of the Indians when they should return and see their fields laid waste, and think of the sufferings that awaited them in the coming winter— the righteous punishment for obeying the orders of a tyrannical king—a text often occurred to him which he one day mentioned to General Sullivan. "*They shall walk through them; be an hungry and curse their God and king, and look upwards.*" The general said, "We will have a sermon from that text, and when we arrive at Easton you shall preach it."

After the return of the army Gano obtained a furlough in order to visit his family. The next winter the division to which he was attached encamped near Newbury, and as his family were at Warwick, not far distant, he was at home a considerable part of the time.

When Washington collected the army in New Jersey, and began to erect large ovens, every one supposed he designed to attack the British in New York. But the combined armies, French and American, suddenly broke up their camps and made that forced march into Virginia, by which Cornwallis was shut up at Gloucester Point and compelled to capitulate. Gano, with others, was so taken by surprise at this sudden movement that he was wholly unprepared to march, having, he said, "but one change of linen." Stating his destitute condition to General Clinton, he asked leave of absence to get more. But the general refused his request, and said he must go on at all events with the division. Luckily, when they arrived in Newark, he found an old lady who had been a member of his church in New York. "I told her," he says, "my situation, and she furnished me what was needful for the campaign." The army was hurried on at the top of its speed, but when Clinton's division reached Baltimore, his aid was taken sick, and he asked Gano to remain behind with him till he was able to proceed. He did so, and in speaking of the event says, "The major's anxiety to follow the army retarded his recovery. However, he attempted it, and set out, but after one or two days he was obliged to lay by. In a day or two we set off again, but did not reach the army before the British capitulated. However, we partook of the joy with our brethren." That "joy of the brethren" was a true "joy." Without were shouts, acclamations and the boisterous exultation of the enthusiastic soldiers, but within, among the noble chaplains of that army were devout thanksgivings, humble, grateful prayers, and tears of joy too deep for utterance.

Mr. Gano returned to Newbury, where the army erected huts to live in during the winter, and one larger than the rest for a place of public worship on the Sabbath. Here three services a day were held, the chaplains from each brigade preaching in rotation.

Thus passed the winter, while rumors of peace filled the land with hope and delight. In the spring the British evacuated New York, and Gano returned to the city, to find his house dilapidated and plundered. His scattered congregation, such as were living, soon returned, and he settled down once more to his pastoral labors. He continued here for some time, but attracted by representations made to him of the growing state of Kentucky, and hoping to relieve himself from debt which he saw no way of canceling in his present position, he removed thither in 1781, much to the disappointment and regret of his church. He settled near Frankfort, where he died in 1804, in the seventy-fifth year of his age. A fall from his horse in 1798, followed by a paralytic shock, rendered him a cripple the last six years of his life, but he never ceased his labors—sometimes preaching while lying on his back. Calm and resigned, he saw death approach without a terror, and to a friend who asked him if he wanted to go home and be with Christ, he faintly, sweetly answered, "Yes." This was the last utterance of his lips on earth, and the Christan and patriot passed to that better land reserved for the people of God.

True to his country, true to his high office, true to his God, he went through the trying scenes of the Revolution, and through life honored, respected and loved by all who knew him, and now sleeps with those whose names are inscribed in the hearts of their countrymen.

CHAPTER XXVI.

CHARLES CUMMINGS.

An Irishman by Birth.—Settles in Virginia.—Enters the Ministry.—Fights the Indians.—Goes armed to his Church.—Takes the Lead in the political Movements of the People.—Chaplain to the Army in the Expedition against the Cherokees.—His Death.

Charles Cummings was an Irishman by birth, but coming in early manhood to this country received his theological education here. He located in Virginia, where he studied divinity, and being licensed to preach in 1767, settled at North Mountain, Augusta county. In 1772 he received a call from the people of Holston, embracing the congregations of Sinking Spring and Ebbing Spring. At this time the Indians were very troublesome in the neighbourhood, and during the summer months the people were obliged to collect in the forts for safety. In 1776 Mr. Cummings' family being in one of the forts, he, with a servant and wagon and three neighbors, went one day to a farm not far distant on an errand, when they were attacked by a party of Indians. The first intimation they had of the presence of the savages was a volley from the woods bordering the road, which tumbled the driver from his seat. Mr. Cummings and his companions immediately returned the fire, and a sharp skirmish followed. In a few minutes, however, two of the neighbors fell mortally wounded. The Indians being under cover, Mr. Cummings saw that to remain longer where they were would be certain death, and turning to his servant told him to follow him, and leading the way, charged boldly into the bushes. The savages, surprised at the sudden onset, broke cover with a fierce yell. They did not flee, however, but turned furiously on their assailants. At this critical moment, when his fate seemed hopeless, Mr. Cummings heard a shout in the road near him. Those in the fort had heard the firing, and knowing at once that the little party was attacked, hastily sent out a detachment to its relief. Coming up on a run it had arrived just as the Indians turned on Mr. Cummings and his servant. It soon finished the unequal fight.

The war with the mother country, which had already commenced, set the entire frontier in a blaze, and the congregation of Mr. Cummings found themselves so surrounded with dangers that when they assembled for worship on the Sabbath they locked up their houses and took their families with them to church. All along the beautiful valley, groups would be seen—(the men armed)—slowly and cautiously gathering to the house of prayer. Last of all came the pastor, mounted on his dun horse, his rifle on his shoulder, and his ammunition belt buckled to his side. Arriving at the meeting-house, he would fasten his horse to a tree and take a short walk by himself wrapped in meditation. When the congregation was all assembled—each man seated with his rifle by his side—he would enter the church, and walking solemnly through the double line of steel mount the steps of the pulpit, and standing his rifle in the corner, lay aside his powder flask, and commence the services of the day.

He took a leading part in all patriotic movements of his congregation, and when the freeholders of Fincastle county met to consult on the measures they should adopt in the perilous condition of affairs, he was the first man named on the committee appointed to draw up an address to the Continental Congress. He was also chairman of the committee of safety, of Washington county. Known throughout the entire region for his daring courage, as well as for his sterling piety, when the first army was organized to penetrate Tennessee and attack the Cherokees, he was chosen its chaplain, and shared all the perils and hardships of that march through the wilderness.

He died in 1812, in the eightieth year of his age.

CHAPTER XXVII.

DANIEL McCALLA.

His Birth.—Graduates at Princeton when eighteen years of age.—Studies for the Ministry.—Settles in Pennsylvania.—Appointed Chaplain under General Thompson.—Is taken Prisoner in the Attack on "Three Rivers."—Thrown into a Prison Ship.—His Sufferings and Fortitude.—Released on Parole.—Flees to Virginia.—Settles in South Carolina.—His Death.

DANIEL McCALLA was born at Neshaminy, Pa., in 1748. Fond of study, and gifted with a fine intellect, he was able to enter Princeton College when only fourteen years of age, and graduated in his nineteenth year. He did not immediately commence the study of his profession, but took charge of an academy in Philadelphia, where he remained for some time. He kept the ministry, however, constantly in view, and in 1772 was licensed to preach, and soon after settled over the united congregations of New Providence and Charleston, in Pennsylvania. But before the year of his ordination closed, blood had flowed at Lexington and Concord, and he saw that the long dreaded conflict had come. He had watched the approaching storm with the deepest interest, and in and out of the pulpit proclaimed the duty of resistance, and aroused the martial spirit of his hearers; and now when the war had actually commenced, he could not remain at home an idle spectator. Offering his services to Congress, he was appointed by that body chaplain to the troops under General Thompson, which had been ordered to Canada.

In the unfortunate attack on the British at Three Rivers he was made prisoner. Gen. Thompson, at the head of fourteen hundred men, had been ordered by Sullivan to join St. Clair, and proceed to this place, and if on a close inspection he should consider it advisable, to attack it. The force, under his command, about two thousand strong, dropped down the river in the night and drifting noiselessly by the British vessels that lay at anchor in the stream, rapidly approached the post. Thompson hoped to reach it before daylight and carry it by surprise, but, contrary to his expectations, he did not arrive till nearly sunrise. He had scarcely commenced landing when the rolling of the drum, beating to quarters, told him that he was discovered. Seeing that an open battle was now inevitable, he hastily marshalled his troops on the shore and prepared to advance. But to move direct on the place, he discovered, would expose his column to a raking fire from some vessels that lay in the stream, and he, therefore, made a circuit to avoid them. In doing so became entangled in a deep morass. While he was floundering through this, the British not only got time to prepare for his reception in front, but also to send a party to the rear and cut off his return to the boats. McCalla waded through the swamp side by side with his General, and when the latter took the desperate resolution to advance to the attack, moved with him into the fire. A sharp conflict followed, but it was plain to the most unpractised eye how it must terminate, and that the enterprise was a failure. They could not advance, while the retreat to the boats being cut off, it was equally impossible to fall back. Finding themselves thus blocked in before and behind, and exposed to a destructive fire, which was rapidly thinning their ranks, the main body plunged into a swamp near by, where the British did not deem it prudent to follow them. Thompson, however, with his chaplain and some two hundred others, were taken prisoners. With their usual hatred of "rebel parsons," (as they called them,) the British threw this accomplished scholar and divine into a loathsome prison ship, and subjected him to a treatment that would have disgraced savages. Crowded into the hold with the sick and dying, breathing the foulest air—made the companion of vermin, and compelled to perform the most menial offices, and asssailed with jibes and insults, he lay for months on board this filthy floating lazar-house. Food fit only for swine was given him, and even this, his brutal captors begrudged him so that he came near dying from starvation. His fate was that of a martyr, and he bore it like one —unsubdued, firm, and noble through all. At length, apparently tired of the attempt to wear out the life of this brave young chaplain, not yet thirty years of age, they, in the latter part of the year, released him on parole. Pale, wan, dirty, and in tatters, but with a spirit unsubdued, he was led forth once more into the free air. His form was bowed, though not with years, but the fire in his eye was undimmed. Leaving the spot where he had so long suffered a living death, he returned to his congregation. He had resumed his charge, however, but a short time when he was accused of having broken his parole, because he publicly prayed for his beloved country, and for the success of its armies. Finding that for this heinous crime he was in danger of again being seized as a prisoner, he left his congregation and fled into Virginia. Chafing under the restrictions his parole placed on his words and actions, he sought, and eventually obtained a release from it by an exchange of prisoners. He continued a warm supporter of the American cause till the close of the war. He afterwards went to South Carolina, and was settled in Christ Church parish, near Charleston, where he remained a "diligent student and faithful pastor to the close of his life." He suffered from a protracted disease, which it is supposed was aggravated by the death of his only child, the wife of Dr. Witherspoon, at the early age of twenty-six.

He lived to see the country, for which he had labored and suffered, on the high road to prosperity, and in the sixty-second year of his age, in perfect peace, and in full confidence of a better life to come, passed to his reward.

CHAPTER XXVIII.

JOHN WITHERSPOON, D. D.

THE CLERGY AS STATESMEN.—WITHERSPOON A SCOTCHMAN BY BIRTH.—HIS EARLY LIFE.—IS LICENSED TO PREACH.—JOINS THE ARMY OF THE PRETENDER.—TAKEN PRISONER AT THE BATTLE OF FALKIRK.—HIS EMINENCE AS A THEOLOGIAN.—IS ELECTED PRESIDENT OF PRINCETON COLLEGE.—FLATTERING RECEPTION IN THIS COUNTRY.—TAKES SIDES WITH THE COLONIES.—ELECTED MEMBER OF THE NEW JERSEY LEGISLATURE.—SCATHING ATTACK OF GOVERNOR FRANKLIN.—ELECTED MEMBER OF CONGRESS.—HIS SPEECH ON THE DECLARATION OF INDEPENDENCE.—HIS GREAT SERVICES IN CONGRESS.—HIS DEATH.

THE clergy of the country were found not only in the pulpit and field upholding the cause of the American Colonies, and in the ranks fighting for it, but also in the counsels of the nation lending both the sanction of their office and the ripened fruit of long years of study to promote its success. Foremost among these was Dr. Witherspoon, a Scotchman by birth, but in every other respect an American patriot. He was born in Yester, near Edinburgh, in 1722. Licensed to preach when scarcely of age, he, in 1744, was presented with the parish of Beith by the Earl of Eglinton. A short time after he was ordained, the Pretender landed in the north of Scotland, and the Highlanders rallying with enthusiasm to his standard he moved southward. Carried away by the general enthusiasm, young Witherspoon raised a corps of militia, and putting himself at its head marched to Glasgow. He was taken prisoner at the battle of Falkirk and confined in the castle of Donne, where he remained till after the terrible overthrow of the Pretender at the battle of Culloden. He was then released, and returned to his ministerial labors. He soon rose to eminence in his native country, and his fame having reached this side of the water he was elected president of Princeton College. Embarking in May, 1768, he, after a long voyage, reached Philadelphia, where he was received with great honor. His arrival at Princeton was celebrated by an illumination of the college and town, and the whole province shared in the general joy felt at the accession of such a man to its seat of learning. Inaugurated president in August, he devoted himself with his accustomed energy to the duties of his position, and soon gave a new impetus to the cause of learning in the country, and elevated to a higher rank at home and abroad the character of the college. He threw himself with his accustomed ardor into the contest between the Colonies and the mother country, and at once took the position of leader of the patriots in New Jersey, which he ever after maintained.

When Congress appointed a day of fasting and prayer in May, 1776, Dr. Witherspoon preached a discourse, entitled "The Dominion of Providence over the Passions of Men," in which he went thoroughly into the great political questions of the day. The sermon being published, it was received with warm encomiums in America, but denounced in Scotland, where it was republished, with notes, and the author stigmatized as a rebel and traitor. A few days after its delivery the provincial Congress of New Jersey met, and

Witherspoon, who had been elected a member, took his seat in it. Among its first acts was the passage of an order requiring the governor to present himself before it to answer for his conduct in opposing the action of the colonists. He came and being escorted into the hall by a military guard, assumed a haughty, overbearing demeanor, and refusing to answer any questions that were put to him, told the representatives of the people that they were an illegal assembly, ignorant, low bred men, wholly unfit and unable to devise any measures for the public good, and deserved to be hung as rebels. Witherspoon fixed his keen eye upon him, and listened in suppressed scorn and indignation to his vulgar, insolent tirade, and the moment he closed sprang to his feet, and unbottling the stores of irony and sarcasm that had been rapidly filling, poured on the astonished representative of the king a rebuke so withering that the boldest held his breath in astonishment. He coolly reminded the governor of his illegitimate origin and the early neglect of his education and well known ignorance of all scientific and liberal knowledge, to show with how little propriety *he* could denounce them as ignorant, incapable men, and concluded by saying, in his tone of bitterest sarcasm: "*On the whole, Mr. President, I think that Governor Franklin has made us a speech every way worthy of his exalted birth and refined education.*" When the vote was finally taken on deposing the governor, his decided aye, left no doubt of the course he meant to pursue. The day after this high handed act he was elected, with five others, to represent New Jersey in the Continental Congress. He joined it a few days before the Declaration of Independence, and among the lofty intellects assembled in Independence Hall, in Philadelphia, he was among the first. No doubt or vacillation marked his course. Intrepid, resolute and far-seeing, he gave the whole weight of his influence to the side of complete independence.

When the "Declaration" was reported and laid before Congress for their adoption and signature, every one felt that a fearful crisis had come. Some true patriots wavered. The step which should forever separate them entirely from the mother country, and plunge the land in a war the end of which no man could foresee, was a momentous one to take, but the hour of decision had arrived, and not only the fate of a great nation, but of man—the world over—hung suspended on it. That august body felt the tremendous responsibility that rested upon it, and a deep and solemn silence reigned throughout the hall. In the midst of it Witherspoon arose and said, "Mr. President—That noble instrument on your table, which insures immortality to its author, should be subscribed this very morning by every pen in the House. He who will not respond to its accents, and strain every nerve to carry into effect its provisions, is unworthy the name of freeman. *Although these gray hairs must descend into the sepulchre, I would infinitely rather they should descend thither by the hand of the executioner than desert at this crisis the sacred cause of my country.*" The venerable man sat down, but those great words continued to vibrate in each heart, strengthening the firm, and giving courage to the wavering. And when a timid member remarked that the country was not ripe for such a declaration of independence, Witherspoon replied, in a voice that rung through the hall, "*In my judgment, sir, we are not only ripe, but rotten.*" With an untremulous hand, and a heart firm and steady, he put his name to that immortal instrument. He continued a member of Congress for six years, and became identified with some of the most important measures adopted by that body. He was a member of the Secret Committee, and of the Board of War, and one of the most active men in the various committees to which he was appointed. He made a report to Congress of the cruel treatment of prisoners by the British in New York, and helped prepare a protest on the subject. He was sent also to the head-quarters of the army to improve the condition of the troops, and was constantly employed in devising measures for the welfare of the colonies. Although a member of Congress, he never laid aside his ministerial character, but preached on the Sabbath, and always wore his clerical robes in Congress during its sittings. He wrote most of the Congressional addresses to the country recommending Fasts, etc. His "Thoughts on American Liberty," and his speeches in Congress against the prodigal issue of paper money, and other State papers, are well known, and can only be referred to here. In the darkest hour his courage never faltered; for, to a high, heroic spirit, he added an unwavering trust in God, and a belief that He would eventually enable us to triumph. Far-seeing and sagacious, he seemed to anticipate evils that escaped the observation of others, and provided against them. When Thomas Paine, though in the fresh popularity of his "*Crisis*" was proposed as Secretary to the Committee of Foreign Affairs, he strenuously opposed his appointment, not deeming him, he said, a safe man for the office. So, also, when Wilkinson made his tardy appearance on the floor of Congress with the standards sent to it by Gen. Gates, and a member moved that the bearer be voted a costly sword for his services, he, seeing through all this delay, and penetrating the contemptible designs of him and Gates, that afterward assumed more definite shape, to unseat Washington as commander-in-chief, arose, and with an emphasis and tone that pierced like a dagger, proposed, in place of a sword, that the messenger should be "*rewarded with a pair of golden spurs.*"

It is impossible in a short sketch to give in detail a history of his career in Congress. It is enough to say that at the time it was the most august body of men that ever sat in deliberation over the fate of a free people, he, in intellect, integrity and influence, ranked among the first; and at a later period, when it became degraded to a miserable cabal, the hot bed of conspiracies and the fountain of all mischief, he stood "faithful among the faithless," one of the few noble columns that towered unshaken amid the disorders and turbulence that for a time threatened to make that body a hissing and bye-word in the nation. While it is well for the reputation of many that composed it and for that of the country at large that the journal for a long period was destroyed, it is a pity, that, for such as he and a few others, it was not preserved, to show their integrity and patriotism in every trial and temptation. With a presence like that of Washington that commanded respect and awe, whenever he arose to address Congress every eye was turned upon him. His sarcasm was withering, and the boldest winced under it, while he possessed a power in argument and a persuasive eloquence which nothing could withstand, and that made him the bulwark of liberty to the last. His duties as a clergyman and those of a legislator he performed with the same conscientiousness, and in them felt he was equally doing God's service. He died the 15th of November, 1794, in full possession of his faculties, and in calm, sublime trust in the Saviour.

He was a voluminous writer and active worker to the last. An edition of his works, comprising three octavo volumes, was published in 1803, in Philadelphia, under the supervision of Rev. Dr. Green, and one of nine volumes duodecimo, in Edinburgh, in 1815. If the pulpit of America had given only this one man to the Revolution, it would deserve to be held in everlasting remembrance for the service it rendered the country.

CHAPTER XXIX.

DAVID AVERY.

His Birth and Character.—Converted under Whitfield.—Leaves his Trade to study for the Ministry.—Enters Dr. Wheelock's Charity School.—Graduates at Yale College.—Studies Divinity.—A Missionary among the Indians.—Settled at Gaysboro, Vermont.—His Patriotism.—Raises a Company and Marches to Boston.—Made Chaplain.—Noddle's Island.—Present at the Battle of Bunker Hill.—Praying for Victory.—Accompanies Washington through the Jerseys.—Wounded at Trenton.—At Valley Forge.—At Ticonderoga.—At Bennington.—His Death.

MR. AVERY was born in that part of Norwich, Connecticut, now called Franklin, April 5th, 1746. His parents, John and Lydia (Smith) Avery, were blessed with a large family of children, though possessing but limited means to provide for their education. Hence David was apprenticed at an early age to a house-joiner in his native town. Gentle and kind in his manners, and with a heart full of tenderness, he had at the same time a bold and fearless nature which, when roused, it was dangerous to oppose. Soon after he commenced his apprenticeship he heard the celebrated Whitfield preach, who was then electrifying the country with his eloquence, and stirring the hearts of men by his solemn appeals and overwhelming application of divine truth to the conscience. Young Avery went at first from curiosity to hear one so distinguished for his eloquence, but soon became deeply impressed with the truths he uttered, and eventually embraced religion. Ardent and resolute in every thing he undertook, he wished to devote his life to the services of his Master in a more direct and efficient manner than he thought he should be able to do by pursuing his trade, and he resolved, if he could obtain the means, to educate himself to become a minister of the gospel. Applying to his parents for aid he was met with the disheartening answer that it was out of their power to help him. He then turned to his elder brothers and begged them to loan him the necessary money to make a beginning, but was again disappointed. Thrown back upon his own resources, he nevertheless did not despair, but went resolutely to work at his trade till he obtained money sufficient to buy himself a stock of clothing, and then entered Dr. Eliezer Wheelock's Indian Charity School, situated in that part of Lebanon now known as Hebron. Applying himself energetically to the task of fitting himself for college, he made the rapid advancement which young men of intellect invariably do who feel that they are to be the artificers of their own fortune. It was here that he became familiar with the Indian character, a knowledge that fitted him so admirably to act, as he afterwards did, as a missionary to the Indians of Central New York. He paid his expenses by spending a portion of the year in teaching the Indians the rudiments of an English education. While at Dr. Wheelock's he made the acquaintance of the notorious Brandt, of whom he afterwards was accustomed to speak as a lad of keen intellectual powers and well fitted to rule the Indians. At that time, however, he said, he gave no indications of the cruelty that subsequently disfigured his character. After remaining at Dr. Wheelock's two years he entered the freshman class of Yale College. This was in 1765. In the same class were the afterwards celebrated Timothy Dwight and Dr. Strong, of Hartford, both of whom became chaplains in the army. Noted for his studious habits, he passed successfully through the first two years of his college life. A portion of his junior year was spent among the Six Nations as a missionary. He stood high in the estimation of all who knew him, and when he graduated received with his baccalaureate an honorary degree from Dartmouth. After finishing his collegiate course he entered on the study of divinity with Dr. Wheelock, of Hanover, New Hampshire. Receiving his ordination in 1773, he spent a year or more with Dr. Kirkland among the Oneida Indians. Leaving here he went to Long Island, where he preached with much success. In his diary kept at this time he says, "Preached at Sag Harbor a New Year's sermon. People solemn. I desire to begin the year with God. Lord! let me spend and be spent for Thee! Dispose of me as Thou pleasest; send me where Thou pleasest. Let me have no will of my own, or let my will be Thine."

He afterwards removed to Gaysboro, Vermont, where he was settled at the breaking out of the Revolution. When the news of the battle of Lexington reached this quiet place the inhabitants were filled with the most intense excitement. To the noble souled pastor, however, it came like a trumpet call to the soldier in battle. He saw at once that the hour big with fate to the Colonies had come, and kindling with the lofty patriotism that filled the hearts of so many, as the tidings of that first fierce conflict was borne with the tap of the drum by swift riders to the remotest limits of the Colonies, he at once decided to do what lay in his power to help on the glorious cause of liberty. The very next Sabbath, to the astonishment of his congregation, he preached his farewell sermon, telling them that God would take care of them—as for himself he was going to join the army. It was a solemn day to all, and when the services were closed each turned away, filled with new thoughts, new fears and new hopes. But the impressive scene was not yet over, the patriotic pastor had no intention of going alone to the army. He knew that beside encouragement in the day of trial and ministrations to the sick, the wounded and dying, it needed stout arms and good muskets for the day of battle. So after the congregation was dismissed, he stood on the steps of the church and summoned them to listen to another address. He had performed the duties of the sanctuary, and he now wished to perform those of a patriot. He spoke of the contest that had begun—of the righteousness of their cause, and the pressing need of soldiers if they would maintain their rights. He said it was God's cause, and haranguing them like a prophet of old summoning the children of Israel to battle, he earnestly besought them to lay off at once the trappings of husbandry, and leaving their untilled fields, gird on the weapons of war and become reapers of men. Their bleeding country, he said, called on them in pleading accents, and he entreated them by every motive of patriotism, and as they valued liberty and abhorred slavery, not to turn a deaf ear to her cry. It was a noble, soul-stirring spectacle, that earnest servant of God calling on his parishioners to leave wives and children and parents and follow him to the field of battle. His burning words fell on hearts already on fire with patriotism, and that quiet Sabbath day among the hills became a scene of thrilling excitement. Twenty of his parishioners responded to his call, and shouldering their muskets started on foot with him for Boston. They chose him captain, and marching rapidly forward reached Northampton Saturday night. The rumor of his coming soon spread through the town, and next day a large congregation assembled to hear him preach. One would give a good deal at this day to possess that sermon. His patriotic fervor was so contagious that volunteers came eagerly forward and enrolled themselves in his little company. In the meantime the clergymen in the vicinity of his parish, sympathizing deeply with him in his devotion to his country, met together and agreed to supply his pulpit while he was absent.

The little band kept on their way, and on Saturday the 29th of April arrived in camp at Cambridge. The troops assembled to receive the "reverend captain and his men," as they were called, for the spirited example encouraged the hearts of all. The next day being the Sabbath, a temporary stage was erected in the area of Cambridge College by turning up a rum hogshead, from which Rev. Dr. Langdon, president of Harvard College, preached a sermon from 1st Timothy, vi. 12, "Fight the good fight of faith," &c. In the afternoon Mr. Avery preached from Nehemiah, iv. 14, "And I looked, and rose up, and said unto the nobles and rulers, and to the rest of the people, Be not ye afraid of them. Remember the Lord, which is great and terrible, and fight for your brethren, your sons and your daughters, your wives and your homes."

With such kind of men and such kind of appeals was the cause of freedom upheld and borne onward; and yet this conduct of Mr. Avery in collecting and leading on troops in person, and of others like him, passes unnoticed or is merely alluded to incidentally, while the action of town committees and the adoption of patriotic resolutions by civilians receive the most earnest consideration. "These things ought ye to have done, and not left the other undone."

Mr. Avery, soon after his arrival at head-quarters, was assigned to Col. Sherburn's regiment, in which he instituted a regular course of daily religious service. Besides the performance of these public duties he used to go from tent to tent and read the word of God— talk with the farmer-soldiers, listen to their tales of distress, and relieve them whenever in his power. The camp and bustle of war were strange to these men— they had come from quiet homes in the valleys and on the hill-sides, and from the family altar and the house of God; and the presence of such a minister was a comfort and a blessing that at this day we can not appreciate. He prayed with them, and helped the youthful to overcome the temptations that always

FIGHT ON NODDLE'S ISLAND. 293

surround the soldier, and boldly rebuked sin, and strove in every way to make the camp a camp of the Lord, like the "tents of Israel," over which God's blessing should hover. He does not tire of his arduous work, but writes home that he is glad that he has espoused the cause of his country.

In his diary he makes the following entry:—"May 11th—A provincial fast—preached on Cambridge common, the troops appeared quite serious. May 29th—Went on a volunteer expedition to Noddle's Island; a brisk skirmish; some of our men killed; stood guard two hours that night after praying and exhorting with the expedition."

This brief note is all that he gives us to show what part he took in it. Noddle's Island, near Boston, and Hog Island were covered with hay and cattle, sheep and horses, and the Americans wished to prevent them from falling into the hands of the enemy. So about eleven o'clock in the forenoon of the 27th, a party of twenty or thirty men passed from Chelsea to Hog Island, and thence to Noddle's Island, and commenced driving off the cattle. The British, observing it, sent a schooner and sloop, with a party of marines in boats, to capture them. The Americans seeing them approach, and finding that they had not time to drive off all the stock, commenced shooting them, and thus destroyed great numbers. As the hostile vessels drew near they retreated to Hog Island, and cleared it of between three and four hundred sheep, and a large number of cows and horses. They then drew up on Chelsea Neck to receive the enemy. In the meantime the American officers at Cambridge had called for volunteers to reinforce the gallant little band that had done so nobly, and now stood at bay. Avery, with the brave Warren, was among the volunteers. Putnam took command of the detachment, and hurrying forward with two four pounders, reached the threatened point at nine o'clock in the evening. A brisk fire was immediately opened on the vessels, which was kept up till eleven, when the crew of the schooner finding it too hot, abandoned the contest. The firing then ceased, and it was thought advisable to make no further movement till day-light should reveal the position of the enemy. Avery took advantage of the cessation of the conflict to exhort the little group of patriots, and pray with them. He then shouldered his musket and kept watch for two hours. At day break they boarded the schooner, and carrying off four four-pounders and twelve swivels set her on fire. In this skirmish the English lost twenty-five in killed and wounded, while the Americans had only four wounded, and those slightly.

In the battle of Bunker Hill, as it is called, but which it is well known took place on Breed's Hill, this brave, godly man stood on Bunker Hill in full sight of the conflict, and as Moses, who stood on the hill, and held up his hands that Joshua might smite the Amalekites, so he, while the adjacent heights and shores were shaking to the thunder of cannon, and the flames of burning Charlestown were rolling heavenward, lifted up his hands and prayed that God would give victory to the Americans. Breed's Hill, dimly seen through the rolling smoke of battle, amid which flashed the deadly vollies, and gleamed the glittering lines, and in the back-ground this patriotic divine, with upraised hands beseeching Heaven for victory, would make an appropriate picture of that bloody prelude to the revolution. He thus notes the event in his diary ;—"Early in the morning of June 18th the enemy attacked our entrenchments, but was driven back. After repeated trials they succeeded in dislodging the troops. In the retreat many of Col. Sherbourne's men were killed. My dear friend, Dr. Warren, was shot dead. I stood on a neighboring hill (Bunker) with hands uplifted, supplicating the blessing of Heaven to crown our unworthy arms with success. To us infantile Americans, unused to the thunder and carnage of battle, the flames of Charlestown before our eyes—the incessant play of cannon from their shipping—from Boston, and their wings in various cross directions, together with the fire of musketry from more than four times our number, all heightened the majestic terrors of the field, exhibiting a scene most awful and tremendous, but amid the perils of the dread encounter the Lord was our rock and fortress."

"The enemy burned Charlestown that they might be benefited by the smoke."

The night that followed this momentous day he spent in dressing the wounds of the soldiers and administering such spiritual consolation as the suffering needed. Day after day he devoted himself wholly to the wounded, and glided from cot to cot cheering the wretched, and pointing those who felt that death was near, to the Saviour of sinners. He notes in his diary that the excessive duties preyed upon his health, but expresses the belief that God will sustain him.

He stood near the great elm tree when Washington drew his sword beneath it and took command of the Continental army. Not long after, Dr. Franklin arrived to make an examination of the army by order of Congress, and Mr. Avery being introduced to him, a warm affection sprung up between the two, which lasted till death. His zeal and patriotism made him a prominent man in the army, and Washington often invited him to dine at head quarters. He was frequently detailed at his own request to accompany expeditions into the adjacent country, for he courted toil and hardship in the cause which lay so near his heart. He stood in the ranks on Dorchester Heights, the morning after they had been occupied, and when he saw the British ships heave their anchors and move down the bay, his exultation burst all bounds, and he exclaimed triumphantly, "Give God the praise, for He hath done it." When the army took up its march for New York he accompanied it, and saw with a breaking heart the defeat of the Americans at the battle of Long Island. After it was over he devoted all his time to the sick, caring for their wants and praying with them ; and many a soul passed from earth on the prayers of this good man.

He was beside Washington in his melancholy retreat through the Jerseys, and says, "The lustre of our commander's presence and magnanimity gave a charm to our gloomy misfortunes—it animated and raised our spirits above the power of undue fear. The people of the country, however, were not so happily fortified against the shock of this sudden change of affairs, and sunk dejected." He accompanied him in his march on Trenton—breasted the snow and hail like the common soldier that wintry morning, and when the thunder of cannon and rattle of musketry awakened the sleeping Hessians, marched with him into the thickest of the fight. Feeling how fearful was the crisis that had come, he, after lifting an invocation to God, seized the musket of a soldier that fell by his side, and mounting a rum hogshead that stood in the street, the contents of which had helped to deepen the slumbers of the foe on that Christmas eve, fired away at the confused and hurrying masses of the enemy. In the darkness and tumult of the fight he received a contusion on the right hip, which laid him up for several weeks; and he who had so long ministered to others was compelled to be ministered unto. On his recovery he rejoined the army, and shared with the soldier the battles and marches that followed. He hutted with it at Valley Forge during all that terrible winter in which troops furnished an example of devotion to their general and a love of country that has no parallel in history—nobly sustained the courage of the men, and showed a spirit of self-devotion that called forth the warmest commendations. Like Washington, he seemed superior to the weakness of common mortals, and exhibited the same serene courage, and wore the same calm aspect in that dark hour, which filled others with despondency, that he did when every thing was promising and hopeful.

He was awhile attached to the northern army, and worked with his own hands in building those fortifications at Ticonderoga that afterwards fell before the advancing legions of Burgoyne.

On his return he was warmly received by Washington, who saw in him the embodiment of all those qualities he wished in a chaplain. Intrepid and fearless in battle, unwearied in his attentions to the sick and wounded—not only nursing them with care, but as faithful to their souls as though they were members of his own parish—with a love for his country so strong that it became a passion—cheerful under privations, and ready for any hardship—never losing in the turmoil of the camp that warm and glowing piety which characterizes the devoted minister of God—he might well have a place near to his great chieftain's heart.

During this period we find him detached from Sherbourne's regiment and joined to that of Colonel Patterson.

He knew Arnold well, and was very active in the efforts made to capture him. He was by the side of Washington when he signed the death warrant of Andre, and saw that ill-fated officer hung on the hill behind Piermont.

In every battle he bore himself so nobly that his conduct elicited universal admiration, while his devotion to the wounded after it was over won the hearts of both friends and foes. At the battle of Bennington, like the good parson Allen, he exposed himself to the hottest of the fire, yet he refers to it only to say, "The **arm of the Lord protected me through dangers seen** and unseen." For his services in and after this bloody engagement, he received a vote of thanks from the Governor and Council of the State.

After the war was over, we find him quietly settled in Bennington, gladly exchanging the turmoil of the camp and the horrors of war for the more congenial pursuits of a pastor.

Thus having nobly helped to wrest the land from the hand of tyranny, he sat down under the tree of liberty, and faithful in his parish as he had been in the field, passed peacefully on to a tranquil death, and the reward of the true patriot and faithful minister of Christ.

CHAPTER XXX.

ISRAEL EVANS.

His Character.—Ordained Chaplain in the Army.—Remains with the New Hampshire Brigade through the War.—Stands beside Washington at Yorktown.—Anecdote of Him and Washington.—His Sermon on the Field of Battle.—Settled at Concord, New Hampshire.—His Death.

THERE is perhaps no chaplain of the Revolution who followed its fortunes so steadily from its commencement to its close, sharing all its perils and its hardships, yet about whom so little is known, as the subject of this sketch. He was a native of Pennsylvania, and at the commencement of the struggle between the Colonies and Great Britain was a warm, uncompromising patriot. Having chosen his profession before the breaking out of hostilities, he did not consider it his duty to relinquish it, though from what is known of his character there is but little doubt that, had he been an ordinary citizen, he would have entered the army as a soldier. He was by nature better fitted for the stern duties of a military life, its strict subordination and exact method, and for the battle field, than for the quiet routine of a pastor's calling. Humility was not a prominent trait in his character, and the exactitude and unbending rules of his military experience did not tend to make him yielding and tractable.

When the war commenced he offered himself as

chaplain to the army, and was ordained as such in 1776, in Philadelphia, at the age of twenty-nine. From 1777 to the close of the war he was attached the whole time to the New Hampshire brigade. Of the fierce battles he witnessed, the long marches he made, and want and privation he endured, he apparently kept no record; and hence the incidents and details of this most interesting portion of his life are forever lost to posterity. We catch a glimpse of him in the fierce conflicts at Saratoga, hear his voice as he addresses the western army after their return from the expedition against the Indians, sympathize with him as he pours his sad lament over the body of his dead commander, Gen. Poor, at Hackensack,—but all between has been swept by the wave of oblivion. He not only shared the sufferings of the army at Valley Forge, but was of great service in encouraging and cheering the soldiers when ready to yield to despair. His imperturbable coolness in battle was proverbial, and he rather sought than shunned the post of danger.

At the battle of Yorktown he was standing beside Washington when a cannon ball in full sweep struck the earth at his very feet and sent a shower of dirt over his hat. Washington glanced at the chaplain to see how he took it, but the latter was as imperturbable as himself. Without stirring from the spot, he took off his hat, and seeing it covered with sand, said quietly as he held it up, "See here, General." Washingington smiled and replied, "*Mr. Evans, you had better take that home and show it to your wife and children.*" The chaplain smiled in return, and replacing it on his head turned his attention once more to the cannonade that was shaking the field like an earthquake.

After the surrender of Cornwallis he preached a sermon in the open air to the assembled brigade, taking the one hundred and fifteenth Psalm for his text, beginning, "Not unto us, O Lord, not unto us, but unto thy name give glory for thy mercy and for thy truth's sake. Wherefore should the heathen say, where is now their God.

But our God is in the heavens, He hath done whatsoever He pleased."

After tracing the hand of God from the commencement of the struggle through all the changing fortunes that followed, he bursts into thanksgiving for the glorious victory they had just achieved, and exclaims :— "For these and innumerable instances of public mercy we desire most heartily to praise God, and say, 'Not unto us, O Lord, not unto the wisdom of our counselors, though their counsels and wisdom have surpassed our most sanguine expectations. Not unto our commanders and armies, though they have behaved themselves so valiantly, and conducted wisely—yet give glory not unto them but unto the name of God, for He it was who taught our Senators wisdom, and girded our soldiers with courage and strength. It is the Lord our God who has fought for us in every successful battle, and has hitherto supported our righteous cause against those who hate us without any just reason. Surely, we may say, O sing unto the Lord a new song, for He hath done marvellous things, His right hand and His holy arm hath gotten Him the victory.

The Lord hath made known his salvation, His righteousness hath he openly showed in the sight of our enemies. He hath remembered His mercy toward us. All the ends of the earth shall see the salvation of our God." He thanks God for the aid of the French—for giving us good men in Congress, and then exclaims, "Oh give thanks to the Lord our God for our brave General, the Commander-in-chief of all our armies. A General possessed of such unparalleled fortitude and patience, and not more patient than meek, and virtuous, and humane. And if I may be permitted to say any thing of a character which so much outshines the brightest encomium that writers can offer, I will venture to say that if you search for faults in the conduct of that true patriot and most excellent hero, you will find none unless you call it a fault to exercise compassion and lenity toward those negligent and guilty offenders, who, by their sloth and inattention to the best orders, counteract the wisest plans, and frustrate the best schemes of military discipline and policy.

"Methinks I see the illustrious Washington, with but two or three thousand men retreating indeed before ten or twelve thousand of the enemy, but checking their progress through the country, and when reinforced by the brave militia, turning upon the enemy, killing some, capturing many, and confining them during the whole winter within narrow bounds. Oh, Americans, give glory to God for such a faithful hero! Then you saw him greatest when most without your aid. Collected himself he greatly resolved with his few **faithful followers to be the barrier of liberty or fall in** its defence." He then speaks of Saratoga, describes Arnold as a thunderbolt on that day, and winds up by referring to the coming winter, which may demand great sacrifices, and exhorts them not to be startled by anticipated sufferings, but bear all like men, and to refrain from profane swearing and all ungodly acts, and live the lives of true Christians.

It was a thrilling spectacle—that war-worn chaplain standing on the bloody field of Yorktown—the wreck of the fight strewn all around him, and lifting his peans of praise to Washington, and his shout of thanksgiving to God. The excited soldiers, fresh from the field of their fame, and elated with their great victory, could scarcely refrain from sending up their thrilling huzzas when the eloquent chaplain, passing from his review of the troubled past, burst forth into an eulogium of their gallant leader.

He published several of his sermons after the war, all of which exhibit his stern, unyielding patriotism.

In 1789 he was ordained pastor of the church in Concord, to which he became known by his connection with the New Hampshire brigade.

His military career did not tend to make him the most conciliating of pastors, and in 1797 he resigned his charge, though he continued to reside in the place till his death, in March, 1807, in the sixtieth year of his age.

CHAPTER XXXI.

COTTON MATHER SMITH.

His Birth and Parentage.—A Teacher among the Indians.—Studies Theology.—Is Settled at Sharon, Conn.—Influence of the Clergy of Connecticut in bringing about the Revolution.—His views of the Struggle between the Colonies and Mother Country.—The Part he took in it.—Patriotism of his Congregation.—Is made Chaplain, and Marches to Ticonderoga.—His Devotion to the Sick.—Seized with the Camp Fever.—Returns Home.—Invasion of Burgoyne.—His Sermon just before the Final Victory at Saratoga.—Thrilling Scene.—His Character.—His Death.

Cotton Mather Smith was born in Suffield, Conn., Oct. 26th, 1731. His father was grandson of Rev. Henry Smith, and his mother grand-daughter of the celebrated Increase Mather. He graduated at Yale College in 1751, after which he went to Hatfield for a while, where he made a public profession of religion, and immediately turned his attention to the ministry. Before, however, he finished his course of theological studies he accepted an invitation to take charge of a school among the Indians in Stockbridge, Mass. Dr. Sprague, in his "Annals of the American Pulpit," says of him in connection with this novel enterprise, "He engaged in it with great zeal, and by his amiable and winning manners, and especially by mingling with the Indians in their athletic sports, he acquired a commanding influence over them, and brought them entirely within his control. He labored for them with untiring diligence and with corresponding success, and became a proficient in their language, while imparting to them a knowledge of his own."

After completing his engagement he returned to Hatfield and resumed his theological studies. He was licensed to preach in 1753, and two years after settled over the church of Sharon, Conn., and continued its pastor through a long and useful life. A distinguished descendant of Rev. Mr. Smith in furnishing me the materials for this sketch, prefaces them with such forcible and true remarks on the "influence of the clergy of Connecticut in making that little State take the gallant stand she did in the revolution," that I quote them entire. After showing that she might well be called the "Lacedæmon of the confederation, since that, small as she was, she furnished thirty-one thousand six hundred troops, or five thousand more than Virginia and Pennsylvania, and far more than New York," and that although she "had a hundred miles of exposed sea coast, only three plundering expeditions ever contaminated her soil, and these made no permanent occupation," and after speaking of the gallantry of her sons at Bunker Hill, in covering the retreat—their efforts in capturing "Ticonderoga with more than two hundred cannon that proved of such vital importance to the American cause in the siege of Boston"—of her brave spirits, such as Knowlton and Hale, and others, early martyrs to liberty—so well calculated to arouse her energy and kindle her heroism, he says, "But the most powerful element of revolutionary strength in Connecticut was her Congregational clergy, and the opinion may be expressed without fear of contradiction, that to no class or order of men is the country so much indebted for its national independence. Had they preached a slavish and cowardly submission to the royal will—had they declared it to be the first of duties to honor the King, we should to-day have been royal colonists of the British crown.

"The immense influence of the clergy for the first century and a half is alike honorable to them and to the people. Most of them who first emigrated into the country were gentlemen of family and station, and had good estates, which they freely spent in assisting their poor brethren and parishioners in the numerous difficulties of making new settlements. They possessed a great proportion of the literature of the colony, and were the instructors of the flower of its youth. They had given a striking evidence of their integrity and self-denial in emigrating from their pleasant homes into this distant land for the sake of religious liberty, and their people reverenced them as exiles and fellow-sufferers for the dearest of causes. No wonder that all these circumstances combined to give them an uncommon influence over their hearers of every rank and character. No wonder that the governors and magistrates and leading men of the land deemed them worthy of all honor. They were consulted by the legislature in all affairs of consequence, civil and religious, and with civilians were appointed on committees to advise and assist them in the most delicate and important concerns of the commonwealth.

"With but little variation this continued down to the epoch of the Revolution, and in all the preparatory movements towards the mighty struggle it was the influence of her clergy more than any thing else that caused the colony of Connecticut to act in one united and harmonious phalanx. To the tyrannical edicts of the throne, and the bitter and barbarous threats of the lords and bishops in the English Parliament, they responded from every pulpit, 'Down with Amalek.' 'The sword of the Lord and of Gideon.' 'Be strong, that ye be not servants; quit yourselves like men, and fight.' It was owing to the clergy that New England was not infested with tories like other provinces."

Of the twenty years of his parochial life—filled up with usefulness—of his labors abundantly blessed—of his kindly charities and devotion to the interests of his people, the limits of this sketch will not allow me to speak. As an instance of his self-sacrificing spirit, it is necessary only to mention that once when the small-pox devastated his parish he never took off his clothes for nearly three weeks, so untiring was his attendance on the sick.

The crisis which the battle of Lexington precipitated had long been foreseen by Mr. Smith. He had watched the slow gathering of the clouds on the political horizon and knew what they portended. Feeling that a struggle between the Colonies and mother country was inevitable, he was not one of those who believed it would result simply in a redress of grievances and a restoration of the old relations. He knew the first resort to arms would rouse the old Puritan blood to a pitch of excitement that would make the restraints of loyalty like threads of gossamer, and he therefore for a long time previous to it, by his pen, in private conversation and in the pulpit, gradually educated his congregation into the belief that when the Colonies should rise in defence of their rights nothing short of a total separation and a national independence must be looked for. Fearful as such an issue seemed, he did not speak of it despondingly, but with high courage and firm faith. Not only was his pen as well as tongue devoted to the cause of freedom in the way of essays, arguments and addresses, but being gifted with poetic talent he is supposed to have composed some of those spirit-stirring odes with which his congregation were wont at times to make the hills of Sharon ring.

> "Let tyrants shake their iron rod,
> And slavery clank her galling chains,
> We fear them not, we trust in God,
> New England's God forever reigns,"

would peal through the old meeting house till the rafters shook with the lofty strain.

At the time the battle of Lexington took place Mr. Smith's parish contained two thousand souls. This number, according to the usual estimate, would give about four hundred men capable of bearing arms, and we find when the news of the battle reached the town four hundred enrolled themselves in the militia, most of whom saw more or less service during the war.

Ticonderoga being captured by Connecticut troops, it was natural she should take pride in maintaining it. Hence, in 1775, a detachment of militia of the State was sent to garrison it, and operate under Schuyler, who had command in Lake Champlain. The General Assembly appointed Mr. Smith its chaplain, and he marched with the troops to the theatre of war. Though unused to a rough life, he endured cheerfully all the hardships of the long march through the wilderness, and during the rigorous campaign that followed shared with the common soldier his privations and self-denials. On the desolate shores of that forest-bound lake he gave himself up to his work with an earnestness and untiring zeal that extorted the admiration of men and officers, and won the lasting affection of General Schuyler. Preaching was but a small part of his labors. He was in constant attendance on the sick, and moved like a good angel among the farmers and mechanics who composed the militia, encouraging the down-hearted, and infusing hope and cheerfulness where despondency and sadness reigned.

He, however, overestimated his powers of endurance, and towards the end of the campaign was seized with the putrid or camp fever, which brought him to death's door. But his good constitution at length triumphed, though for a long while he either lay helpless or was able only to creep around the fortress. Finding himself a confirmed invalid, he was compelled, to his great regret ; to leave the army, and returned to his parish. Although he soon afterwards resumed his parochial duties, he never fully recovered from the effects of this terrible illness. It did not, however, quench the fire of his patriotism, and he saw that every draft for men, money and provisions made on his parish was promptly met. When the news of

Burgoyne's formidable invasion filled the land with so much dread, he appealed to the patriotism of his congregation, and urged them to rally en masse to the call of New York for volunteers.

Instead of sharing in the general despondency he spoke of sure victory, and told them the time had now come to do or die, and if every man put his shoulder to the work, God would make bare his arm for the deliverance of His people. His hearers caught his spirit, and seizing their fire-locks, streamed toward the northern wilderness. So universal was the patriotic response, that every man in the parish capable of bearing arms volunteered; and the good pastor found his congregation composed only of old men, women, and children. It brought tears to many eyes as they looked over the half-filled pews, in which not an erect, manly form was visible, when "the *absent*" were remembered in the fervent prayers of the pastor.

At length the news of the drawn battle of the 19th of September was received. Then followed the long and anxious interval between it and the final conflict of the 7th of October, during which the country was in a state of the most painful suspense. The next breeze that swept from the north might bring the news of the overthrow of the American army. The fears as to the final result were greatly increased by the knowledge that Sir Henry Clinton, at New York, was fitting out a formidable expedition to force the passage of the Hudson, and effect a junction with Burgoyne, at Albany. Should this succeed, the struggle to all human appearance would be over, and the sun of liberty set.

The summer verdure slowly changed to its autumnal tints, and October spread its dreamy atmosphere over the mountains, and robed woods and fields with the untold glories of the dying year, yet an ominous silence brooded over the north. The crisis still delayed, and the hours, so big with the fate of the colonies, dragged wearily on, yet strong prayers ascended the heavens daily and nightly for the untried farmers and mechanics, who, in their homely apparel, were standing resolutely in the Britons' path. Nothing was thought of but the coming battle, and at the first dawn of morning and in the last twilight of evening, anxious eyes were strained along the road, down which the messenger of good or evil tidings would come.

While public feeling was in this state of painful excitement, Mr. Smith, one Sabbath day, took for his text a part of Isaiah, xxi, 11, 12: "*Watchman, what of the night? The watchman said, The morning cometh.*" The question in the first part of this passage had been the daily, almost hourly, mental inquiry for nearly a month of every one of that congregation, and hence its appropriateness was keenly felt, but the startling announcement, "the morning cometh," took them by surprise, and they could not at first comprehend its significance, or how it could be adapted to the present gloomy prospect. Had he heard any good news? What *had* happened that he could say so confidently, "*the morning cometh?*" No, he had nothing new to tell them, only to proclaim over again his unshaken confidence in God's promises. He did not attempt to conceal or lessen the calamities that had befallen the country, nor deny that a fearful crisis was at hand. He acknowledged that to human appearance "clouds and darkness were round about God's throne," but said that the eye of faith could pierce the gloom. The *throne* was there, though wrapped in impenetrable darkness. In all the disasters that had successively overwhelmed them, he traced the hand of God, and declared that to his mind they clearly indicated some striking interposition of divine providence about to take place in their behalf. "Man's extremity was God's opportunity." *Our* extremity had come, and now was the time for Him "to make bare His arm for the deliverance of His people."

Prophet-like, kindling with the vision on which the eye of his faith rested, he boldly dropped the general subject of God's faithfulness, and told his astonished hearers that he believed they were on *the point of hearing extraordinary news of victory to our arms.* He would not wait for an indefinite future to prove his faith to be well founded—he was willing to bring it to the test of the present. They might judge whether he was right or wrong, for, said he, "'*The morning now cometh.*' I see its beams already gilding the mountain tops, and you shall soon behold its brightness bursting over all the land." One cannot imagine at this day the effect of such language uttered by the minister of God in such a time of doubt and anxiety and suspense. He ceased, and as he closed the Bible, and exclaimed, "Amen! so let it be," a silence profound and death-like rested on the audience. Each one seemed to feel as if an invisible presence was there and some weighty announcement was at hand. Suddenly the deep hush was broken by the distant clatter of a horse's hoofs along the road. The sharp and rapid strokes told of fierce riding and of urgent haste. They knew at once what it meant. For days and weeks their eyes had strained up the street that led northward to catch sight of the messenger of good or evil tidings that was hourly expected. He had come at last, and as nearer, clearer, rang the sound of that wild gallop on the listening ear, each one looked in mute and earnest inquiry into his neighbor's face. Right on through the place, straight for the meeting house, darted the swift rider, and drawing rein at the door leaped from the saddle, and leaving his foam-covered steed untended, strode into the main aisle. On the deep silence that filled the building, like a sensible presence, his armed heel rang like the blows of a hammer. As he passed along, a sudden paleness spread over the crowd of faces turned with a painful eagerness towards him. But looking neither to the right hand nor the left, the dread messenger passed on, and mounting the pulpit stairs handed the pastor a letter. Notwithstanding the good man's faith, his hand trembled and an ashy hue overspread his face as he reached out to receive it. "BURGOYNE HAS SURRENDERED" were the first words that met his eye. He staggered under them as under a blow. The next moment a radiance like that of the morning broke over his countenance, and he burst into tears. Rising to read the incredible tidings, such a tide of emotion flooded his heart that he could scarcely utter them aloud. The audience sat for a moment overwhelmed and stupefied, then, as their pastor folded his hands and turned his eyes toward heaven in thankful prayer, impelled by a simultaneous movement they fell like one man on their knees and wept aloud. Sobs, sighs and fervidly murmured "amens" were heard on every side, attesting the depth of their gratitude and the ecstasy of their joy. "The morning had come," bright and glorious, and its radiance filled all the heavens.

The arrival of such news at the close of that sermon was a strange coincidence, but the Revolution is a history of just such coincidences.

Mr. Smith was somewhat above the medium height, of graceful bearing and an attractive personal presence. Dr. Robbins, of Hartford, in a letter to Dr. Sprague, said of him : "His manners were remarkably polished, so that he might have appeared to advantage even in a court. They were a delightful compound of simplicity, gracefulness and dignity ; while, on the other hand, they were entirely free from hauteur or ostentation, and he could make the humblest man in the community feel at home in his company. In his intercourse with his people and with society at large he was distinguished for his prudence—he never performed an act or uttered a word that was fitted needlessly to wound others, or to impair the dignity or lessen the influence of his own character. He possessed an exquisite sensibility, which was sometimes a source of great pleasure to him, and not unfrequently of no inconsiderable pain. His sense of right and wrong was exceedingly nice, and with all his mildness he was capable of dealing out severe reproofs to obstinate offenders. An illustration of this remark now occurs to me. He was sent, as were several of his brethren, at an early period, by the Litchfield County Association as a missionary to Vermont, which was then but sparsely settled, and in some parts by a population of rather an equivocal character. Some of the inhabitants—I think Ethan Allen of infidel notoriety was among them—took it in high dudgeon that he should have come on such an errand, as if there was some implication that they needed to be converted from a state of heathenism. They even attacked him in the most rude and opprobrious manner in the public papers, and he replied to their wanton attacks with dignified severity. I remember that the closing words of his answer, which certainly showed an indignant sense of injury, were—'The Lord rebuke thee, Satan.'"

After the Revolution Mr. Smith continued his parochial duties, a "devout and earnest Christian, and an instructive and animated preacher." In 1805 he preached his Half Century sermon to his people, from the text, "Lord, now lettest thou thy servant depart in peace, for mine eyes have seen thy salvation." In this sermon he stated that during his ministry he had delivered "upwards of four thousand public discourses, and more than fifteen hundred on funeral and other special occasions." The next year he preached his last sermon. A disease which had been gradually undermining his constitution at length laid him prostrate. He, however, lingered on for several months, suffering at times the most excruciating torture, yet he bore all with the patience and calm resignation of a Christian martyr. Two days before his death, in an interval of pain, he spoke at length of the value of the Bible, declared what he believed to be its essential doctrines, concluding his remarks with, "These things I have preached to others, and these things I believe as fully as that the Bible is the word of God, and this I believe as fully as that the Son of God was made manifest in the flesh, and this I believe as fully as that God governs the world, and this I believe as fully as I believe in my own present existence and approaching dissolution. Lord, help mine unbelief." He spoke but little after this, and on the morning of the 27th of November, 1806, in the seventy-sixth year of his age, peacefully and without a struggle sunk to rest.

He had six children, one of whom, John Cotton, has borne a prominent part in the history of the nation.

CHAPTER XXXII.

JUDAH CHAMPION.

JUDAH CHAMPION, THE PASTOR OF LITCHFIELD, CONNECTICUT.—HIS PRAYERS FOR HIS COUNTRY.—EXTRAORDINARY SCENE IN CHURCH ON THE ARRIVAL OF NEWS FROM THE ARMY.—WOMEN WORKING ON THE SABBATH TO PREPARE GARMENTS FOR THE SOLDIERS.—THE PASTOR ON THE FIELD OF BATTLE.

JUDAH CHAMPION was born in Haddam, Connecticut, May 21, 1724. From his youth he was distinguished for his integrity, truthfulness and scrupulous performance of duty. During his college course at Yale, he missed morning prayers *but once*, and then his delinquency was occasioned by a senior, who purposely imposed on him a duty that he could not perform without being absent from chapel exercises. When he made his explanation to the professor, the latter said, "Champion, you never need give any excuse for absence from prayers again." He was ordained pastor of the Congregational Church of Litchfield, Connecticut, July 4, 1753, when that parish comprised Northfield, South Farms and Milton. Short, erect, with an elastic step and dignified gait; he had a frank and open countenance, and a clear, straightforward look, that bespoke both his sincerity and fearlessness. Earnest and eloquent, he exercised unbounded influence over his parish, and was looked up to with love and reverence by young and old. His power in prayer was so remarkable that whenever any one within his extensive parish felt it necessary to send for a physician, he sent also for the pastor to pray with the sick, having an almost superstitious belief in the efficacy of his "fervent prayer." A thorough scholar, many distinguished men fitted for college under him, among whom may be mentioned Gov. Oliver Wolcott and Hon. Frederick Wolcott.

Ardent in his feelings, and hating every form of oppression, he lent the weight of his personal character and his eloquent tongue to the cause of the Colonies. His prayers for their success in the conflict on which they had entered, were so fervent and thrilling as at times completely to electrify his congregation. On one occasion Major Tallmadge was passing through Litchfield with a regiment of cavalry. Reaching the village Saturday night, they remained over the Sabbath and attended Mr. Champion's church. The presence of the armed troopers in the house, brought before the patriotic pastor more vividly than ever the struggle that was wasting the land, and the more terrible conflicts awaiting it when the veteran hosts reported to be on their way to conquer them should arrive. In his morning prayer he referred to the prospective hostile invasion; the overwhelming numbers that composed it, the cruel purpose for which it was set on foot, and the haughty, scornful spirit of those who carried it on. He spoke of their enmity to the American church, and the ruin to religion which their success would accomplish; of congregations scattered, churches burned to the ground, and the Lord's people made a hissing and a by-word among their foes, till his own feelings and those of his hearers were roused into intense excitement in view of the great wrongs and sufferings designed for them and the Church of God, and he burst forth:

"O Lord, we view with terror and dismay the enemies of our holy religion; wilt thou send storm and tempest to toss them upon the sea, to overwhelm them in the mighty deep, or scatter them to the utmost parts of the earth. But, peradventure, should they escape thy vengeance, collect them together again, O Lord, as in the hollow of thy hand, and let thy lightnings play upon them. We beseech thee, moreover, that thou do gird up the loins of these thy servants, who are going forth to fight thy battles. Make them strong men, that one shall chase a thousand, and two put ten thousand to flight. Hold before them the shield with which thou wast wont in the old time to protect thy chosen people. Give them swift feet, that they may pursue their enemies, and swords terrible as that of thy destroying angel, that they may cleave them down. Preserve these servants of thine, Almighty God, and bring them once more to their homes and friends, if thou canst do it consistently with thy high purpose. If, on the other hand, thou hast decreed they shall die in battle, let thy spirit be present with them that they may go up as a sweet sacrifice into the courts of thy temple, where are habitations prepared for them from the foundation of the world."

In these days of peace and security one is apt to look on such a prayer with profound surprise, if not with condemnation; but the patriotic clergy of the revolution never practised self-deception; they did not wish for one thing in their hearts and pray for another with their lips. When they wanted the destruction of their foes, they did not pray about something else, and wait to see if their desires might not be accomplished through the agency of wicked men, or chance, or the devil. They came boldly to the very Holy of Holies, and *asked* for it. Their enemies were the enemies of God; their foes those of the Church, who were coming to lay waste and destroy God's heritage, and they wished their overthrow, and honestly, and with strong crying and tears, prayed for it. Like Cromwell's Ironsides, who first invoked God's right arm to strike with them, and then with the fearful war-cry "Religion" on their lips swept like a thunder-cloud to battle; like the Covenanters, who prayed that their swords might be like that of Gideon, that turned not back from the slaughter, and then fell in fury on their pursuers; like David, praying for the overthrow of his enemies, and Moses, and Joshua, and the prophets, whose earnest supplications swelled the heaps of the slain; so these puritan divines, without rancor or vindictive hate, prayed in this fashion, and with an honest, earnest purpose, "Thy kingdom come."

At this remote period it is impossible to imagine the state of excitement in which the country was thrown by the opening scenes of the revolution. Important news traveled at that time by couriers, and eyes were constantly turned up and down the streets for swift riders bearing intelligence big with the fate of the colonies.

One pleasant Sabbath morning, the inhabitants of Litchfield had gathered to the sanctuary, the streets were deserted, and not a living thing broke the serenity and stillness that reigned in the quiet village. The services had already commenced, and the solemn strains of the morning hymn had just died away, and the clear tones of Mr. Champion's voice were echoing through the consecrated place, when the clatter of a horse's hoofs, coming at a furious rate down the street, arrested every ear. The animal was covered with foam, but the eager rider spared not the spur as he pressed straight for the meeting-house. Alighting at the door, he flung the bridle on the horse's neck, and entering the porch, walked rapidly up the centre aisle, and amid a hush like that of death, ascended the pulpit steps and handed Mr. Champion a paper. The excited pastor cast his eye over it, and then arose and announced to the still more excited congregation, that St. John's had been taken by the American troops. "St. John's is taken,"* exclaimed the patriot, and lifting his eyes to heaven burst forth, "Thank God for the victory!" The chorister, who sat opposite in the gallery, could not contain his joy, but clapping his hands, vigorously shouted, "Amen, and amen!"

After the first excitement was over, the pastor proceeded to read the entire communication. It stated

---

* It must be remembered it had been besieged six weeks, and was regarded as the key of Canada.

that our army was in a suffering condition, destitute of clothing, without stockings or shoes, while in that latitude, the latter part of November had brought all the rigors of winter, and that with bare, lacerated feet they were soon to march to Quebec. Sorrow and pity took the place of exultation, and generous sympathetic eyes filled with tears on every side. There was scarcely a dry eye among the females of the congregation. As soon as the audience was dismissed, they were seen gathered together in excited groups, and it was evident some scheme was on foot that would not admit of delay. The result was, that when the congregation assembled in the afternoon, *not a woman was to be seen.* The men had come to church, but their earnest, noble wives and daughters had taken down their hand-cards, drawn forth their spinning-wheels, set in motion their looms, while the knitting and sewing needle were plied as they never were plied before. It was a strange spectacle to see that puritan Sabbath turned into a day of secular work. The pastor was at the meeting-house performing those duties belonging to the house of God, and the voice of prayer and hymns of praise ascended as usual from devout and solemn hearts; but all through the usually quiet streets of Litchfield the humming sound of the spinning-wheel, the clash of the shuttle plying to and fro were heard, making strange harmony with the worship of the sanctuary. But let it not be supposed that these noble women had gone to work without the knowledge of their pastor. They had consulted with him, and he had given them his sanction and blessing.

Nor was their toil enlivened by pleasant conversation and light talk. Swimming eyes and heaving bosoms were over their work, and lips moved in prayer for the destitute and suffering soldiers. The pastor's wife contributed eleven blankets from her own stores to the collection. Many years after, when speaking of this event, a grand-daughter asked the venerable man how such a desecration of the Sabbath could be justified. He turned on her a reproving look, and replied, "Mercy before sacrifice."

Is it wonderful that a cause which called forth such efforts and such prayers should succeed? How superficially has the American historian studied the revolution, who leaves out of his narrative the pulpit and clergy, or fails to give them a prominent place? The express-rider dashing through Litchfield was guilty of no such mistake. Driving the rowels in his panting steed, he dashed straight for the house of God and the pulpit. He knew that the clergy were a committee of one in every parish to whom all other committees, aye, and Provincial Congresses too, looked for sympathy and support.

Not long after Mr. Champion received, on the same morning, from various parishioners, who were ignorant of each other's intentions, a great many quarters of veal. Mrs. Champion, alarmed at the extraordinary supply, informed her husband of it, and wanted to know what to do, as it would be impossible to preserve such a large quantity of fresh meat till it was consumed. "Never mind," said the good pastor, "Providence has a meaning in it. There will be occasion to use it in some way we do not think of." Scarce two hours had passed before a letter was put in his hand from his nephew, Henry Champion, quarter-master in the army, stating that a regiment of soldiers would pass through Litchfield that day, and wishing he would see that a dinner was prepared for them. He immediately sent word round to the inhabitants, who assembled, and soon tables were set all through the main street, and bountifully provided. Before night Mrs. Champion found that the quantity of veal that had distressed her so much had all disappeared.

When the news of Burgoyne's invasion sent consternation over the land, this patriotic pastor could no longer remain at home an idle spectator of the contest. Offering his services as chaplain, he was ordered to Ticonderoga. He was there during the siege of that fortress, and fled at midnight with the retreating army through the wilderness. Sharing the perils and hardships of that disastrous retreat, he at length saw with joy and thankfulness the army make its determined stand at Saratoga. After the first battle, he devoted himself night and day to the sick and wounded. The same attention was shown to the wounded British, after the surrender of Burgoyne. He made the hospitals his home, for the wretchedness and suffering around him so moved his heart that he could not rest. The sick and dying of whatever nation were to him as brothers, and such was his zeal and self-sacrifice that the British officers, as well as our own, returned him their warmest thanks.

He witnessed the close of the great drama, and

when the British evacuated New York, he returned once more to his parish to share in the general joy that swelled the hearts of a ransomed people. He died October 8, 1810, in the fifty-seventh year of his ministry, and eightieth year of his age.

CHAPTER XXXIII.

ALEXANDER McWHORTER.

His Early Life.—Zeal in the Cause of Liberty.—Sent South by Congress to rouse the Inhabitants.—Accompanies Washington in his Retreat through New Jersey.—Made Chaplain of Knox's Brigade.—Leaves the Army.—Settles in North Carolina.—His Library and Furniture destroyed by the British.—Flees to Pennsylvania.—Sent to England to raise Funds for Princeton College.—Revisits his Native Place.—His Death.

Although the subject of the following sketch moved amid some of the most stirring scenes of the Revolution, and was identified with many of its leading events, the details and incidents necessary to a proper appreciation of his services are sadly wanting.

He was born in Newcastle, Delaware, July 15th, 1734, though his parents removed when he was a mere boy to North Carolina. He was licensed to preach in 1758, and continued to discharge his duties as pastor with great success till the breaking out of the Revolution. He was at the North in search of health when the battle of Bunker Hill set the land in a blaze, and immediately flung himself with such zeal into the struggle that Congress sent him to North Carolina to rouse the people to take sides with the other Colonies. His enthusiastic appeals kindled the hate of the Tories of that State, and he was pursued with the utmost malignity, and met with such determined opposition that he at length abandoned the effort and returned North.

In the summer of 1776 he received the degree of Doctor of Divinity from Yale College. The next winter found him by the side of Washington in the gloomy retreat through the Jerseys, and on the frozen banks of the Delaware, concerting with him on what was to be done for the salvation of the state. On the night of the 26th of December he marched through the driving sleet to Trenton, and with a heart full of joy and devout thanksgiving heard the shout of victory that lifted the land from the abyss of despair, and shed a bright though transient gleam of light on the all enshrouding darkness. He gave his whole time and effort to the army, encountering hardships and making sacrifices for the common good with a cheerfulness and zeal that endeared him to Washington and the other officers. In the summer of 1778 General Knox made an urgent request that he should become the chaplain of his brigade, then encamped with the main army at White Plains. He consented, and frequently in his sermons to the troops had Washington for a hearer. The latter esteemed him highly, and often invited him to headquarters. During the summer his wife was struck with lightning, and although not killed received such a shock to her constitution that he felt it his duty to resign his chaplaincy and return home to attend to her and the family. In 1779 he received a call from the congregation of Charlotte, Mecklenburg county, North Carolina, and at the same time an invitation to be president of Charlotte Academy. Both of these he accepted. He had not been settled here long, however, when the approach of Cornwallis, spreading devastation on every side, compelled him to flee with his family. On his return he found that his library, furniture and other property had become the spoil of the invaders, and fearing repeated attacks he left the place and set his face northward. He preached afterwards for a few years in Abingdon, in Pennsylvania, but in 1802, after Princeton College was burned, he, at the earnest request of the trustees, went to England to solicit aid for its reërection.

In his old age, feeling a strong desire to visit his native place in Delaware, he took a colored servant, and in a light carriage traveled slowly to Newcastle. Dr. Murray, of Elizabethtown, thus relates the following incident of this visit, obtained from Dr. Miller, of Princeton: "Driving up to the door of the house in which he was born—now old and dilapidated—he asked the woman who came to the door who lived there. Being answered, he asked again who lived there before *them*. Having received a reply, he again asked, 'Who lived there before *them?*' The woman could not tell. He then asked her if she had ever heard of a family who once lived there by the name of McWhorter. 'What name did you say?' said the woman. 'McWhorter,' replied the doctor. 'I never heard of such a family,' said she. He then drove to a neighboring house, where an uncle, a brother of his father, used to live. He asked the same questions, and received the same answers. Returning to the house of his birth, he left his carriage and asked for a tumbler, saying, 'There is one place here that knows me and that I know.' And leaning on the arm of his servant he hobbled to a spring at the bottom of the garden from which he used to drink when a boy. He stood over it for some time, and drank of its waters until he could drink no more. He then hobbled back to his carriage, repeating these words as he entered it—the tears streaming from his eyes—'The places that now know us will know us no more forever.'"

He died the 20th of July, 1807, calm, patient, and at times triumphant, and passed to his reward. The noble patriot, however, lived to see his country not only free, but rapidly advancing to that rank among nations which she has since taken.

CHAPTER XXXIV.

MOSES ALLEN.

His Early Life.—A Friend of Madison.—Settles in Midway, Georgia.—His Patriotic Efforts.—Chaplain in the Army.—His House and Church Burned.—In the Battle before Savannah.—Is taken Prisoner.—Confined on board a Prison Ship.—His Sufferings.—Brutality of his Captors.—Attempts to Escape.—Is Drowned.—Denied Decent Burial.

There were not two nobler, more devoted patriots in the revolution than the two brothers, Thomas and Moses Allen. The latter was born in Northampton, Mass., Sept 14th, 1748. He received his education at Princeton College, where he graduated in 1772, and two years after was licensed to preach by the presbytery of New Brunswick. A friend and classmate of young Madison, he, soon after receiving license, made a visit to him at the house of his father, Col. Madison, where he spent several days, and by whom he was invited to preach at the Court House. His discourse delighted the people so much that he was requested to spend the winter there. In the March following he preached at Christ's Church, twenty miles from Charleston, South Carolina. Having received ordination, he remained here till 1777, when he removed to Midway, Georgia. Though surrounded by tories in his new home, some of whom formed a part of his congregation, he took open ground against the mother country. He thought it no sacrilege to preach rebellion from the pulpit, and though remonstrated with and threatened, he continued to denounce the aggressive measures of Great Britain as insulting and tyrannical, declaring they never should be submitted to, and called on his people to arm in defence of their country and its most sacred rights. During the winter and spring of 1778 the tories, aided by the Indians, became so formidable, and gathered in such threatening numbers on the southern frontier, that an expedition was fitted out against them. Gov. Houston, of Georgia, furnished three hundred and fifty militia, and led them in person. Young Allen, whose eloquent tongue had never ceased to plead with the hesitating and denounce the tories as traitors, no sooner heard the trumpet of war sound than he left his parish, and joined the Georgia brigade as chaplain.

The entire force was under the command of Gen. Robert Howe, who immediately pushed southward to St. Mary's river, and driving the affrighted tories from Fort Tonin, made preparations to move against St. Augustine, at that time in the hands of the enemy. The latter immediately began to concentrate his forces, and if Howe expected to do any thing, prompt and energetic action was necessary. But instead of this, divided councils and disputes respecting the rights of the several commands prevailed—the commander of the naval force refusing to obey a land officer, and Gov. Houston asserting the right to the control of his own troops, so that nothing at all was done. In the meantime, the troops being without tents, were compelled to encamp on the damp ground, curtained at night with the pestiferous exhalations of swamps, which soon prostrated the militia unaccustomed to such exposures, with sickness. Disheartened by this state of things, Col. Pinckney took the fragments of his command and returned by water to Charleston, while Howe, his force of eleven hundred being reduced to three hundred and fifty, marched back to Savannah.

The patriots were much disheartened by the disgraceful failure of this expedition, but young Allen, whose courage and enthusiasm nothing could shake or dampen, grew bolder as the prospects darkened, and devoted his entire energies to keep up the spirit of the inhabitants, urging them by every argument, and the most impassioned eloquence to arm in defense of the State. This was the more necessary, as the failure of this grand attempt to invade Florida had emboldened the enemy to invade in turn. Savannah was selected by them as the point of attack, and arrangements were made to have a naval force from the north enter the Savannah river and invest it on the water side, while Provost, with his heterogeneous horde of regulars, tories, and Indians from Florida, should advance against it over the country. The whole region was thrown into a state of the wildest alarm by the imposing forces that now threatened to sweep away every vestige of opposition. The tories were elated, and the hitherto timorous and wavering, were inclined to accept the terms of mercy that had been offered. It was in this crisis that the eloquent voice and fearless bearing of young Allen stayed the ebbing tide of patriotism. His presence and appeals so arrested disaffection that the tories cursed his very name. He became more obnoxious to them than the military leaders of the patriotic forces, and the most deadly threats were uttered against him.

In the meantime Provost, with his rabble hordes, was advancing in the direction of Midway. Mr. Allen's congregation was, of course, broken up, part fleeing into the surrounding country, while most of the able-bodied men rallied around their pastor, who hastened to join the patriots under General Scriven. The latter had frequent skirmishes with the enemy, in one of which the tory general, McGirth, was killed. The enemy continued to press forward, however, until they came within three miles of Ogeechee ferry. Mr. Savage, a patriotic planter, hearing of their approach, and ascertaining they were marching in the direction of the ferry, hastily called his slaves together, and repairing thither threw up a breastwork. He kept the terrified blacks steadily at their work until the sound of fife and drum in the rear announced the approach of help. Soon Colonel Elbert, with two hundred continentals, arrived and took possession of the works. The enemy coming in sight of this unexpected obstacle in their path, immediately retreated towards the Altamaha, lighting their way with burning dwellings and stacks of rice, which at that season dotted the fields. Midway, the hot bed of rebellion, and the home of Mr. Allen, was the first object of revenge. The tories told the British officer that this rebel parson did more injury to the cause of the king than a dozen colonels, and that the hornet's nest should be utterly destroyed.

To his shame, he ordered the torch to be applied, not only to his house, but also to the church where they said so much treason had been preached, and they were both burned to the ground. These outrages were not calculated to cool the pastor's patriotism, or cause him to slacken his efforts, nor did they. Between this time and December, when Savannah fell, he labored incessantly to rouse the inhabitants to defend their capital. The people of the city turned out, and seizing the spade and pickaxe toiled side by side with the soldiers and negroes in erecting defences. In the meantime, Howe, with only a little over seven hundred men, hastened thither. The militia were called upon by the governor, but they came in slowly, so that when Provost arrived before the place, the army, all told, amounted to only nine hundred men.

The British fleet at length entered the river, and Howe prepared for battle. The disposition of his forces, however, was injudicious, and the British commander by outmaneuvering him, virtually won the battle before a shot was fired. Among other errors he neglected a bye-path which led to his rear, although Walton, the commander of the Georgia brigade, pointed it out to him. Howe replied that it was of no consequence, for the British would never notice it. The result was, Sir James Baird, with a body of infantry and New York volunteers left the main body, and under the guidance of an old negro named Quomino Dolly, traversed this obscure path and fell on the rear of the army at the same time the British commander attacked in front. The Georgia militia, taken by surprise, were thrown into confusion, but their officers rallied them to meet the onset firmly. Young Allen, seeing the unsteadiness of the troops, rushed to the front of the battle and called on the men to follow him. Wherever the fire was hottest, there he hurried, unconscious of fear, and strove heroically to impart courage to others. The reckless exposure of the unarmed minister of God, again and again shamed the wavering troops back to their duty. But the flank movement had, from the outset, decided the battle, and though each man had been determined and fearless as Allen, defeat was inevitable and resistance only increased the slaughter. Walton, the commander, at length fell wounded, when all order was lost. A few escaped, but the greater part were taken prisoners, and among them Mr. Allen. The line in front now gave way, and the fight became a rout. A few escaped through the rice fields, and some by swimming a creek in the rear, but a hundred were killed or drowned, and four hundred and fifty-three taken prisoners. The enemy now occupied Savannah without further resistance. The continental officers were sent on parole to Sunbury, but the privates were placed on board prison ships in the river, and among them the chaplain. It seems hardly conceivable that an officer, commanding Christian troops, should be guilty of such an outrage upon a minister of God. One would think, if any distinction at all was made in the prisoners, it would have been in his favor, and not against him. Were the sacredness of his profession set aside altogether, it is not easy to see by what right he, an officer in the army, was denied the parole extended to all the others. It seems the more strange in this case as the British commander, Col. Campbell, had the reputation of being both humane and generous. It can be explained only on the ground that the tories represented his case as a peculiar one—that by his influence, his preaching and example he inflicted more injury on the royal cause than any other man. Besides, his bold denunciations of King George, and irreverent language used not only toward his majesty but the government, lost none of their bitterness and treasonable character in being repeated to the commander. In short, he was the head rebel of the entire region, whose bold, free tongue cut deeper than the sword. On this account the young, educated, accomplished divine was thrown into a loathsome prison-ship, and placed under the tender mercies of the brutal commander, Parker. Here, crowded between the confined decks, suffocated for want of air, and fed like brutes, the men fell sick, and the atmosphere almost unendurable before, became tainted with disease.

Young Allen, however, bore up like a Christian and a hero under the sufferings and degradation of his position. He prayed with the sick, and spoke cheering words to the desponding. Some of them were his parishioners, whose wives and families were wanderers like his own amid their desolate homes. To filth, disease, and dirty, unfit food, were added insults and profanity. Emaciated, pale and ragged, this young clergymen, the friend and class-mate of Madison, dragged out the weary weeks, with a brave, unyielding heart.

But as the warm weather of spring approached the sickness increased, and his loathsome den became intolerable. To shed additional gloom on their fate, their inhuman captors surrounded death, which otherwise would have been hailed as a happy release, with the most repulsive, horrible associations. The dead bodies of the prisoners were not allowed a resting place even beneath the waters of the Savannah, but carried like common carrion to a swamp on the shore and thrust into the mud. The brutal soldiery did not always take pains to force the corpses below the surface of the ooze, but left arms and legs and heads exposed to rot in the sun. Here the wan, ghastly face of a young man, and there the gray hairs of an aged farmer, whose only crime was defending his home from invaders, appeared on the slimy surface. The buzzards, attracted by the stench that arose from the decomposed bodies, came from the surrounding region and swept in slow, melancholy circles, above the swamp where the patriots lay, ere they descended upon their human repast.

Surrounded with such sights and sufferings, exposed to constant insults, with no prospect of release, Mr. Allen, though his spirit remained unbroken, determined to make an attempt to escape. The inhuman treatment he received, and to which there seemed no termination but death, had made him look on any fate as preferable to the one he was then enduring. He had noticed a point some distance down the river, from which, if he could reach it, he might, he thought, effect his escape, and he resolved on the first favorable occasion to make the attempt. It was true he might be detected in the act of plunging overboard and shot, but this did not deter him for a moment, for to the desire of escaping from his intolerable prison was added the anxious longing to be with his wife and infant child, now without a protector in a land overrun by malignant tories. The thought of them gave greater fixedness to his determination to remain in that living grave the scoff and by-word of the brutal soldiers no longer. Watching, therefore, a favorable opportunity, when the guard was turned away, he slipped overboard and boldly swam for the distant point. At first he struck out strong and vigorous, but he soon found that he had overrated his strength. Starvation and long confinement in the pestilential air of the prison had taken away all his powers of endurance, and his strokes gradually became slower and feebler. His fearless courage could not supply the place of strength, and he soon saw that he would never reach the shore. He struggled on, however, manfully to the last, and then, without lifting one cry for help, sunk beneath the surface. His body was thrown ashore on Tybee Island, and some of the prisoners who were his old friends and parishioners, went to Commodore Parker and asked for a few rough boards that they might make a box, at least, in which to place the remains of their pastor. But this man, who was a disgrace to his profession and to the nation whose commission he bore, returned a brutal refusal, saying that the rebel preacher deserved only a traitor's grave ; and he was thrust unceremoniously into the mud with the others. Thus at the early age of thirty died this intellectual, accomplished man, eloquent divine and earnest patriot. It is a shame to the State for whose defence he gave his life, that she has not reared a monument to his memory.

CHAPTER XXXV.

BENJAMIN POMEROY.

His Early Life.—Becomes a "New Light."—Is Persecuted by the State, and Finally Deprived of his Salary.—Becomes Chaplain in the French War.—His Letter to his Wife describing the Execution of a Criminal.—At Seventy becomes Chaplain in the Revolutionary Army.—His Venerable Appearance.—Touching Appeals.—His Death.

A FEW of the New England clergy who served as chaplains in the French war lived to act in the same capacity in the revolutionary struggle. Among these was Benjamin Pomeroy, who was born in Suffield, Connecticut, in 1704. Having graduated at Yale College in 1733, with the highest honors of his class, he devoted a short time to the study of theology, and two years after was ordained pastor of the church in Hebron, Connecticut. Having identified himself with the great religious excitement which commenced about 1740, he was called a "new light," and as such became obnoxious to the bigoted, intolerant act of 1742, passed by the State to prevent, it was said, the great disorders caused by these revivalists. Being arraigned before the Assembly, he was tried and acquitted, though he narrowly escaped personal violence at the hands of the excited crowd who had assembled to witness the trial. Two years after, he was brought again before the Assembly for having denounced its intolerant edicts, especially for saying on Fast-day that "great men had fallen in with those that were on the devil's side, and enemies to the kingdom of Christ—that they had raised such persecution in the land, that if there be a faithful minister of the Lord Jesus he must lose his estate—that if there be a faithful man in civil authority he must lose his honor and usefulness, and that there was no colony so bad as Connecticut for persecuting laws." For this bold declaration he was condemned to pay the cost of the prosecution, give bonds to the amount of fifty pounds for his peaceable behavior till the succeeding May, and then appear again before the Assembly to take up his bond. This surveillance of the State caused him much annoyance, but he retained the confidence and love of his entire parish. Subsequently he was again arraigned and suffered still severer punishment. A lecture having been advertised for him in the adjoining town of Colchester, with the consent, as he supposed, of the pastor, he went at the appointed time, to the church where it was to be delivered but found it closed against him. Finding a crowd, however, assembled to hear him, he was unwilling to disappoint them, and so adjourned to a neighboring grove, and gave his lecture. For this violation of the law he was deprived of his stated salary for a period of seven years.

On the breaking out of the French war he became a chaplain in the army. Whether the annoyance to which he was subjected by the oppressive laws of the State, or his own ardent spirit prompted him to this course, we are unable to say. We are left in equal ignorance of the incidents that marked his career during the campaigns in the wilderness. A single waif has drifted down to posterity in the shape of a letter to his wife, which gives us a glimpse of his life as chaplain.

"LAKE GEORGE, July 23, 1759.

"MY DEAR,

"Saturday last, at break of day, our troops, to the number of twelve thousand, embarked for Cabrillons, all in health and high spirits. I could wish for more dependence on God than was observable among them, yet I hope God will grant deliverance unto Israel by them. Mr. Beebe* and I, by the advice of our colonel, stay behind, but expect soon to follow. A considerable number of sick are left here in the hospitals. Five died last night. I have been well in general. Want very much to hear from you—our dear children, the people, the neighboring ministers, etc. I would mention, did time permit me to describe it, the affecting scene of last Friday morning. A poor, wretched criminal, Thomas Bailey, was executed. Mr. Brainard and myself chiefly discoursed with him, but almost all his care was to have his life prolonged—he pleaded with us to intercede with the general for him, but there was no prospect of succeeding. His crime was stealing or robbing, whereof he had frequently been guilty. Once received one hundred lashes, and once reprieved from the gallows, but being often reproved, he hardened his heart, and was suddenly destroyed. Several prayers were made at the place of

* Assistant Chaplain.

execution—the poor creature was terrified, even to amazement and distraction, at the approach of the King of Terrors. An eternity of sinful pleasures would be dear bought with the pains of the last two hours of his life. He struggled with his executioners, I believe, more than an hour ere they could put him in any proper position to receive the shot. The captain of the guard told me since, that he verily believed that the Devil helped him. I was far from thinking so, yet his resistance was very extraordinary.

"I am, with increasing love and affection, my dear, your most affectionate, loving husband.

"BENJ. POMEROY.

"MRS. ABIGAIL POMEROY, Hebron, Conn."

A man of his fearless, independent nature, and who had suffered from oppressive laws would not be likely to be a mere spectator of the struggles of the colonists against the tyrannical acts of Great Britain. Though his ardent, impetuous spirit had become somewhat tempered by age, he entered into the quarrel with all the energy and enthusiasm of youth. His impassioned eloquence and impressive appeals that were so wont to move his audience in the time of Whitfield, were now devoted to a cause equally worthy of his fervent sympathy and great powers. Preaching extempore, those addresses, which would melt his hearers to tears, have never come down to posterity. He had reached his three score and ten years, and as he stood before his audience and spoke of the coming struggle, and declared that God would make bare His right arm for the deliverance of His people, and the discomfiture of His foes, and foretold the coming glory of the nation free and independent; he seemed some ancient seer, whose aged eye pierced the clouds that wrapped the future from the gaze of ordinary mortals. When the news of the battles of Lexington and Concord reached Hebron, though he was seventy-one years of age, it stirred the sluggish blood in his aged veins so that he hastened to the army, and volunteered his services as chaplain. The venerable divine, with his thin locks white as the driven snow, was looked upon almost with veneration by the soldiers. His addresses to them were mostly earnest appeals to fight manfully the battles of freedom, assuring them that the cause was God's, and that ultimate victory was as certain as that God's promise could not be broken. It was an affecting sight to see that prophet in Israel standing on the tented field, surrounded by young soldiers, urging them as Ephraim Macbriar of old did the Covenanters, to let " every man's hand be like the hand of Sampson, and every sword like that of Gideon that turned not back from the slaughter."

He was too infirm to follow the army in its long and toilsome campaigns, and after a while returned to his people. The war passed on with its vicissitudes, but in the gloomiest hour, when hope could scarcely see a single gleam of light through the all-enclosing darkness, his faith never shook, and he spoke as confidently then, as amid the exultation of a great victory, that God would deliver His people. He lived to see his predictions verified, and sat like a patriarch of old and listened with tearful eyes and overflowing heart to the shouts of joy that rolled over the ransomed land.

He died Dec. 22nd, 1784, in the eighty-first year of his age.

CHAPTER XXXVI.

JOHN ROGERS.

His Reputation Abroad.—His Patriotism.—Introduction to Washington.—Chaplain in Heath's Brigade.—Resigns and goes to Georgia.—On his Return made Chaplain to the New York Provincial Assembly.—Becomes Member of the Legislature.—Chancellor of the Regents of the University.

As I remarked in a previous chapter the career of some of the chaplains, like that of many of the officers, was marked by striking events, while the history of others has perished with them, and their immediate descendants. There are others, also, whose patriotic, efforts and sacrifices are known only as general facts, but not sufficient details have been preserved to make an extended biography.

Of this class was John Rogers, of Boston, who was so honored even in Europe for his talents and learning, that in 1768 he received the degree of Doctor of Divinity from the University of Edinburgh. From the commencement of the revolution his whole heart was given to the cause of the colonies, and all the aid which his great abilities and exalted position enabled him to furnish was cheerfully rendered. Before hostilities had actually commenced, he, with several other clergymen, held a weekly prayer meeting in behalf of their country, and strong supplications ascended to the throne of grace that in the conflict which they clearly foresaw to be inevitable, God would give victory to the oppressed colonies. These meetings were kept up until those composing it were compelled to flee before the approaching enemy. When Washington, on the 19th of April, took possession of New York for its defense, Dr. Rogers, with several other gentlemen, called to pay him their respects. Washington received him with marked attention, and when he took his leave followed him to the door, and remarked that persons in Philadelphia had mentioned him as one who could render him important service, and asked if he would allow him to apply to him for information whenever he desired. The Doctor assured him that he would gladly do anything that lay in his power to serve him and his country. Washington *did* often consult him afterwards, and found him an ally not only devoted to his country, but gifted with rare intelligence and foresight.

In May, 1776, having been appointed chaplain in Heath's brigade, he removed his family to Greenfield, Conn., where they could be out of danger, and then returned to the army and entered on the duties of his office. In the autumn, having private business to transact in Georgia, he resigned his chaplaincy. In April, the next year, as he was returning north, he was informed that he had been elected chaplain to the New York State Convention then in session at Esopus. Paying a flying visit to his family in Greenfield he crossed over to New York State and entered on his duties, which he continued to perform till the power of the State was lodged in a council of safety, when he served as chaplain in that body. He brought his family on to Esopus, and remained there till it was burned by the British, when he removed to Sharon, Conn. He afterwards became a member of the Legislature, and served for three successive years. At the close of the war he was enabled to return to his congregation in New York city, but he found the parsonage burned to the ground and the sanctuary in ruins. The vestry of Trinity Church, with generous liberality, offered him the use of St. George and St. Paul's Churches till another place of worship could be erected, and he preached alternately in them through the winter. The subject of one of his first discourses after his return to the city was "The Divine Goodness displayed in the American Revolution," which was published. When the Legislature established the board of "Regents of the University" he was chosen Vice-Chancellor, and held that office till his death, in May, 1811, in the eighty-fourth year of his age.

CHAPTER XXXVII.

GEORGE DUFFIELD.

DESCENDED FROM THE HUGUENOTS.—STUDIES FOR THE MINISTRY.—IS SETTLED IN CARLISLE.—HIS PARISHIONERS GO ARMED TO CHURCH.—HIS PATRIOTISM.—SETTLES IN PHILADELPHIA.—KING'S MAGISTRATE ATTEMPTS TO STOP HIS PREACHING.—IS BROUGHT UP BEFORE THE MAYOR ON CHARGE OF RIOT.—EXCITEMENT OF THE PEOPLE.—HIS POPULARITY WITH MEMBERS OF CONGRESS.—STIRRING ADDRESS.—BECOMES CHAPLAIN IN THE ARMY.—PREACHES TO THE SOLDIERS FROM THE FORKS OF A TREE.—BURIES A BROTHER CHAPLAIN WHO HAS BEEN MURDERED.—NARROW ESCAPE.—EXAMPLE OF HIS FAITH.—HIS DEATH.

THE descendants of the French Huguenots that were living in America at the time of the revolution were almost without exception staunch patriots. Among these none took a firmer and nobler stand than George Duffield, of Pennsylvania. His ancestors fled from France to England to escape religious persecution, and thence to Ireland, from which country his immediate parents emigrated to America and settled in Pequea, Pennsylvania. He was born October 7th, 1732, and received his education at Princeton College. Graduating in 1752 he studied theology in his native town under Dr. Robert Smith, and was licensed to preach in 1756. He married the daughter of General Armstrong, and in 1761 was ordained and settled over the congregation at Carlisle.

At this time the Indians were numerous in the vicinity of the Church, and often assumed such a hostile attitude that the male members attended the Sabbath services fully armed. Sometimes it was necessary to go in pursuit of them to chastise them for acts of violence, and Mr. Duffield always accompanied the expeditions, sharing with his parishioners their privations and dangers.

At Monahan, one of the associate churches over which he presided, they were compelled from the exposed position of their place of worship to surround it with fortifications, and men were stationed on the ramparts during service to give notice of the approach of the savages.

In such a stern school was this ardent apostle of liberty reared. The readiness with which he shared the perils of the frontier with the inhabitants, and the dauntless courage he exhibited on all occasions of danger, made him known far and wide, and bound him to the hardy yeomanry of the country in the warmest attachment.

In the dispute that arose between the colonies and mother country, he took sides at once and fearlessly, with the former. And when an open conflict and a long and wasting war were seen to be inevitable, he preached rebellion as a duty, and declared that he had no doubt that God would carry them triumphantly through the struggle. Before his patriotic addresses and stirring eloquence, despondency gave way to hope, and the spirit of determined resistance was kindled in hearts that before thought only of submission.

At this time, he was sent in company with Rev. Charles Beatty on a missionary tour to the scattered settlements along the frontiers of Virginia, Maryland and Pennsylvania. Returning from his arduous journey, he received a call to the Third Presbyterian Church of Philadelphia. The Colonial Congress was then in session in the city, and consequently the greatest excitement prevailed among the inhabitants. He immediately took a bold stand on the side of Congress, and denounced sternly and fearlessly the encroachments of the mother country. The people flocked to hear him, and he soon became an object of dread and hate to the Tories, who sought in every way to injure him. On one occasion, the congregation of the First Presbyterian Church invited him to preach in their large place of worship on Sunday evening when the officers of the church hearing of it closed the doors, so that neither minister nor people could enter. The latter, however, determined not to be baffled, and prying open a window, lifted Mr. Duffield through it. They then unbolted the doors, and the eager crowd poured in and filled the edifice. The news soon spread that Mr. Duffield was addressing the people on the Sabbath evening. The king's magistrate being applied to, hastened thither, and forcing his way through the crowd, interrupted the speaker and began to read the riot act. A military officer among the congregation, by the name of Knox, rose and sternly ordered the magistrate to stop. The latter replied that he would not, and again commenced reading. A second time the excited officer, in a voice of thunder, bade him hold his tongue; but the magistrate paid no attention to the order, and went on with his reading. The officer was a powerful man, and seeing his orders so contemptuously disobeyed, cleared his way through the multitude, and seizing the astonished magistrate, bore him bodily along the crowded aisle, and thrusting him out of doors, bade him begone. Astounded at this summary ejection, the discomfited minion of the king took himself off, and Mr. Duffield went on with his sermon. The next day, however, he was brought before the mayor's court and required to plead to the charge of aiding and abetting a riot, and give bail for his appearance for trial. He politely, but firmly, refused to do either, asserting his rights as a minister of Christ, and denying that there was any riot whatever, except such as the king's magistrate himself had created. The mayor, a kind-hearted man, said if he took such a course, the court would be compelled to send him to prison; and urged him to get bail, saying he would take as such any of his numerous friends then in court. Mr. Duffield promptly but courteously declined. The mayor then offered to be bail himself. He thanked him for his kindness, and assured him he felt grateful for this exhibition of his good will, but declared that he considered it his sacred duty to assert the rights of a minister of Christ and a worshiping assembly that had been ruthlessly invaded by a king's magistrate. The mayor was in a quandary, for he knew that if he remanded him to prison there would be another kind of a riot—one which all the king's magistrates in the colony could not put down. He finally said he would postpone his decision for a few days, and in the meantime Mr. Duffield might return home. The news that the king's government was going to put Mr. Duffield, the patriot clergyman, in prison, spread like wild fire, creating the most intense excitement. It flew on the wings of the wind over the country, and reaching the region where he had formerly lived, the volunteer forces there called the "Paxton Boys," though a hundred miles distant, met and passed a resolution, that if the king's government dared to imprison Mr. Duffield, they would march arms in hand to Philadelphia and liberate him at the point of the bayonet. The worthy mayor, however, seeing the serious course things were taking, never called him into court to receive judgment, and the affair was hushed up.

The patriots of the first Congress flocked to his church, and John Adams and his compeers were often his hearers, for he preached as Jonas Clarke had before preached at Lexington.

In a discourse delivered before several companies of Pennsylvania militia and members of Congress, four months before the Declaration of Independence, he took bold and decided ground in favor of that step, and plead his cause with sublime eloquence, which afterwards made him so obnoxious to the British that they offered a reward of fifty pounds for his capture. He declared that Heaven designed this western world as the asylum for liberty, and that to raise its banner here their forefathers had sundered the dearest ties of home, friends and native land, and braved the tempests of the ocean and the terrors of the wilderness. Not through the fostering care of Britain, he said, had they grown and flourished, but her "tyranny and oppression, both civil and ecclesiastical," had driven noble souls hither "to enjoy in peace the fair possessions of freedom." " 'Tis this," he exclaimed, "has reared our cities, and turned the wilderness, so far and wide, into a fruitful field. And can it be supposed that the Lord has so far forgotten to be gracious, and shut up His tender mercies in His wrath, and so favored the arms of oppression, as to deliver up their asylum to slavery and bondage? Can it be supposed that *that* God who made man free, and engraved in indefaceable characters the love of liberty in his mind, should forbid freedom already exiled from Asia and Africa, and under sentence of banishment from Europe—that He should *forbid* her to erect her banners *here*, and constrain her to abandon the earth? As soon shall He subvert creation, and forbid the sun to shine. He preserved to the Jews their cities of refuge, and whilst *sun and moon endure America shall remain a city of refuge for the whole earth*, until she herself shall play the tyrant, forget her destiny, disgrace her freedom, and provoke her God. When that day shall—if ever come—then, and not till then, shall she also fall, *slain with them that go down to the pit.*" In such strains of impassioned eloquence did he sustain his high argument for liberty, and pour his own brave, glowing soul into his excited listeners, till they were ready, when he ceased, to shout, "*To arms! to arms!*" So great was his zeal in the cause of the Colonies, and so wide was his influence known to be, that his services in the army were sought for at the earliest moment, and four days after the Declaration of Independence he received his commission as chaplain in the Pennsylvania militia. Although he had great influence with members of

Congress, he was needed especially among the troops. This, too, was the place for him, for his heart was with those struggling on the battle field more than with those debating in Congress. Whenever any perilous undertaking was attempted, he could not remain behind. Accustomed to the habits and peculiarities, as well as the privations of a camp life, he wielded great influence over the soldiers. He could infuse courage in the hour of danger, and cheer the disheartened in disaster, by example, precept and prayer. Bold and confident himself, he inspired confidence in others. He was well known in camp, and his visits were always welcome, for the soldiers loved the eloquent, earnest, fearless patriot.

When the enemy occupied Staten Island, and the American forces were across the river on the Jersey shore, he repaired to camp to spend the Sabbath. Assembling a portion of the troops in an orchard, he climbed into the forks of a tree and commenced religious exercises. He gave out a hymn, and as the soldiers, like the troops of Cromwell at the battle of Dunbar, "uplift it to the tune of Bangor or some still higher score, and rolled it strong and great against the sky," the British on the Island heard the sound of the singing, and immediately directed some cannon to play on the orchard from whence it proceeded. Soon the heavy shot came crashing through the branches, or went singing overhead, arresting for a moment the voices that were lifted in worship. Mr. Duffield, to avoid the danger and escape such rude interruption, proposed they should adjourn behind an adjacent hillock. They did so, and continued their worship while the iron storm hurtled harmlessly overhead. The deep thunder of the heavy cannon, shaking the ground on which they stood, and the hissing shot filling the air with their mysterious sounds, were not calculated to lessen the eloquent patriot's fervor, or quench the glowing zeal that inspired him. It was a strange, solemn scene, yet, withal picturesque, which that group of soldiers presented—listening with upturned faces to the man of God as he urged them to fight manfully the battles of the Lord, while the deep voiced cannon uttered between each sentence their angry notes of defiance.

When the army, reduced to a handful, fled through New Jersey, and night starless and rayless, and to human seeming, endless, lay on the land, his great sympathizing heart would not let him stay at home, and he kept with it, sharing its hardships and exposures, and striving in every way to encourage the hearts of the soldiers. In this disastrous retreat he had a forewarning of his own fate should he, by the chances of war, fall into the hands of the British. In a skirmish, near Trenton, John Rossburgh, a brother chaplain, lost his horse and was taken prisoner. Seeing his prayer for life refused, he knelt down and committed his soul in prayer to his Maker—and while in this attitude was thrust through with the bayonet, and left weltering in his blood. Mr. Duffield found the body hurriedly buried by the neglected way-side, and had it removed to a neighboring grave-yard and decently interred. A similar fate would be his own should he be taken, for the British knew that every such rebel parson was more dangerous to the cause of the King than a whole regiment of militia.

A short time after, he had a narrow escape from it. Washington, continuing his retreat, abandoned Princeton and Trenton—destroying the bridges over the stream near the latter place to delay the enemy's pursuit. Mr. Duffield, worn out with fatigue, and not being apprised of this movement, had retired to a private house near by to snatch a moment's repose. In the meantime, the bridges were being rapidly destroyed. A Quaker, who knew him, for he had once befriended him when in danger from his principles, seeing what was going on, endeavored to seek him out and warn him of his danger. He had by some means ascertained that he was not with the army already on the farther side of the river, and hence knew he must be somewhere in the place. Alarmed at the imminent danger to his benefactor—for he was aware that the British had set a price on his head—he hastened hither and thither, and at last found him quietly taking his repose, wholly unconscious of the departure of the army. Informing him, in a hurried manner, of the position of things, he told him that in a few minutes his escape would be hopelessly cut off. Warmly thanking the Quaker for the timely information he had taken such trouble to give him, he hastened to the door, and mounting his horse, dashed away on a gallop for the nearest bridge and overtook the rear just as they had crossed, and were making preparations to destroy it.

Many incidents and details of this part of his life are lost forever, while others are but indistinctly and partially remembered, serving only to make us regret that a complete account of his career as one of the chaplains and patriotic clergy of the Revolution can not be given. His zeal for his country, however, never abated, and his patriotic efforts never ceased till peace and liberty blessed the land. He was a man of great humor and exuberant spirits, yet withal deeply religious in his feelings, and possessing an unwavering trust in the promises of God. Whether it was his suffering country or his suffering family that weighed on his heart, he turned with an undoubting faith to his Heavenly Father, feeling that He would send help in His own good time. He did not escape the privations which all more or less suffered, and often his family were left without any apparent means of subsistence. On one occasion his son came to him on Saturday night and said they were nearly out of provisions, and unless some could be purchased early Monday morning they would be entirely destitute. But he had not a cent in his pocket, and knew not where to apply for aid, for all around him were as destitute as himself. Instead, however, of allowing his mind to be distressed at the prospect before him, and diverted from the duties of the Sabbath, he dismissed the subject, saying, "*My son, the Lord will provide.*" During the day a sealed letter was put in his hands, which, in accordance with a rule he invariably practised, he did not open till Monday morning. On opening it the next day he found it to contain a sum of money sufficient to relieve all his present necessities. He never knew who sent it.

The same grand, unwavering faith that God would finally make us victorious in our efforts to be free, never forsook him through all the vicissitudes of the long and eventful struggle of the revolution.

Faith is never allowed a place in the philosophy of history, when events are being traced to their causes or probable results, though from creation till now it has proved stronger than all physical force. But that it had something to do with the success of our Revolution, none but a disbeliever in the Christian religion can doubt.

With the return of peace, Mr. Duffield was again quietly settled over his congregation in Philadelphia, where he remained till his death, in February, 1790, in the fifty-eighth year of his age.

CHAPTER XXXVIII.

DAVID SANDFORD.

His Patriotism.—His Personal Appearance.—His Eloquence.—Gives his Salary to the Cause of Liberty.—Becomes Chaplain.—Expressive Countenance.—Anecdote Illustrating It.—Stern Rebukes.—His Piety.—His Death.

David Sandford was born in New Milford, Connecticut, December 11, 1737. He graduated at Yale College in 1755, and after finishing his theological education was licensed to preach, and settled in Medway, Massachusetts. Previous to the commencement of hostilities he was an earnest advocate of the cause of the Colonies, and when war actually began he launched at once and with all his heart into the struggle. Mingling with the assemblies of the people, he took a leading part in every measure adopted for a vigorous defence against the encroachments of Great Britain.

With a form almost perfect in its symmetry and majestic bearing, and a countenance of rare beauty and power of expression, his presence always arrested the attention of the beholder. But when the full, rich tones of his voice fell on the ear—now ringing, clear, like the call of a bugle, and now melting into the sweetest and most plaintive accents, his hearers were held as by fascination.

Impassioned, fearless, and knowing well how to use

the rare gifts with which nature had endowed him, he mastered all who came under the spell of his eloquence. His high courage and strong will made him restive under temporizing, timorous counsels, and when he arose to denounce them, his face was like a thunder cloud charged with wrath, and his powerful voice broke in startling accents on the audience. With such a man in every parish in the land, not a tory would have been found bold enough to have lifted his head in opposition. Patriotism became a passion with him, and when he called on his people to bear without murmuring their proportion of the expenses of the war, he showed them an example of self-sacrifice by throwing in his entire salary to swell the public treasury. But even this did not content him. Not only did he devote his rare eloquence and yearly stipend to the common cause, but as the sound of war rolled over the land, hastened to the army and volunteered his services as a chaplain. He gave all he had to the service of his country, and no doubt if he had not been restrained by his profession would have been one of the most daring officers in the army. Indeed, nature had endowed him with rare gifts for a military leader. His commanding personal appearance, his impulsive, fearless spirit, and that power of expression in mere look, which will carry men farther than words, eminently fitted him to be one. This power of the countenance can never be described any more than it can be resisted. Washington had it.

As an illustration of it in Mr. Sandford, he was once preaching to the troops in a somewhat dilapidated church, when a board, which had been placed in one of the shattered windows, blew down. The soldiers in putting it back made so much noise that he was compelled to stop in his sermon. The board again being blown in, the soldiers, the second time, replaced it, arresting the services by the confusion they made. The third time it fell in, and the soldiers rushing to put it back, he thundered out *"let that board alone."* One look at the pulpit and they slunk back to their places. After the services were over a citizen asked the commanding officer how he liked the eloquent preacher. He replied, "Very well, but I should have liked him better if he had'nt sworn so." "Sworn, Captain," exclaimed the man, "I did'nt hear any oath." "Yes, he did," replied the former, "he said (repeating a fearful oath) *let that board alone.*" "You certainly are mistaken, he uttered no oath whatever." "Well," replied the Captain, "if he did not say those very words he *looked* them." This became a bye-word, and in after years whenever his brother ministers saw the frown of displeasure darkening his open, manly brow, they would say good-naturedly, "*don't swear so.*" His features had the same power to express the softer emotions, and when moved with pity, or pleading with sinners, would melt the most stubborn heart. The soldiers not only reverenced him for his devoted piety, and loved him for his lofty patriotism, but they admired him for his personal presence. Not an officer in the brigade rode his horse with such incomparable grace and ease as he. His known inflexibility of purpose, abrupt and often stern manner, also pleased them. These traits sometimes caused him to be charged with want of courtesy. Once a clownish, shabbily dressed licentiate asked him what system of divinity he would recommend him to study, he replied, with his stern expression of countenance, "Lord Chesterfield to *you*." So on another occasion, a young preacher telling him that he had refused a call to a certain place on account of an extensive pine swamp in the vicinity, he turned upon him, "*Young man, it is none of your business where God has put his pine swamps.*" Notwithstanding these peculiarities he was a devoted minister, and one who knew him well says, "His name was associated with early attempts to propagate the gospel in the new settlements, and every fresh effort that was put forth for the promotion of Christianity, no matter on which side of the water, met with his cordial and grateful approval.

As a counsellor he was sought after by the churches, and was not unfrequently called away a great distance to aid in healing ecclesiastical divisions. In 1807 he was struck with paralysis, from which he never recovered, and after languishing three years, a suffering invalid, he died, being in the seventy-fourth year of his age.

CHAPTER XXXIX.

NATHAN KER.

His Birth and Ancestry.—Anecdote of his Grandfather.—His Patriotism.—Abjures all Allegiance to Great Britain.—Tories and Indians.—Massacre at Minisink.—Slaughter of Mr. Ker's Congregation.—Anecdote of Him and Lafayette.—A Friend of Washington.—Loans the Government Eight Thousand Dollars, for which He received Nothing but "Old Liberty."—Celebration at the Close of the War.

Nathan Ker, of Goshen, Orange County, hardly comes under the head of chaplains, because he received no special commission in the army, yet he had a general permit to pass through the forces and fortresses scattered over West Point, Fishkill and Newburgh, as a minister to exercise his functions as he saw proper.

He was born in Freehold, New Jersey, September 7th, 1736, and embraced religion under the preaching of the celebrated William Tennent. Devoting himself at once to the gospel ministry, he entered Princeton College, and completing his education was licensed in 1763. For some years he labored as an itinerant, the field of his duties extending over a thousand miles along the continent. Subsequently he settled in Goshen, where he remained till his death in 1804. He took decided ground against the mother country in her unjust demands on the Colonies, and when hostilities commenced, and American blood was shed, he called together his entire family, and making it an act of religious worship, solemnly abjured all allegiance to the British king and government, and took an oath before God to stand firm and true to his country. Tall and commanding in person, he bore so strong a resemblance to Washington that he was often called "the General." Of a firm and fearless spirit, he exerted the wide influence he wielded, zealously and successfully for the cause of liberty. He came honestly by his love of freedom and unyielding opposition to tyranny, for his grandfather before him suffered persecutions in Scotland for exhibiting the same noble spirit. The latter being asked one day (when such a question tested to the utmost the courage of a man), "Who was the head of the Church?" fearlessly replied, "The Lord Jesus Christ." That same night he received warning that he had better leave the kingdom. He immediately fled to the mountains and hid himself in caves. But hunted from one place of concealment to another like a beast of prey, he finally made his escape to America. It was but natural that the descendant of such a sire should be a bold and uncompromising advocate of both civil and religious liberty.

The whole region around Goshen was for a long time subject to the ravages of the Indians and Tories, and Count Pulaski was stationed at Minisink, near by, with a body of cavalry to protect it. When, in February, 1779, this gallant officer was ordered to South Carolina to aid General Lincoln, the Indians and Tories once more took the field; and in the following July made a descent upon the town, killing and scattering the inhabitants, and burning their dwellings. When the news reached Goshen, Dr. Tusten, colonel of the militia, ordered his troops to meet him at Minisink, the next day, with as many volunteers as would join him. The congregation of such a fearless patriot as Mr. Ker would not hesitate in a crisis so alarming, and a hundred and forty-nine were at the rendezvous the next morning. The flower of his flock were all there. After a short consultation, the intrepid little band started in pursuit of the Indians and were joined on the way by a small force from Warwick, which swelled their number to a hundred and sixty or seventy men.

Ascertaining from some of the inhabitants who had escaped the massacre, that the marauding party was too large for the small, undisciplined force under him, Colonel Tusten advised to give over the pursuit, but Major Meeker mounting his horse, and waving his sword and shouting, "Let the brave men follow me, the cowards may stay behind," swept away all caution and prudence, and amid shouts of excitement they streamed forward on the trail of the savages.

Continuing their march all night they came, at sunrise, upon the smouldering camp-fires of the Indians, which the latter had apparently but just left. The number of these, showing clearly how large the force was, again brought the officers to a stand, and a council was called to decide whether to continue or abandon the pursuit. The majority were in favor of the latter course, but the minority scoffing at the decision as cowardly, the majority yielded, and the march was resumed. Brandt, who commanded the tories and

Indians, being made aware by his scouts of the number and movements of the Americans, resolved at once on their destruction. At nine in the morning, the latter having ascended a high hill overlooking the Delaware, saw the enemy below them making toward a ford of the river. They immediately determined to intercept them there, and made their dispositions accordingly. But the moment they descended the heights, and some intervening hills shut them from sight, Brandt wheeled his column, and plunging into a deep, narrow ravine, marched rapidly back until he got in their rear, and then burst with his fearful war-cry upon them. The Americans, though taken completely by surprise, met the onset of the savages firmly, but, overwhelmed by numbers, were gradually borne back until they occupied scarce an acre of ground on the top of a rocky hill. Here, in a hollow square, they withstood their assailants hour after hour, until the hot July sun stooped behind the western wilderness. Darkness was now coming on, and their ammunition began to give out. No longer able to keep at bay their savage assailants, their firm formation was broken, and the battle became a massacre. The night was made hideous with frantic yells, while the gleaming tomahawk descended on the strong and helpless alike. Of all that gallant little band, only thirty remained to tell the story of how they fought, and how they fell. Mr. Ker's congregation the next Sabbath was clad in mourning, for most of the young men that composed it had been slain, while thirty-three widows present, told how fearful the blow had fallen on heads of fam-

ANECDOTE OF LAFAYETTE.

ilies. He himself repaired to the bloody field, and spent the whole night with one of his aged parishioners searching for the dead body of his son.

The remembrance of this massacre made the troops of Sullivan look with grim exultation afterwards on the burning paradise of the Senecas and Cayugas, to which they had applied the avenging torch.

A curious anecdote of Lafayette, in connection with Mr. Ker, has been related to me by one of the descendants of the latter. While Washington lay at Brandywine he had occasion to despatch Lafayette with orders to a portion of the army in New York State. The latter stopped on his way at an inn in Sussex Co., N. J., where he was compelled to sleep in the same room with another traveler. When he awoke in the morning he found his fellow lodger gone, and on dressing himself discovered that some valuable jewels and a miniature had been abstracted from his pockets. Being entrusted with important despatches, he could not stop to take any measures for the recovery of his property, and hastened on his way. He made efforts, however, at every place through which he passed, to obtain tidings of the robber. Reaching Goshen, he endeavored to make the landlord of the tavern where he halted, acquainted with his troubles, but being unable to speak English was wholly unsuccessful. The only sentence he could utter so as to be understood was, "De picture of de lady," "De picture of de lady," and 'De picture of the lady' was constantly on his tongue, accompanied with many anxious gestures. No one in the place understanding French the rest of his language could not be made out. They saw he was an officer of rank, and hence were exceedingly anxious to understand his wants, and as a last resort took him to their pastor, thinking that he might be able to comprehend him. Mr. Ker did not understand French, but inferring from the appearance of the stranger that he was an educated man, addressed him in Latin. The countenance of the latter brightened at once, for he had at last found a medium through which he could make his troubles and wishes known. Mr. Ker soon understood the whole case, and drawing from him an accurate description of his fellow lodger, he sat down and wrote several placards, describing the man and stating the robbery. These he told the stranger to distribute freely on his route. The latter thanked him profusely, and taking his departure, mounted his horse and hastened forward. A fortnight after, Mr. Ker was surprised by a second visit from the stranger, who, after warmly thanking him for his kindness, stated that through it he had been able to secure the robber and recover his property. He then, to the astonishment of the clergyman, introduced himself as Lafayette, and added, that the miniature, the loss of which affected him more than that of his jewels, was a portrait of his wife.

Mr. Ker's second daughter married the son of the hero patriot and martyr, Rev. John Caldwell, whom Lafayette took to his home at La Grange, and educated as a son of his own.

During the latter part of the war, Lafayette, Rochambeau, and Count de Grasse were accustomed to visit the patriotic divine as personal friends. Washington, also, was warmly attached to him, and when at West Point and Newburgh frequently invited him to dinner at head-quarters.

Out of his moderate fortune, this good man loaned the government eight thousand dollars, for which he received nothing in return except an old blind horse, which he caused to be tenderly cared for, and which, as a memento of the past, was christened " Old Liberty."

When the war was over he had a celebration on the 4th of July in his parish, at which thirteen young ladies dressed in white, with green sashes, and crowned with laurel wreaths, appeared, representing the thirteen States. As the venerable man looked over the crowded seats, radiant with joyful faces, his heart overflowed with devout thankfulness and he recounted the past, and told how the Lord had led His people, as He did Israel of old, to the promised land, till the tears of his audience were mingled with his own.

CHAPTER XL.

JOHN HURST.

His Patriotism.—Sermon to the Soldiers.

John Hurst was chaplain to the 4th, 5th and 6th battalions of Virginia troops that served in New Jersey in 1777. He was a fearless man and an ardent patriot, while no one more faithfully discharged his ministerial duties than he. No incidents of his life have come to my knowledge that require a particular notice. The character of the man, however, and the manner in which he performed the duties of chaplain, may be gathered from the following extracts from a sermon preached by him to the Virginia battalions, April 20th, 1777. The sermon is dedicated to General Stephens—the dedicatory note closing with the following. pithy sentence: " For after all the definitions of patriotism that ever was or ever will be given, this is the quintessence of it, *the opposing ourselves foremost in the field of battle against the enemies of our country.*" He took for his text, Psalm cxxxvii. 5, 6 : " If I forget thee, oh Jerusalem, let my right hand forget her cunning. If I do not remember thee, let my tongue cleave to the roof of my mouth ; if I prefer not Jerusalem above my chief joy."

" Reflections upon past enjoyments tend only to the

aggravation of present sufferings, and yet I know not how—the mind of man is ever fondly disposed to draw the painful parallel betwixt the happiness he once possessed and the misery he now feels. This was true of the captive Israelites, as is pathetically described in the Psalm before us. 'By the rivers of Babylon there we sat down, yea, we wept when we remembered Zion. We hanged our harps upon the willows in the midst thereof.' As the soul in affliction is ever apt to dwell upon any circumstance which heightens the sorrow, he here represents the harp, that sacred instrument devoted to his God, now laid aside, silent and neglected, for how indeed could he 'sing the Lord's song in a strange land.' Oppression and servitude throw a damp upon every noble faculty, no wonder, then, the sacred musician could ill exert the heavenly harmony under the dispiriting pressure of a foreign tyranny. 'How shall we sing the Lord's song,' &c. Here the faithful patriot turns by a very natural transition from lamenting over his country's fate to the strongest professions of preserving his affections forever inviolate towards her. 'If I forget her, may my right hand forget her cunning. If I do not remember thee, let my tongue cleave to the roof of my mouth; if I prefer not Jerusalem above my chief joy.'"

Starting from this point he discourses eloquently of the love of country as acknowledged and honored in all past times among the Romans, and the obligations each one is under to act for his country, and of the motives that prompt him to it, and then says: "Let us change the scene and take a cursory view of our own case. Thanks and praise be to the Lord God of armies, it is our felicity not to be members of such a society, not to be in so abject and humiliating a state as those Roman colonies were. We have never yet been conquered—we never yet tamely received laws from a tyrant, nor never will while the cause of religion, the cause of nature and of nature's God cry aloud, or even whisper resistance to an oppressor's execrated power. The gloomy cloud that has long been gathering and hovering over Jerusalem is indeed still formidable, and demands our utmost exertions to effect its dispersion, and this great and wished-for good is, in all human probability, the most likely to be accomplished by firmness, unanimity, perseverance and a fixed determination, strenuously to execute and defend what our Continental Congress, provincial assemblies and commanding officers, and so forth, shall wisely and prudently resolve.

> " 'Let fools for modes of government contest,
> That which is best administered is best.' "

He then describes the kind of liberty for which they are contending. "It is not," he says, "licentiousness, nor a war of conquest," but a struggle for "their rights, the very liberty England always contended for, and which has made her glorious."

His sermons were always well adapted to inspire the soldiers who listened to them with the deepest attention. A good man, and an earnest patriot, he, with the thousand other clergymen of the land, presented a noble front in the cause of freedom, and helped to swell the lofty enthusiasm that seven long years of toil and suffering could not quench.

CHAPTER XLI.

WILLIAM McKAY TENNENT.

UNCERTAINTY AS TO HIS IDENTITY WITH THE SUBJECT OF THE FOLLOWING SKETCH.—PATRIOTIC SERMON DELIVERED BEFORE THE TROOPS AT TICONDEROGA.—HIS CAREER AFTER THE WAR.—HIS DEATH.

THERE were several Tennents who were clergymen at the time of the Revolutionary war, and who took an active part in the struggle of the Colonies. One was a chaplain in the army at Ticonderoga, and though I can not positively ascertain *which*, circumstances all seem to point to William McKay Tennent, who was born in 1741. He graduated at the college of New Jersey in 1763, and was ordained to preach in 1772. He married the daughter of Dr. Rodgers, of New York, a distinguished patriot, and a chaplain in the army, and was settled in Greenfield, Connecticut. He was a man of polished manners, and distinguished for his amiability of temper and generous hospitality. Nothing is known of his career as chaplain except the following sermon :

"Delivered at the head of Cols. Mott's and Swift's regiments when under arms, expecting the approach of the enemy hourly, at Mount Independence, Sunday, October 20th, 1776.

"Be not ye afraid of them : remember the Lord, which is great and terrible, and fight for your brethren, your sons, and your daughters, your wives, and your houses." Nehemiah, iv. 14.

"No exultation can be more applicable and pertinent for us, my dear countrymen and fellow-soldiers, at this time, and under our circumstances, than this which was delivered by good Nehemiah to the Jews, when their proud, their haughty, and oppressive enemies were coming upon them for their destruction.

"When danger approaches it is natural for man to be afraid, and our fears generally increase in proportion to our dangers, and sometimes by indulging the former we are rendered incapable of escaping the evil which impends. It is, therefore, necessary to keep a guard upon this passion lest, in its excess, it should prove ruinous. This is necessary in an especial manner for the soldier. 'Be not ye afraid of them' is the voice of Heaven, the voice of your bleeding country, the voice of the Church, and the voice of all who are dear to you—with respect to the approaching foe. The hour is expected when, with the blessing of Heaven, you will have it in your power to do the most signal, important, and lasting services to your native land. She asks, she entreats, she calls with a solemn, but pathetic tone—yea, she demands your service, your most vigorous exertions to save her from ruin. Let her not be disappointed, but, as she has honored you with martial attire for her defense, do her honor, do yourselves honor by using the weapons of your warfare with that heroism, firmness, and magnanimity which the cause requires. When our enemy approaches, be ye not afraid of him; let not your spirits sink, but rather rejoice that you have an opportunity to contribute your whole might for the deliverance of your country from the disturbers of the common peace, and robbers of the rights of mankind. I mean not that you should entertain a contemptible idea of the strength of your enemy. They will no doubt come strong prepared to the battle, and will fight valiantly. But they fight in an unrighteous cause—they are armed to deprive us of our liberty and property, they are armed to ruin our families, to murder both them and us, or to reduce us to the most abject slavery. And will not you, gentlemen, under these circumstances, fight valiantly, too. Shall your courage be less than theirs when all is at stake. Consider they are made of the same materials with yourselves. Though transported from foreign climes, they are flesh and blood. They are but men, subject to the like hopes and fears with yourselves, and a ball well directed will humble them as quick as any, even the feeblest of you. Be not ye, therefore, afraid of them, for they are not invincible. Be not afraid of them, because they are engaged in a wicked and unrighteous cause, which the righteous Lord abhorreth. Be not afraid of them though their numbers should be superior to yours, because you are possessed of advantages which they have not—you have the ground, and all the works you have made on it. Be not afraid of them, because the want of courage will prove your ruin. There is nothing but victory, or an honourable death before you. There is no retreat for you, and if you are taken prisoners, no doubt you will soon be discharged as our friends who were lately captured were, with their baggage and a few days' provision, but with this additional and horrid circumstance, that before you are two miles from this encampment you will be overtaken in your disarmed condition by savages, Canadians, and Hessians, who will at once plunder you, and sacrifice your lives with a barbarity which can not be described. Gen. Carleton's late conduct was only designed to deceive—his clemency is to be dreaded. Expect not mercy from an enemy, who is fighting in support of tyranny; it can not, it will not be shown any longer than it is for his interest. The scheme of this cunning man is evidently this—he supposed that you would conclude from what was past, that if you were compelled to a hot engagement, you would rather submit, expecting the same lenity which your captive friends have had, than fight as the sons of freedom ought to fight. Let the fox be catched in his own trap. Believe him to be your bitter enemy, and according to Scripture language, reward your enemies, and your country's enemies even as they have rewarded you, and render double to them. Be not afraid of them: remember the Lord, which is great and terrible. Call to remembrance His Almighty name. Let the strength of Israel be your trust. Implore His aid and assistance. Under His banner go forth to battle. In His name and strength meet the approaching foe, determined to conquer or gloriously die. Remember His name, which is great and terrible—sufficiently great and terrible to vanquish your enemies, and cause them to flee before you: and fight for your brethren, your sons, and your daughters, your wives, and your homes. Do the work of the Lord faithfully. Play the men for your kindred and your estates, which are in jeopardy. So shall those of you who fall in battle be immortalized for your valor : your names shall be had in grateful remembrance by America's latest posterity ; and those of you, whose lives shall be spared in the bloody conflict, shall return with great joy to your friends, and be received with the high honor of conquerors and deliverers of this oppressed land. Your officers, I doubt not, will set you an example, and I hope you will all be engaged to support the honor of New England, and of the State, in a particular manner, which has employed you. Your wives and children, your aged parents, your brethren and sisters, look to you, under God, for salvation. The peace of all our frontier inhabitants depends upon your success. You have the prayers of thousands for victory, and be assured, if you are victorious, the enemy will from henceforward cease to expect a submission from these United States. If you are victorious, the virgins of our land, and all your dear connexions will hail you welcome upon your return with high applause and great joy, yea, Zion herself will be glad. May the Lord inspire you all with that magnanimity which makes the great and successful soldier. May He cover your heads in the day of battle, and crown our arms with victory, and the glory shall be given to Father, the Son, and Holy Ghost, world without end. Amen."

Such sermons, on the verge of an expected battle, had a powerful effect on the soldiers.

At the close of the war Mr. Tennent removed to Abingdon, near Philadelphia. He afterward became trustee of Princeton College, and in 1794 received the degree of Doctor of Divinity from Yale College. He died in 1810, after a protracted illness, which he bore, without murmuring, to its close.

CHAPTER XLII.

MR. BOARDMAN.

Chaplain to Durkee's Regiment.—His Diary.

A STRONG doubt exists as to the proper name to be placed at the head of this sketch. My utmost efforts have failed to discover who was the "chaplain of Durkee's regiment," from whose diary the following extract is taken. I have been able to learn only that his name was probably Boardman.

"Powle's Hook, Sept. 15th, 1776. After Long Island was evacuated, it was judged impossible to hold the city of New York, and for several days the artillery and stores of every kind had been removing, and last night the sick were ordered to Newark, in the Jerseys, but most of them could be got no farther than this place and Hoebuck, and as there is but one house at each of these places, many were obliged to lie in the open air till this morning, whose distress, when I walked out at daybreak, gave me a livelier idea of the horrors of war than any thing I ever met with before. The commandant ordered them every thing for their comfort that the place afforded, and immediately forwarded them to the place appointed and prepared for them.

"About eight this morning three large ships came

to sail and made up towards the Hook. The garrison, consisting of the 20th Continental regiment (Col. Durkee's), and a regiment of Jersey militia (Col. Duyckinck's), were ordered into our works. Soon after they had taken their posts, the ships came up near Jersey shore to avoid our shot from the grand battery (the removal of the cannon from which they were ignorant of), and as they passed up the North River kept up an incessant fire upon us, their shot (a great part of which was grape) raked the whole Hook, but providentially one horse was all the loss we sustained by it. The fire was briskly returned from our battery by Capt. Dana, who commanded a company of the train on this station. It gave me great pleasure to see the spirit of the troops around me, who were evidently animated by the whistling of the enemy's shot, which often struck so near them as to cover them with dust.

"About eleven o'clock a furious cannonade was heard a little above New York, and before night numbers came over from the city and informed us that it was evacuated by our troops, and about sunset we saw the tyrant's flag floating on Fort George.* Having received intelligence that a number of our troops were in the city, and the enemy spread across the island above, two small parties were ordered to assist them in making their escape. Two captains, with about forty men, two brass howitzers, and about two tons of military stores, were brought off by one

* On the Battery.

of them; the other party, consisting of five men only, were fired upon by the enemy (supposed to be Tories, who have committed a number of robberies on the friends of America), when one Jesse Squire, of Norwich, was wounded, who, together with another, fell into their hands.

"16th. About two o'clock this morning an attempt was made to burn the ships that passed up the North River yesterday, and anchored about three miles above us, one of them (the Renown, of fifty guns) was grappled, but broke her grappling, and came down by us again. Another cannonade ensued, but no damage was received on our side. The brave Col. Duyckinck, who did all he could to retain his men, could now keep his regiment no longer, but was obliged to retreat to Bergen, from which time Col. Durkee was left on the Hook with only a part of his regiment, consisting of about three hundred effective men.

"17th. An express arrived with information that Col. Williams, from Connecticut, was ordered to reinforce us, and might be expected next day, but was not able to join us till our retreat to Bergen. This day a quantity of lead, musket ball and buck shot was discovered in a suspected house about a mile and a half above us, and brought down to this place and properly secured for the United States. Towards night the Renown returned back to her station up the North River, but kept near the eastern shore to avoid the shot from our battery, which, however, kept up a brisk fire upon her as long as she was within reach.

"18th. Nothing material happened here—just at

evening intelligence was received that the brave Lieutenant Col. Knowlton, of our regiment, was killed in the action that happened a little below Kingsbridge, on Monday, as he was fighting, with undaunted courage, at the head of a body of rangers, the command of which was assigned him. The joy of the success that action would have occasioned was greatly lessened in this department by the loss of an officer so greatly respected and beloved.

"20th. The Renown returned back again to the fleet, and though she passed close in with the New York shore, yet, as there was very little wind, about forty shot from our battery were fired at her, many of which took effect. She lay all next day upon a careen to repair.

"21st. At two we were waked up by the guards, who informed us that New York was on fire. As the fire began at the south-east end of the city, a little east of the grand battery, it was spread by a strong south wind, first on the East River, and then northward, across the Broadway opposite to the old English church (if I mistake not the name), from thence it consumed all before it between Broadway and the North River, near to the college, laying about one third part of the city in ashes (in the opinion of those best acquainted with it), and had not the wind, as it veered to the west died away, the remainder of that nest of vipers would have been destroyed.

" This evening a seaman, who said he belonged to Providence, and that he was taken and was obliged to fight against his countrymen on board the Roebuck, made his escape by swimming from New York to this place. He informed, that the men on board the Roebuck were very sickly; that they had lost one hundred since they left the capes of Virginia. He also gave notice that preparations had been made to attack this post; that a large body of troops in boats (which we discovered on the opposite shore above us this afternoon) were to make a descent above us, and endeavor to cut off our retreat; that it was to have been executed this morning, but the fire prevented.

"22nd. As no reinforcements could be sent us, we received orders this morning to remove our artillery, stores, and baggage, and hold ourselves in readiness to retreat; before night most of them were removed.

"About nine A. M., we saw the enemy embarking in flat bottomed boats about two miles above us, who appeared in large numbers on the shore after they (about forty) were full. Four ships at the same time came to sail below and stood up towards us, but they soon came to anchor again, and the boats which had pushed off, returned back. Had they come at this time we might either have retired and left them large quantities of artillery and stores, or fought their army and navy at the same time with our small detachment, and that under every disadvantage—but they saw fit to retire to get more strength, as appeared afterwards, though they could not be ignorant of our weakness, as our men were paraded every day in full view of them.

"23rd. At one o'clock, P. M. having removed every thing of value, we were ordered to retreat from the

Hook. As soon as we began our march, four ships came up and anchored near the shore around the Hook. At the same time a number of boats and floating batteries came down from just above New York—the latter run up into the cove opposite the causeway that leads to Bergen. After taking considerable time to see that there was nobody to hurt them, they began a most furious cannonade on our empty works, which continued till they had wearied themselves. In a word, they dared to come much nearer, and displayed the boasted British valor in much brighter colors than ever they had while there remained a single man to oppose them. Meanwhile, our little battalion retreated with drums beating, and colors flying to Bergen, and before night the brave Britons ventured on shore and took possession of our evacuated works, where they have taken every precaution to prevent our formidable detachment from returning, and driving them from a post, which, with so great a display of heroism, they have got possession of.

"The post we now possess covers the Jerseys. Here we are reinforced by a number of regiments—more are daily coming in—the sick are recovering—the troops in high spirits, and we have no fear, but we shall be able to maintain our ground against all the banditti of George the Third."

The subsequent overthrow of the American army dispelled this brave chaplain's immediate hopes, and what become of him in the turbulent events that followed I have been unable to ascertain.

Such waifs, drifting down to us from the past, show us how many valuable incidents respecting the revolutionary war might have been saved from oblivion had efforts been made a half century ago to have collected them together.

CHAPTER XLIII.

MR. MAGOON.

In the absence of details respecting this noble clergyman, I cannot give a better idea of his patriotic course in the Revolution than by presenting the following extracts from an address delivered by him to Haslett's battalion on its parade in Dover, Delaware, May, 1776. After speaking in general terms of the necessity of public spirit—how it made a people great and prosperous—and showing how righteousness "exalteth a nation" and sin degrades it; and the importance of cherishing good and patriotic sentiments, he turned directly to the soldiers and said: "You love your country, I venture to affirm, and are not strangers to the full meaning of that honorable word. A Roman orator and patriot of celebrated fame mentioning the subject expresses himself thus: 'Our parents are dear, our children are dear, our relations, our near acquaintances, but our country comprehends every endearment and the tender ties and charities of all, for which what good man would hesitate to dare to die.' And doth not the great St. Paul's declaration breathe a like patriotic spirit, 'None of us liveth to himself, and no man dieth to himself.' It is really grand, it is solemnly pleasing to behold at a perilous, alarming conjuncture so many stepping forward voluntarily as thousands and thousands in these United Colonies have done, prepared to face any danger, ready to encounter any difficulties, rather than that the free should become enslaved, and the once happy be reduced to wretchedness. * * * Perhaps never were freemen or patriots or warriors or heroes called forth for nobler purposes than we have now in prospect. We are contending for no other prize than that we may continue to be free, that the fruits of our honest labor may be our own, that we may be delivered from the hands of those who would oppress us—that our civil and religious happiness may be secured, and that we may be able to transmit those blessings on a firm foundation to our children and generations after them. It is not in rebellion, it is not in the violation of the spirit of law and contempt of the constitution, that we arise and join with such amazing unanimity. No, ye illustrious shades of our pious ancestors, and ye martyrs of of whatever age or clime who have shed your tears and your blood for dying freedom! Ye cloud of witnesses with which we are encompassed about, we declare as in your presence, and we declare to the whole earth, that such are not our aims, that our public measures result from a dreadful necessity—that America hath resisted purely on the footing of self-preservation."

The closing sentiment of this address applies with peculiar force to our own times. It lies at the bottom of the terrible uprising of the North to put down the rebellion that threatens the integrity of our government. The President of the United States, every officer and every chaplain in the army might say with truth : "*It is not in rebellion, it is not in violation of the spirit of law and contempt of the Constitution, that we arise and join with such amazing unanimity. No, ye illustrious shades of our pious ancestors, and ye martyrs of whatever age or clime, who have shed your tears and your blood for dying freedom. Ye cloud of witnesses with which we are encompassed about, we declare as in your presence, and we declare to the whole earth, that such are not our aims---that our public measures result from a dreadful necessity— that America hath resisted purely on the footing of self-preservation.*"

CHAPTER XLIV.

THOMAS COOMBS.

Sermon on Fast-day and Patriotic Sentiments.

This patriotic chaplain being called upon to preach a sermon on the occasion of a fast proclaimed by Congress, took for his text, 2d Chronicles, xx. 12, 13: "O our God, wilt thou not judge them? for we have no might against this great company that cometh against us; neither know we what to do: but our eyes are upon thee. And all Judah stood before the Lord, with their little ones, their wives and their children." After describing the circumstances which produced this prayer, and speaking of the certainty of God's assistance to those who call on Him in truth, he passes to the consideration of our own country, and says:

"We have asked but for peace, liberty and safety derived from Heaven and the Constitution—sanctified by the faith of charters, and which no power on earth, without our own consent, hath authority to disannul, and since I am called to the office of speaking before you on this subject, it is my duty to declare that they are privileges which, had we been so tame as to have surrendered without a struggle, we should have been guilty of treason to posterity."

Again: "We have the authority of God's own declaration, 'that all things shall work together for good to them that love God;' and under the influence of this cheering thought we may reasonably indulge the expectation that out of the present jarring interests a new and more perfect system will arise which, rescued from the capricious mutilations of arbitrary men, shall perpetuate the liberties of these United Colonies to the end of time: for God will take our cause into his hand, and will help the oppressed unto their right, that the men of the earth be no more exalted against us, and though Assur come out against us with ten thousands of his army, the multitude whereof hath *stopped the torrents*, and their horsemen have covered the hills—though he boasteth that he will burn up our borders, and kill our young men with the sword, the Almighty Lord shalt disappoint them and confound their impious devices."

CHAPTER XLV.

A ROMAN CATHOLIC CHAPLAIN.

CATHOLICS HAVE FOUGHT WITH PROTESTANTS FROM THE FIRST FOR LIBERTY.—CAUSE OF THIS SINGULAR COINCIDENCE.—FOURTH OF JULY ADDRESS.

IT is a curious fact that in our first struggle for liberty, and in all the wars that the republic has since waged, even till now, when the North is struggling against a monstrous rebellion, Roman Catholic chaplains have sent up their prayers side by side with protestant ones. Though so far apart in every other enterprise, they have presented the anomalous spectacle of working together to support free institutions. In the revolution we were emphatically a purely protestant people, but our French allies were Roman Catholics, and the chaplains they brought with them, though not governed by the same motives and spirit that actuated our clergy, manifested the deepest interest in our struggle for independence, and expressed the warmest hopes for our success. Since then the large number of foreign born citizens in our army have made them in times of war a necessary part of its organization. Whole regiments would be without chaplains entirely were it not so.

In the revolution the religious exercises were, of course, in French, and hence we know little of their character ; but the following translation of an address,

delivered in a Roman Catholic church in Philadelphia, on the 4th of July, 1779, is a fair illustration of the spirit they exhibited throughout. After a Te Deum was chanted, the chaplain came forward and said:—
"Gentlemen, we are assembled to celebrate the anniversary of that day which Providence had marked in His eternal decrees to become the epocha of liberty and independence to the thirteen United States of America. That being, whose Almighty hand holds all existence beneath its dominion, undoubtedly produces in the depth of His wisdom those great events which astonish the universe, and of which the most presumptuous, though instrumental in accomplishing, dare not attribute to themselves the merit. But the finger of God is still more peculiarly evident in the happy, the glorious revolution which calls forth this day's festivity. He hath struck the oppressors of a people, free and peaceable, with the spirit of delusion, which always renders the wicked the artificers of their own proper misfortunes. Permit me, my dear brethren, citizens of the United States, to address you on this occasion. It is God, the all-powerful God, who hath directed your steps when you knew not where to apply for counsel—who, when you were without arms, fought for you with the sword of eternal justice—who, when you were in adversity, poured into your hearts the spirit of courage, of wisdom, and of fortitude; and who has at length raised up for your support a youthful sovereign, whose virtues bless and adorn a sensible, a faithful, and a generous nation. This nation has blended her interests with your inter-

ests, and her sentiments with yours. She participates in all your joys, and this day unites her voice to yours at the foot of the altars of the eternal God to celebrate that glorious revolution, which has placed the sons of America among the free and independent nations of the earth.

"We have nothing to apprehend but the anger of heaven, or that the measure of our guilt should exceed the measure of His mercy. Let us, then, prostrate ourselves at the feet of the immortal God, who holds the fate of empires in His hands, and raises them up at His pleasure, or breaks them to dust—let us conjure Him to enlighten our enemies, and to dispose their hearts to enjoy that tranquillity and happiness which, the revolution we now celebrate, has established for a great part of the human race—let us implore Him to conduct us by the way which His providence has marked out for arriving at so desirable an end—let us offer unto Him hearts imbued with sentiments of love, consecrated by religion, by humanity, and patriotism. Never is the august ministry of His altars more acceptable to His Divine Majesty than when it lays at His feet homages, offerings, and vows, so pure, so worthy of the common parent of mankind. God will not reject our joy, for He is the author of it, nor will He reject our prayers, for they ask but the full accomplishment of His decrees that He hath manifested. Filled with this spirit, let us, in concert with each other, raise our hearts to the Eternal—let us implore His infinite mercy to be pleased to inspire the rulers of both nations with the wisdom and force necessary to perfect what it hath begun. Let us, in a word, unite our voices to beseech Him to dispense His blessings upon the counsels and arms of the allies— that we may soon enjoy the sweets of a peace which will cement the union, and establish the prosperity of the two empires. It is with this view we shall cause the canticle to be performed, which the custom of the Catholic Church hath consecrated, to be at once a testimonial of public joy, a thanksgiving for benefits received from heaven, and a prayer for the continuance of its success."

CHAPTER XLVI.

A CHAPLAIN AT BRANDYWINE.

Address before the Battle.

There are contradictory opinions about the following sermon said to be delivered on the eve of the battle of Brandywine. Hence I give it without comments, just as I find it. The name of the chaplain is said to have been Trout.

"*They that take the sword shall perish by the sword!*"—Matt. xxvi. 52.

"Soldiers and countrymen! We have met this evening, perhaps, for the last time. We have shared the toil of the march, the peril of the fight, the dismay of the retreat—alike we have endured cold and hunger, the contumely of the infernal foe, and outrage of the foreign oppressor. We have sat night after night, beside the same camp fire, shared the same rough soldiers' fare;—we have together heard the roll of the reveille which called us to duty, or the beat of the tattoo which gave the signal for the hardy sleep of the soldier, with the earth for his bed, and his knapsack for a pillow. And now soldiers and brethren, we have met in the peaceful valley, on the eve of the battle, while the sunlight is dying away behind yonder heights, the sunlight that to-morrow morn will glimmer on scenes of blood. We have met amid the whitening tents of our encampment; in times of terror and gloom have we gathered together. God grant it may not be for the last time.

"It is a solemn moment. Brethren, does not the solemn voice of nature seem to echo the sympathies of the town? The flag of our country droops heavily from yonder staff. The breeze has died away along the green plain of Chadd's ford—the plain that spreads before us glistening in sunlight—the heights of the Brandywine arise dark and gloomy beyond the waters of yonder stream, and all nature holds a pause of solemn silence on the eve of the uproar of the bloodshed and strife of to-morrow.

"'They that take the sword shall perish by the sword,' and have they not taken the sword?

"Let the blood-stained valley—the desolated homes —the burned farm house—the murdered farmer—let the whitening bones of our own countrymen answer! Let the starving mother with the babe clinging to her withered breast, let her answer—with the death rattle mingling with the murmuring tones that mark the last struggle for life; let the dying mother and her babe answer!

"It was but a day past, and our land slept in the light of peace. War was not here, wrong was not here. Fraud, and woe, and misery and want dwelt not among us. From the eternal solitude of the green woods, arose the blue smoke of the settler's cabin; and golden fields of corn looked forth from amid the waste of the wilderness, and the glad music of human voices awoke the silence of the forest.

"Now! God of mercy! Behold the change. Under the shadow of a pretext, under the sanctity of the name of God—invoking the Redeemer to their aid, do these foreign hirelings slay our people. They throng our towns, they darken our plains, and now they encompass our posts on the lonely plain of Chadd's Ford.

"'They that take the sword shall perish by the sword.' Brethren! think me not unworthy of belief, when I tell you that the doom of the Britisher is near! Think me not vain when I tell you that beyond the cloud which now enshrouds us, I see gathering thick and fast, the darker cloud and the blacker storm of Divine Retribution! They may conquer us on the morrow!—might and wrong may prevail, and we may be driven from the field—but the hour of God's vengeance *will* come! Aye, if in the vast solitudes of eternal space, if in the heart of the boundless universe, there throbs the being of an awful God, quick to revenge and sure to punish guilt, there will the man, George of Brunswick, called King, feel in his brain and in his heart the vengeance of the eternal Jehovah! a blight will be upon his life—a withered brain, an accursed intellect; a blight will be upon his children, and his people. Great God! how dread the punishment!·

"Soldiers! I look around upon your familiar faces with a strange interest. To-morrow we will all go forth to battle—for need I tell you that your unworthy minister will march with you, invoking God's aid in the fight. We will march forth to battle. Need I exhort you to fight the good fight for your homesteads, your wives, and your children.

"And in the hour of battle when all around is darkness, lit by the lurid cannon glare, and the piercing musket flash, when the wounded strew the ground and the dead litter your path. Then remember, soldiers, that God is with you. The eternal God is with you, and fights for you. God! the awful, the infinite, fights for you and you will triumph.

"'They that take the sword shall perish by the sword.'

You have taken the sword; but not in the spirit of wrong and revenge. You have taken the sword for your homes, for your wives, and for your little ones. You have taken the sword for truth, for justice, and for right, and to you the promise is, be of good cheer, for your foes have taken the sword in defiance of all man holds dear. They shall *perish by the sword*.

"And now, brethren and soldiers, I bid you all farewell. Many of us may fall in the fight of to-morrow. God rest the souls of the fallen—many of us *may* live to tell the story of the fight of to-morrow, and in the memory of all will rest the quiet scenes of this autumnal night.

"Solemn twilight advances over the valley; the woods on the opposite heights fling their long shadows over the green of the meadow—around us are the tents of the continental host—the suppressed bustle of the camp, the hurried tread of the soldiers to and fro among the tents, the stillness that marks the eve of battle.

"When we meet again, may the long shadows of twilight be flung over a peaceful land. God in heaven grant it! Amen."

Other Solid Ground Titles

In addition to the book in your hand, Solid Ground is honored to offer other uncovered treasure, many for the first time in more than a century:

THE COMMUNICANT'S COMPANION by Matthew Henry
THE CHILD AT HOME by John S.C. Abbott
THE LIFE OF JESUS CHRIST FOR THE YOUNG by Richard Newton
THE KING'S HIGHWAY: *10 Commandments for the Young* by Richard Newton
HEROES OF THE REFORMATION by Richard Newton
FEED MY LAMBS: *Lectures to Children on Vital Subjects* by John Todd
LET THE CANNON BLAZE AWAY by Joseph P. Thompson
THE STILL HOUR: *Communion with God in Prayer* by Austin Phelps
COLLECTED WORKS of James Henley Thornwell (4 vols.)
CALVINISM IN HISTORY *by Nathaniel S. McFetridge*
OPENING SCRIPTURE: *Hermeneutical Manual by Patrick Fairbairn*
THE ASSURANCE OF FAITH *by Louis Berkhof*
THE PASTOR IN THE SICK ROOM *by John D. Wells*
THE BUNYAN OF BROOKLYN: *Life & Sermons of I.S. Spencer*
THE NATIONAL PREACHER: S*ermons from 2nd Great Awakening*
FIRST THINGS: F*irst Lessons God Taught Mankind* Gardiner Spring
BIBLICAL & THEOLOGICAL STUDIES *by 1912 Faculty of Princeton*
THE POWER OF GOD UNTO SALVATION *by B.B. Warfield*
THE LORD OF GLORY *by B.B. Warfield*
A GENTLEMAN & A SCHOLAR: *Memoir of J.P. Boyce by J. Broadus*
SERMONS TO THE NATURAL MAN *by W.G.T. Shedd*
SERMONS TO THE SPIRITUAL MAN *by W.G.T. Shedd*
HOMILETICS AND PASTORAL THEOLOGY *by W.G.T. Shedd*
A PASTOR'S SKETCHES 1 & 2 *by Ichabod S. Spencer*
THE PREACHER AND HIS MODELS *by James Stalker*
IMAGO CHRISTI: *The Example of Jesus Christ by James Stalker*
LECTURES ON THE HISTORY OF PREACHING *by J. A. Broadus*
THE SHORTER CATECHISM ILLUSTRATED *by John Whitecross*
THE CHURCH MEMBER'S GUIDE *by John Angell James*
THE SUNDAY SCHOOL TEACHER'S GUIDE *by John A. James*
CHRIST IN SONG: *Hymns of Immanuel from All Ages by Philip Schaff*
COME YE APART: *Daily Words from the Four Gospels by J.R. Miller*
DEVOTIONAL LIFE OF THE S.S. TEACHER *by J.R. Miller*

Call us Toll Free at 1-877-666-9469
Send us an e-mail at sgcb@charter.net
Visit us on line at solid-ground-books.com
Uncovering Buried Treasure to the Glory of God

www.ingramcontent.com/pod-product-compliance
Lightning Source LLC
Chambersburg PA
CBHW021957160426
43197CB00007B/159